The Contemporary British Novel Since 2000

The Contemporary British Novel Since 2000

Edited by James Acheson

EDINBURGH
University Press

Edinburgh University Press is one of the leading university presses in the UK. We publish academic books and journals in our selected subject areas across the humanities and social sciences, combining cutting-edge scholarship with high editorial and production values to produce academic works of lasting importance. For more information visit our website: edinburghuniversitypress.com

© editorial matter and organisation James Acheson, 2017
© the chapters their several authors, 2017

Edinburgh University Press Ltd
The Tun – Holyrood Road
12(2f) Jackson's Entry
Edinburgh EH8 8PJ

Typeset in 10/12 Goudy Old Style by
Servis Filmsetting Ltd, Stockport, Cheshire

A CIP record for this book is available from the British Library

ISBN 978 1 4744 0372 6 (hardback)
ISBN 978 1 4744 0374 0 (webready PDF)
ISBN 978 1 4744 0373 3 (paperback)
ISBN 978 1 4744 0375 7 (epub)

The right of James Acheson to be identified as the editor of this work has been asserted in accordance with the Copyright, Designs and Patents Act 1988, and the Copyright and Related Rights Regulations 2003 (SI No. 2498).

Published with the support of the University of Edinburgh Scholarly Publishing Initiatives Fund.

Contents

Acknowledgements   vii

Introduction   1
James Acheson

Part I Four Voices for the New Millennium

1. Ian McEwan: Lies and Deceptions   17
   David Punter
2. David Mitchell: Global Novelist of the Twenty-First Century   27
   Brian Finney
3. Hilary Mantel: Raising the Dead, Speaking the Truth   37
   Lisa Fletcher
4. Zadie Smith: The Geographies of Marriage   48
   Gretchen Gerzina

Part II Realism and Beyond

5. Maggie O'Farrell: Discoveries at the Edge   61
   Susan Strehle
6. Sarah Hall: A New Kind of Storytelling   70
   Sue Vice
7. A. L. Kennedy: Giving and Receiving   79
   Alison Lumsden
8. Alan Warner: Timeless Realities   88
   Alan Riach

Part III Postmodernism, Globalisation and Beyond

9. Ali Smith: Strangers and Intrusions — 99
    Monica Germanà
10. Kazuo Ishiguro: Alternate Histories — 109
    Daniel Bedggood
11. Kate Atkinson: Plotting to Be Read — 119
    Glenda Norquay
12. Salman Rushdie: Archival Modernism — 129
    Vijay Mishra

Part IV Realism, Postmodernism and Beyond: Historical Fiction

13. Adam Foulds: Fictions of Past and Present — 143
    Dominic Head
14. Sarah Waters: Representing Marginal Groups and Individuals — 153
    Susana Onega
15. James Robertson: In the Margins of History — 163
    Cairns Craig

Part V Postcolonialism and Beyond

16. Mohsin Hamid: The Transnational Novel of Globalisation — 177
    Janet Wilson
17. Andrea Levy: The SS *Empire Windrush* and After — 188
    Sue Thomas
18. Aminatta Forna: Truth, Trauma, Memory — 199
    Françoise Lionnet and Jennifer MacGregor

Notes on Contributors — 209
Index — 213

Acknowledgements

I would like to thank, first and foremost, the contributors to this volume. They all wrote their essays specifically for this collection; their professionalism, intellectual energy and enthusiasm ensured that the project was a thoroughgoing pleasure for me as editor.

I also wish to thank my wife Carole for her stimulating conversation and many insightful suggestions.

Finally, I would like to thank Professors John Fletcher, Suzette Henke, Bruce King, Brian McHale, John Pilling and Sidonie Smith for their support and encouragement, and my editor at Edinburgh University Press, Jackie Jones, for her unfailingly helpful advice every step of the way.

Introduction

James Acheson

Where is the twenty-first-century British novel headed? The answer to this question depends on which contemporary novelists are taken into consideration, and this in turn depends on the view one takes of the contemporary British literary scene. Certainly it is very different from the scene described by David Lodge in 1971, when he pictured the British novelist at a crossroads, one choice being to continue within the realist tradition, and the other to further the modernist experiments of James Joyce, Virginia Woolf and Dorothy Richardson. Lodge expected the British novel to follow one road or the other, but on re-examining the British novel in 1992, he found that the crossroads no longer existed. Its place had been taken by an 'aesthetic supermarket' where novelists could choose from a number of available options.[1]

From this it is clear that an increasingly complex contemporary world has given rise to increasingly complex contemporary novels – novels that members of the reading public, as well as students in schools, colleges, polytechnics and universities around the world, often find daunting. Those who write about contemporary fiction are not always clear what they mean by key terms like 'realism', 'postmodernism', 'postcolonialism' and 'globalisation'. *The Contemporary British Novel Since 2000* seeks, like its predecessor, *The Contemporary British Novel Since 1980*,[2] to define (or identify the problems involved in defining) these terms not only for students but also for teachers and interested members of the reading public. In addition, it reveals the extent to which the practice of eighteen leading British novelists embodies, exemplifies or modifies the theories that these terms represent.

The present collection of eighteen hitherto unpublished chapters examines the work of some of the leading British novelists of the past sixteen years. By virtue of winning major literary prizes, these novelists have become the most widely taught at educational institutions in Great Britain and elsewhere in the English-speaking world. They have also become the most widely bought by public libraries worldwide, and have thereby become known to members of the reading public wanting to keep up with 'serious' fiction. When the inevitable objection is raised that other novelists should also have been included in the present volume, the answer is that many novelists have been omitted simply because there is a limit to the number who can be accommodated in a work of this length. In any case, the present volume includes thirteen novelists not discussed in *The Contemporary British Novel Since 1980*, in recognition of the fact that many talented writers have recently come to the fore.[3]

About half of the writers considered here had their first novels published in the year 2000 or later, while the other half started prior to the turn of the century, and have continued to write fiction of a high standard since then. There has been an increase in the number of women novelists in the past twenty years, and it is interesting that many of them are writing about gender issues that existed in the past but no longer exist in the present. It is also interesting that lesbian novelists are no longer being charged with indecency, as Radclyffe Hall was in 1928, even though her novel *The Well of Loneliness* contained no explicit sex scenes.[4]

The Contemporary British Novel Since 2000 is in five parts, with the first part examining the work of four particularly well-known and highly regarded twenty-first-century writers: Ian McEwan, David Mitchell, Hilary Mantel and Zadie Smith. It is with reference to each of these novelists in turn that the terms 'realist', 'postmodernist', 'historical' and 'postcolonialist' fiction are introduced, while in the remaining four parts, other novelists are discussed and the meaning of the terms amplified. From the start it must be emphasised that these terms and others often mean different things to different novelists, and that the complexity of their novels often obliges us to discuss their work with reference to more than one of the terms.

It is as well to begin with the concept of realist fiction, realism being the oldest of the terms under consideration. Ian Watt notes in *The Rise of the Novel* that it was first used in France in 1835, but that some of the earliest English novels – those by Defoe, Richardson and Fielding, especially – anticipate in practice certain aspects of nineteenth-century French theory.[5] In particular, Defoe and the others seek to create the illusion that their characters are real people living in the real world. As David Punter observes in Chapter 1, Ian McEwan is a realist in this sense, though his novels are self-conscious in a way that most eighteenth- and nineteenth-century novels are not. Implicit in his fiction, says Punter, is the question, why tell stories, knowing that stories are lies? The answer is that we need to tell them in order 'to turn the world into a place in which we can live', into a version of reality that 'will allow us to flourish; or, at least, to survive'.

Significantly, in *Atonement* (2001) the narrative viewpoint employed in much of the novel is itself a lie: though much of what happens is presented from the point of view of an omniscient narrator – an analogue to God who knows everything about the ostensibly 'real' people who serve as the novel's characters – in the end we discover that the narrator is actually a character herself, Briony Tallis. Years before writing the narrative, Briony has testified in court that she saw a neighbour, Robbie Turner, rape one of her cousins, Lola, though it was dark and she was unable to see the rapist clearly. Much later she admits to herself that she may have been mistaken, and feels that she must do something to atone for sending an innocent man to prison; writing the narrative is her act of atonement. The problem is that she has had to question what she really saw, and this reminds us that reality is a concept that is hard to define.

In Chapter 5, Susan Strehle says that Maggie O'Farrell's six novels 'bring an updated psychological realism to bear on the tangled lives of contemporary British characters'. The realism is 'psychological' in that O'Farrell dwells at length on the thoughts of her characters, and is 'updated' in that she presents us with variations on established fictional conventions 'in complex, layered plots'. Her aim is to appeal to both a broad audience and the cultivated reader alike. In her best-known novel, *The Vanishing Act of Esme Lennox* (2006), O'Farrell focuses on three women for each of whom reality means something completely different. The eponymous Esme has been confined to a psychiatric hospital for sixty-one years, not because she is mentally ill but because she had a baby out of wedlock. Hidden away there by a scandalised Edwardian family, she has lost the baby to her sister Kitty, who is unable to have children of her own. By the end of the novel we see that for Kitty reality has been an unhappy marriage, for Esme the injustice of lifelong incarceration, and for her granddaughter Iris the recognition of how lucky she has been to grow up in the era of women's liberation. Though O'Farrell is, in Strehle's view, not a 'programmatic feminist' – a feminist who advocates ways of improving the lot of women in the twenty-first century – she is a feminist in that she deplores the way women have been treated in the past.

At the start of Chapter 6, Sue Vice notes that Sarah Hall's novels are all different from each other, Hall being a writer who seeks to represent reality by a variety of means. Especially interesting is *The Electric Michelangelo* (2004) which, although narrated from a traditionally omniscient point of view, is in other respects self-consciously unconventional. 'I threw everything at it: language, rhyming sentences, nonexistent plot,' Hall has been quoted as saying, and it is clear from this statement that she is deliberately challenging the reader's concept of what a novel should be like. Her main character, Cyril Parks, is an unlikely figure, a tattoo artist who has 'eyes for the grotesque things of life'. At the start of the novel he is living in his mother's establishment for consumptives, and although he is constantly exposed to the ugliness of bowls of tubercular fluids and the spectacle of the dead and dying, he manages to create imaginative 'dreamscapes' suitable for etching into his clients' skin. Having trained in Britain, Parks moves to Coney Island, where he works as a fully fledged 'electric Michelangelo' and accepts a commission from Grace, a young circus performer who wants her whole body tattooed with images of black-rimmed green eyes. Shockingly, she is subjected to an acid attack that leaves her looking like 'a fresco with a jar of paint stripper knocked over her'. Clearly Hall is asking us to reflect on what we mean not only by a novel but about beauty as well. We may believe that a novel should feature heroic characters seeking to make the world a better, more beautiful place, in which case *The Electric Michelangelo* will hold little appeal. On the other hand, we may wish to concede that there is something of value in its presentation of the real world in a way that includes the ugliness of illness and accident.

In Chapter 7 Alison Lumsden discusses A. L. Kennedy's three twenty-first-century novels, *Paradise* (2005), *Day* (2008) and *The Blue Book* (2012). All three are concerned with the difficulties involved in living a solitary life and forming lasting relationships. For Lumsden, however, *Day* is especially interesting because it is Kennedy's only foray into historical fiction. The main character, Alfred Day, is a tail-gunner on a Lancaster bomber during World War II; he comes from a dysfunctional family, and finds for the first time a sense of community in the camaraderie that the air force has to offer, though this is disrupted when various members of his crew are killed in action. Taken prisoner by the Germans, he yearns at war's end for the friendship he enjoyed with his fellow inmates; since he cannot go back to the camp, he takes a job as an extra in a film about escaping from one. 'It had seemed', says Kennedy, 'not unlikely that he could work out his own little pantomime inside the professional pretence and tunnel right through to the place where he'd lost himself, or rather the dark, the numb gap he could tell was asleep inside him . . . So it could possibly make sense that he'd turn up here and at least work out what was missing, maybe even put it back.' For Lumsden this is a sign that Day is starting to see, however dimly, that it was something that happened in the past that is interfering with his ability to form lasting relationships. 'Kennedy's foray into the historical novel', she says, 'suggests that revisiting the past may offer one mechanism by which characters can break the cycle of entrapment that her earlier characters encounter.' For Kennedy the real world is a place that makes serious demands on us, denying happiness to many; returning to the past may help to break the solitude/lasting relationship cycle, but then again it may not.

The novels of Alan Warner present us with a different kind of realist fiction, dwelling for the most part, as Alan Riach observes in Chapter 8, on what it is to be young. In *The Stars in the Bright Sky* (2010), we observe a group of women in their twenties waiting for a flight out of Gatwick in 2001. They are excited, free of responsibilities and content with a range of trivial pleasures until the end of the novel, when the sobering news is announced that the twin towers of the World Trade Centre in New York have been brought down by terrorists. It is 9/11, and we are left in the final sentence on a note of suspense: 'They all waited to see what would happen next.' Here we are reminded that reality takes many forms, for at the end of the novel, one kind of reality – the reality of worldwide terrorism – has intruded onto another, that of feckless youth.

Very different from this novel is *The Deadman's Pedal* (2012), set in the 1970s and 1980s, in which the main character, Simon, leaves school and finds work driving diesel locomotives. The Thatcher era is approaching, and Simon must make the transition from a time when the unions and workers' rights are in the ascendant to one in which laissez-faire capitalism is the order of the day. Partly through its structure – it is divided into twenty-one unnumbered, not altogether chronological episodes – the novel conveys to us that Simon's life is a succession of massive changes of widely varying kinds. The deadman's pedal of the title is a safeguard, a mechanism for slowing a train should its driver have a heart attack and die. The question Warner raises is whether there is some counterpart to the pedal in real life – some safeguard protecting society against economic calamity through the loss of proper political guidance.

Postmodernism has been defined in a number of ways by a number of different commentators. Frederic Jameson, Jean-François Lyotard and Brian McHale, however, are often referred to where a concise definition is needed. For Jameson, postmodernism represents a 'radical break' in the 1950s and 1960s from the certainties, aims and ideals of modernity, resulting in the development of new cultural forms in areas as diverse as architecture, film, advertising and literature.[6] Lyotard similarly expresses his distrust of 'metanarrative' or 'grand narratives' – the theories of Marx or Hegel about the course of history, for example, or the modern concept of 'Progress'.[7] McHale sees the modernist movement, extending from about 1900 until the mid-1960s, as having been subject to an epistemological dominant, a prevailing tendency on the part of writers to address themselves to epistemological questions – questions of how much we know and how we know it. By contrast, he says, the postmodernist movement that followed, from the mid-1960s through to the early twenty-first century, has been governed by an ontological dominant, a compulsion to ask 'Which world is this? What is to be done in it? Which of my selves is to do it?'[8]

In Chapter 2, Brian Finney reveals that such questions as these arise repeatedly in David Mitchell's fiction. Our sense that *Ghostwritten* (1999), Mitchell's first novel, is a succession of different worlds arises from the fact that its nine chapters are set in nine different places: Okinawa, Tokyo, Hong Kong, China, Mongolia, St Petersburg, London, Ireland and New York. Eventually we discover, however, that each of the nine locations resembles the others. In the first chapter, a Japanese terrorist observes that '[h]igh streets are becoming the same all over the world', and this statement is repeated word for word by a character in the sixth. What we are witness to here, says Finney, is globalisation, a term Anthony Giddens defines as 'the intensification of worldwide social relations which link distant localities in such a way that local happenings are shaped by events occurring many miles away and vice versa'.[9] *Ghostwritten* represents what it is to live in a globalised civilisation rather than in a national one, a world in which lives are ghostwritten by globalised forces.

Cloud Atlas (2004), Mitchell's best-known novel to date, was inspired by Italo Calvino's *If on a Winter's Night a Traveler* (1979). 'Mitchell not only interrupts each of his six narratives with another,' says Finney, 'as Calvino does; he picks each up again and completes it in reverse order, so that the second half of the novel mirrors the first half in reverse order.' The complexity of the narrative is meant to correspond to the complexity of our globalised world, and its preoccupation with human predation is meant, as Mitchell revealed in a *Guardian* interview, to endorse Nietzsche's theory of the will to power.[10] Like Nietzsche, Mitchell believes that there will always be predators and prey the world over, and that it would be naïve to imagine that good will eventually triumph over evil. Finney finds in Mitchell's novels an ambivalent attitude to postmodernism, and characterises him as 'a self-consciously post-postmodern novelist',[11] a novelist who, in McHale's words, devotes him- or herself to 'the intensification and mutation of features and tendencies *within* postmodernism'.[12]

In Chapter 9, Monica Germanà describes Ali Smith as a postmodern novelist who favours the use of multiple first-person narrators. In *Hotel World* (2001), Smith presents us with four first-person narrators associated with the fictional Global Hotel, and, by extension, with the globalised world at large. The first narrator is the ghost of Sara Wilby, a hotel maid who has died after falling down a dumb-waiter shaft, while the other narrators are a homeless woman (Else), an unhappy employee (Lise) and a bereaved teenager (Clare). When pictured talking on their mobile phones the four characters appear to each 'occupy a world of their own', and this, says Germanà, is a reminder of the 'post-millennial intensified virtuality McHale regards as a feature of the post-postmodern era'.[13] However, she adds that there is also a sense, 'strongly linked to language and its redemptive powers', that it may be possible for the characters to '[reconnect] the centre with the margins'. Key to the novel, Germanà emphasises, is the word 'rebegot', from John Donne's poem 'A Nocturnal upon St Lucy's Day'. When Else draws attention to the idea of being 'rebegot', which Donne invents to describe every imaginable kind of remaking – 'fathering, conceiving, the very deepest place of thought' – she is suggesting that this kind of regenerative action 'is a way of . . . re-establishing new, invisible bonds with the others'.

Like *Hotel World*, *The Accidental* (2005) is narrated from four points of view, those of four members of the dysfunctional Smart family. Framing the novel's three sections is another first-person narrator named Amber. Smith is concerned with the family's lack of authentic bonds because she sees, says Germanà, that there is now an increasing 'sense of fragmentation, solipsism and isolation' shared by all four of its members. What she wants to emphasise is that this dysfunctional family is 'a microcosmic projection of the contemporary condition' worldwide. Amber acts as a 'saviour' in bringing the family back together, helping individual members to discover new words within themselves and also to understand in a new way the word 'and'. 'The word *and*', one of the characters reflects to himself, 'is a little bullet of oxygen.'

In Chapter 10, Daniel Bedggood examines Kazuo Ishiguro's postmodern turn away from realist fiction. He begins by discussing *Remains of the Day* (1989), a realist novel whose main character is Stevens, butler during the 1930s to Lord Darlington, a man he considers to be beyond reproach. Eventually Stevens discovers that his master is not the man he thought he was but is instead a Nazi sympathiser, and he is deeply troubled; yet his response is dignified, restrained and well within the bounds of realist fiction.

By contrast, Ishiguro's first twenty-first-century novel, *When We Were Orphans* (2000), is strangely dream-like, its first-person narrator, Christopher Banks, being a young man who appears unable to think clearly about either the past or the present. Though he claims to be a great detective, it quickly becomes clear that in fact he is self-deluded: sent from China to Britain as a child, he is returning to China as a young adult to find his parents. What he discovers is that his father has disappeared altogether and his mother is a concubine of the warlord who has paid for Banks's education in Britain. When he meets her he discovers that she is too mentally incapacitated to recognise him. Ishiguro's use of the detective story form initially suggests that there will be a ready solution to the mystery of what has happened to

Banks's parents, but the reader's expectations are thwarted. *When We Were Orphans* begs the questions that McHale identifies as characteristic of postmodernism: 'Which world is this? What is to be done in it? Which of my selves is to do it?' The world that Ishiguro presents us with is the real world as refracted through a lens or seen in a distorting mirror. Banks sees that what is to be done is to engage in a quest for his parents, but the self who plays the part of detective is someone with a troubled mind, a mind that is unequal to completing the task he has set himself.

'From her early fiction onwards', says Glenda Norquay in Chapter 11, Kate Atkinson 'has demonstrated a "postmodern" interest in the ontological' – in what Brian McHale refers to as 'world-making and modes of being'.[14] To this Norquay adds that 'although her novels have been described as combining an interest in "history, family and identity within a postmodern aesthetic", the increasing sophistication of that dynamic has made them both more complex and more commercially successful'.[15] In a series of detective novels featuring Jackson Brodie – *Case Histories* (2004), *One Good Turn* (2006), *When Will There Be Good News* (2008) and *Started Early, Took My Dog* (2010) – Atkinson seeks to defamiliarise an established literary mode and create an unsettling experience for readers through disrupted chronology. Brodie seeks to solve the mysteries in these novels, but, like Ishiguro's detective, Banks, he must contend with the fact that the lines of demarcation between victims, perpetrators and innocent bystanders often become blurred and uncertain.

The Brodie novels move backwards and forwards in time, and in *Life After Life* (2013) Atkinson begins with an epigraph voiced by one of her characters – 'What if we had a chance to do it again and again until we finally got it right?' – which becomes the central question in the book. Beginning in 1910 and ending in about 1967, the novel corresponds to McHale's concept of postmodernist literature, which presents us with differing worlds and selves. The main character of Atkinson's novel, Ursula Beresford Fox, finds that she is able to learn from past mistakes: in an early version of her life she is raped by a visiting American, leading to an unwanted pregnancy, a disastrous marriage and problems with alcohol. In later versions of the incident, however, she finds the courage to beat off her aggressor, escape and live her life more satisfactorily. This creates a sense that women are free to improve their lot, and that it is as important for women as for men to appear in the history books. On the other hand, we are told that Ursula's memories do not proceed in 'a straight line', as the memories of another character do, but behave instead 'like a cascade of echoes'. As Norquay observes, *Life After Life* 'not only presents a challenge to gendered versions of history but begins to interrogate progressional versions of temporality'. Here we are reminded that Jean-François Lyotard is dismissive of the idea of Progress.

One of the features of literary postmodernism that distinguishes it from the high modernist literature of the 1920s and 1930s is the difference in attitude to popular culture taken by its practitioners. Where the literary high modernist alludes in his or her writing to only the very best literature, art and music, the postmodern writer readily calls attention to various aspects of popular culture, including comic books, cartoons, films, television, pop art and pop music. We see this in the novels of Salman Rushdie, who in *Fury* (2001) writes in part about the classical Furies, while at the same time alluding to Monty Python's *Life of Brian* (1979), Woody Allen's *Husbands and Wives* (1992) and the work of pop artist Andy Warhol.

Rushdie's references to pop culture are easily identified, but his many allusions to classical European literature, and also to medieval Islamic and European literature, are not. As Vijay Mishra demonstrates in Chapter 12, Rushdie makes extensive use of these sources, drawing on them as though from a private archive for inclusion in his novels. This is especially clear in *The Ground Beneath Her Feet*, which is informed not only by the classical version of the myth of Orpheus as found in Virgil and Ovid, but also by the medieval and late modern versions of the story (the Middle English *Sir Orfeo*, Henryson's *Orpheus and Eurydice*, Cocteau's *Le Testament d'Orphée*, 1950, and the carnivalesque *Orfeu Negro*, 1960). In brief, the myth tells of the descent into the underworld made by Orpheus in search of his departed wife; he is allowed to take her back to the land of the living, but only if he will not look back. Unable to hear Eurydice following behind him, he turns and loses her forever. Mishra traces the parallels between the myth and *The Ground Beneath Her Feet*, commenting that '[f]or Rushdie the myth that informs the novel raises a number of questions about love and art'. The novels he wrote after *The Ground Beneath Her Feet* similarly raise a variety of questions about love, art and other topics as well.

The historical novel, says Richard Bradford in *The Novel Now: Contemporary British Fiction*, has proved to be 'the most popular and fascinating subgenre' of recent years.[16] Many contemporary historical novels are set in the nineteenth century, and this is largely because the strictures of the Victorian era have for many years been a source of fascination for today's permissive society. Of the historical novels published from the 1960s onward, John Fowles's *The French Lieutenant's Woman* (1969), set in 1867, is one of the best known and most widely read. The appeal of Fowles's novel lies partly in its irreverent view of mid-nineteenth-century rectitude, and partly in its artistic self-consciousness, for *The French Lieutenant's Woman* is a clear example of what Linda Hutcheon describes as 'historiographic metafiction' – historical fiction that comments self-consciously on the writing of history and/or fiction.[17] Fowles's self-consciousness is nowhere more apparent than in chapter thirteen, where he draws attention to the inappropriateness of making use of an omniscient narrator – an analogue to God – at a time when the existence of God has been widely questioned.

Historiographic metafiction is a postmodernist kind of fiction, and twenty-first-century historical novels, notes Richard Bradford, are often postmodernist, or, if not, make 'unapologetic, manipulative use of the conventions of realism'.[18] This is not always the case, however, and in Chapter 3 Lisa Fletcher notes that Hilary Mantel's two best-known novels, *Wolf Hall* (2009) and *Bring up the Bodies* (2012), are both conventional realist fictions written almost entirely in the present tense. 'The novelist Margaret Atwood', says Fletcher, 'sees Mantel's use of present-tense narration as a strategy to avoid one of the "pitfalls" of historical fiction, the exaggeration of the strangeness of the past so that readers feel alienated.'[19] Mantel wants readers to feel as though they are on the scene, witnessing historical events as they take place: she is committed to presenting us, in *Wolf Hall* and *Bring up the Bodies*, with as accurate a picture of Thomas Cromwell and the court of Henry VIII as possible. Cromwell, comments Fletcher, is 'her vehicle to the distant past. Like his twenty-first-century creator, Cromwell is a rare person in that he likes "everything squared up and precise" *and* "will allow some drift at the margins".'

Another conventional historical novelist is Adam Foulds, who turned to historical fiction after writing a novel set in the present, *The Truth about These Strange Times* (2007), and also a narrative poem, *The Broken Word* (2008), about the Mau Mau uprising in Kenya in the 1950s. His first historical novel, *The Quickening Maze* (2009), is set in nineteenth-century England and focuses on the poet John Clare, whose mental instability led to his confinement to a mental asylum in the country. In Chapter 13 Dominic Head argues that the restriction of Clare's movements to within the grounds of the asylum is emblematic of 'the historical circumstance of enclosure – or, rather, that final stage in a centuries-long process of enclosure that was modernity's final *coup de grâce* for the traditional rural community'. 'Clare's significance is, then, not just that he is [in Foulds's words] "a key figure of ecological literature" – indeed, "our greatest ecological poet" – but that his plight anticipates our plight, in a continuum of ecological disaster.'

Foulds's second historical novel, *In the Wolf's Mouth* (2014), is similarly concerned with the relationship between man and nature. Throughout, frequent reference is made to Kenneth Grahame's *The Wind in the Willows* (1908), which is used, says Head, to bring to mind 'the idealism of classical pastoral' in a novel concerned with the horrors of modern warfare. Much of the action of the novel takes place in Sicily, where Allied troops free the local farmers from Mussolini's oppression, but at the same time create an acute shortage of food. Young Sicilian women find that they have no choice but to prostitute themselves to the Allied soldiers in return for tins of meat, prompting the main character, a young soldier named Will Walker, to reflect that 'this was the whole thing. You killed people with guns and machines, smashed homes to bits, and in the ruins you fucked hungry survivors in exchange for [food].'

Sarah Waters's historical novels display, says Susana Onega in Chapter 14, 'a striking generic hybridity, with elements of the sensational novel, the historical romance, the war novel, the London novel and the trauma novel, among others'. Waters's doctoral thesis was on lesbian and gay historical fiction, and her own novels are concerned with homosexual characters who live in a predominantly heterosexual world. *Fingersmith* (2003), comments Onega, is 'a bawdy lesbian picaresque intrigue that combines elements of the "seduced and abandoned maiden" romance, the "rags-to-riches tale", and the classical topos of the exchange or confusion of identical children'. There are also elements of Dickens in the novel, and in particular a clear debt to *Oliver Twist*. For the most part Waters's historical novels situate her, says Onega, 'as a feminist writer with a thematic focus on lesbianism and as a postmodernist writer of historiographic metafictions'.

To this she adds, however, that Waters's most recent novel, *The Paying Guests* (2014), is an example of conventional realist fiction, 'a pastiche of "the domestic novel", a deceptively transparent type of novel created by early feminist writers like Elizabeth Taylor and . . . Elizabeth Bowen'. Set in 1922, the novel describes the lesbian relationship that develops between a young woman named Frances Wray and her lodger, Lilian Barber. The two women accidentally kill Lilian's husband Leonard, and when a young man is unjustly charged and put on trial, they shrink from confessing their guilt. Frances reflects that the jury 'had no idea how decency, loyalty, courage, how it all shrivelled away when one was frightened'. Nevertheless, there is a fairy-tale ending: the young man is found not guilty, thanks to the testimony of a man who comes forward at the last minute.

Like Sarah Waters, James Robertson wrote a doctoral thesis on historical fiction, though his was on the construction and expression of Scottish patriotism in the works of Sir Walter Scott (1989). Here, says Cairns Craig in Chapter 15, Robertson argues that 'Scott created a version of *Scottish* patriotism that was contained safely in the past so that it would not conflict with the *British* patriotism of a Scotland now committed [after the Battle of Culloden in 1745] to Union and Empire'. His first novel, *The Fanatic* (2000), is set partly in the seventeenth century and partly in 1997, in the weeks before the establishment of a Scottish Parliament, when the question of Scotland's continuing relationship to England was being widely discussed. The two periods are linked by Andrew Carlin, a history student who discovers a secret book containing a vivid description of what happened; however, before Carlin can finish reading it, both the book and the librarian who provided it disappear. If this seems an odd feature of the novel, its purpose is to remind us – as the librarian does before disappearing – that history is a ghostly affair. 'What's real, Mr Carlin?' asks the librarian. 'We say history's real. It really happened. But we can't prove it. We can't touch it.' In his Introduction to *Scottish Ghost Stories*, Robertson comments that 'it may be our ancestors had access to doors now locked and bolted to all but a few of us. The "ghost" opens a door which empirical, realist narrative does not know exists and points to possibilities that are excluded by the mode in which modern history is written.'[20]

While there is often a historical dimension to the work of postcolonial novelists, Zadie Smith's *White Teeth* (2000) is set in the present. *White Teeth* attracted considerable media attention when it was first published, not only because Smith was only twenty-four when she was paid an advance of £250,000 for it, but also because it represented a new and different kind of postcolonial fiction. In the past, postcolonial fiction had been taken to mean the writings of people whose countries had at one time been colonised by Western imperial powers. Some postcolonial writers were concerned with life in their home country, both before and after it had been granted its independence, while others dwelt on emigration to the country that had wielded power over their homeland.[21] Often the novels written by postcolonial immigrants dwelt on the prejudice that the British exhibit against non-white people from former colonies. What is different about *White Teeth* is that it pictures Britain not in postcolonial but in multicultural terms. Smith has 'a perfect ear for speech', says Gretchen Gerzina in Chapter 4; she presents us with an 'assemblage of cultures, argots, races and classes', speaking 'to a contemporary audience of a London that had been irrevocably altered by immigration and multiculturalism'. Smith's is a new voice for the new millennium: she is of a generation of people who think of themselves as British, and consider their colonial past to be irrelevant.

Another postcolonial novelist-with-a-difference is the Pakistani-born Mohsin Hamid, whose first novel, *Moth Smoke*, was published in 2002. Hamid writes not about Britain's colonisation of Pakistan, but instead about the concept of globalisation, the idea (in this context) that, under American influence, the world is moving closer and closer to a state of cultural homogeneity. Of greater interest than Britain's colonial influence, says Janet Wilson in Chapter 16, is 'the impact of changing post-imperial US politics, economics and educational opportunity upon the transnational youth of Pakistan'. The youthful, privileged party set of Lahore are clearly devoted to making money in the same aggressive way as their counterparts in the United States. Though Daru, the main character, initially has a good job in international banking, he is abruptly dismissed and finds it impossible to secure a new position. He has an affair with his best friend's wife, starts using heroin and finally becomes a drug dealer. In a postmodern turn, Hamid makes a judge, wigged and robed, of the reader, inviting us to conclude that globalisation is of no greater benefit to Pakistan than was British colonisation.

Andrea Levy focuses on the relationship between Britain and Jamaica. In her most recent novel, *Long Song* (2010), Levy presents us with the reminiscences of a fictional black Caribbean slave, and in the novel that preceded it, *Small Island* (2004), with the story of two people who arrive from Jamaica in 1948 on the SS *Empire Windrush*, the ship that is 'usually seen', as Sue Thomas comments in Chapter 17, 'as marking the beginning of post-war West Indian emigration to Britain, and the bicentenary in 2007 of the British abolition of its slave trade respectively'. Amongst its passengers are two characters, Gilbert and Hortense, who arrive in Britain in the expectation of beginning a new life in a land of milk and honey, only to come up against the racist hostility of the white British public.

In recognition of the fact that there are still racial tensions in Britain, *Small Island* was made the focal point of a unique mass-reading project in 2007. This 'involved the distribution of 50,000 free copies of Andrea Levy's novel, along with 80,000 copies of a glossy A5 readers' guide. It generated 100 separate events (including library talks, book group discussions, competitions, exhibitions), and 60 school workshops.'[22] To date it is one of Britain's best-known twenty-first-century postcolonial novels.

In the novels of Aminatta Forna, who was born in Scotland but grew up in Sierra Leone, we find another aspect of postcolonial writing. Although she has written about her experience of Africa in several of her books, Forna stands out from other recent postcolonial novelists in that her novel *The Hired Man* (2013) is set neither in Britain nor in a former British colony, but instead in Croatia. Its first-person narrator, Duro Kolak, is the hired man of the title, and the story he tells is of agreeing to help a visiting English tourist and real estate investor, Laura, restore a cottage in the fictional village of Gost. The authors of Chapter 18, Françoise Lionnet and Jennifer MacGregor, find in Laura's motives for buying the cottage an impulse to colonise. Oblivious, as colonisers often are, to local history and customs, Laura wants to ready it for rental to British tourists. It might seem that Duro benefits from the work she brings him, since it is a good source of income; however, she is unaware that he has an ulterior motive for working for her. In the recent Serbo-Croatian civil war,

Duro's lover, a woman named Anka, has been killed, and the opportunity to renovate what was originally Anka's cottage is also a way of reminding the local community of the civil war, something most would like to forget. Forna's overall purpose in *The Hired Man* is to reveal not only the exploitative character of those who colonise but also the way in which the colonised seek to redress the balance – to compensate for the fact that they are being exploited.

While it would have been desirable to include more contemporary British novelists in this collection, it was especially important to supply the reader with a range of writers to supplement the selection discussed in the predecessor to this volume, *The Contemporary British Novel Since 1980*. Considerations of space made it impossible to supply a list of each author's novels at the end of each essay, together with a list of the literary prizes they have won. Instead I have referred readers in every case to the British Council website (https://literature.britishcouncil.org/writers), and have asked each contributor to supply a list of books and/or articles at the end of each essay for those who wish to read at greater length about the novelists represented in this volume.

NOTES

1. For a fuller discussion of Lodge, see Richard Bradford's excellent *The Novel Now: Contemporary British Fiction* (Oxford: Blackwell, 2007). On p. 3 Bradford says that one of the objects of his book will be to 'test Lodge's thesis and to give an account of what has happened to the novel from the 1970s to 2005'.
2. I am referring here to an essay collection I co-edited some years ago with Sarah C. E. Ross, entitled *The Contemporary British Novel* (Edinburgh: Edinburgh University Press, 2005). The collection was co-published in the US as *The Contemporary British Novel Since 1980* (New York: Palgrave Macmillan, 2005). In the interests of clarity, I have used the American title throughout.
3. Included in *The Contemporary British Novel Since 2000* but not in the earlier volume are: Kate Atkinson, Aminatta Forna, Adam Foulds, Sarah Hall, Mohsin Hamid, Andrea Levy, Hilary Mantel, David Mitchell, Maggie O'Farrell, James Robertson, Ali Smith, Alan Warner and Sarah Waters.
4. At trial, Radclyffe Hall's lesbian novel was found to be obscene, and all copies of it were ordered to be destroyed. For further information see <https://en.wikipedia.org/wiki/Radclyffe_Hall> (last accessed 9 June 2016).
5. Ian Watt, *The Rise of the Novel* (1957; Harmondsworth: Penguin, 1968), p. 10. For a fuller introduction to French realism, see Damian Grant, *Realism in Literature* (London: Methuen, 1970).
6. Frederic Jameson, 'Postmodernism, or the Cultural Logic of Late Capitalism', in K. M. Newton (ed.), *Twentieth-Century Literary Theory: A Reader*, 2nd edn (New York: St. Martin's Press, 1997), p. 267.
7. Jean-François Lyotard, 'The Postmodern Condition', in Keith Jenkins (ed.), *The Postmodern History Reader* (London: Routledge, 1997), p. 6.
8. Brian McHale, *The Cambridge Introduction to Postmodernism* (Cambridge: Cambridge University Press, 2015), pp. 14–15.
9. Anthony Giddens, *The Consequences of Modernity* (Cambridge: Polity, 1990), p. 64.
10. David Mitchell, 'Genesis', *The Guardian*, 16 April 2005, <http://www.guardian.co.uk/books/2005/apr/16/featuresreviews.guardianreview23> (last accessed 9 June 2016).

11. McHale, *Introduction*, p. 176, draws attention to Jeffrey T. Nealon's *Post-Postmodernism, or the Cultural Logic of Just in Time Capitalism* (Stanford: Stanford University Press, 2012).
12. McHale, *Introduction*, p. 178.
13. Ibid., p. 180.
14. Ibid., p. 15.
15. Fiona Tolan, ' "Everyone Has Left Something Here": The Storyteller-Historian in Kate Atkinson's *Behind the Scenes at the Museum*', *Critique: Studies in Contemporary Fiction*, 50 (2009), 275–92; 276.
16. Bradford, *The Novel Now*, p. 80.
17. Linda Hutcheon, *A Poetics of Postmodernism: History, Theory, Fiction* (London: Routledge, 1988), p. 105.
18. Bradford, *The Novel Now*, p. 99.
19. Margaret Atwood, '*Bring up the Bodies* by Hilary Mantel – Review', *The Guardian*, 4 May 2012, <http://www.theguardian.com/books/2012/may/04/bring-up-the-bodies-hilary-mantel-review> (last accessed 13 June 2016).
20. *Scottish Ghost Stories*, ed. James Robertson (London: Warner Books, 1996), p. ix.
21. For a fuller discussion of the term 'postcolonial', see Bruce King, in Acheson and Ross (eds), *The Contemporary British Novel*, p. 85.
22. Danielle Fuller and James Procter, 'Reading as "Social Glue"? Book Groups, Multiculture, and the *Small Island* Read 2007', *Moving Worlds: A Journal of Transcultural Writings*, 9.2 (2009), 30.

FURTHER READING

Bradford, Richard, *The Novel Now: Contemporary British Fiction* (Oxford: Blackwell, 2007).
De Groot, Jerome, *The Historical Novel*, The New Critical Idiom Series (London: Routledge, 2010).
Grant, Damian, *Realism in Literature* (London: Methuen, 1970).
Hutcheon, Linda, *A Poetics of Postmodernism: History, Theory, Fiction* (London: Routledge, 1988).
King, Bruce, *The Internationalisation of English Literature* (Oxford: Oxford University Press, 2004).
Lukács, Georg, *The Historical Novel*, trans. Hannah and Stanley Mitchell (London: Merlin, 1974).
McHale, Brian, *The Cambridge Introduction to Postmodernism* (Cambridge: Cambridge University Press, 2015).
Nealon, Jeffrey T., *Post-Postmodernism, or the Cultural Logic of Just in Time Capitalism* (Stanford: Stanford University Press, 2012).
Watt, Ian, *The Rise of the Novel* (1957; Harmondsworth: Penguin, 1968).

PART I

Four Voices for the New Millennium

CHAPTER 1

Ian McEwan: Lies and Deceptions

David Punter

Since 2000, Ian McEwan has published six novels: *Atonement* (2001), *Saturday* (2005), *On Chesil Beach* (2007), *Solar* (2010), *Sweet Tooth* (2012) and *The Children Act* (2014). To separate off this body of work from his previous publications is inevitably somewhat arbitrary; nevertheless, especially considering McEwan's frequently close involvement with historical events, it can fairly be suggested that these novels represent a sustained attempt to refract, as through a many-sided prism, some of the key concerns of the twenty-first century, as well as some of the major themes which have reverberated through his work since the days of *First Love, Last Rites* (1975), *The Cement Garden* and *In Between the Sheets* (both 1978).

The theme on which I want to concentrate here is the characterisation of the past by lies and deceptions. These are often not intentional lies: they are not told, or enacted, with the express purpose of deception, but their texture is slippery, they participate in a more general unreliability of language, and here surely lies one of the crucial paradoxes of McEwan's work: that a writing so precise, so elegantly textured, so minutely detailed, so regularly exquisite in its dealings with inner states, should simultaneously be devoted to an exposition of how language itself has continually distorting effects. As in Edgar Allan Poe's 'The Purloined Letter' (1845), the hiding place is in plain sight; but also plain sight itself has its hiding places, it can be revisited, rewritten, the word, whether spoken or written, is never stable, it is only an attempt to make still those floods of language and history which are continually restless: like the pebbles washing up on the shore of Chesil Beach.

Can writing, McEwan asks, put history 'straight' in some way, or does it serve only further to confound those moments in the past which continue to set the parameters for the stories we tell ourselves in the present? Perhaps equally important is the question as to whether such writing can actually produce or encourage real communication, or whether it is permanently in-turned, self-justifying: why do we need to tell stories in the first place if not to turn the world into a place in which we can live, which requires that the world accepts, at least to a degree, the version of it which will allow us to flourish; or, at least, to survive?

In a review of *Saturday*, Zoe Heller refers to what she calls 'vintage McEwan nightmare';[1] of course, we could further refer this back to old tropes about history as a nightmare from which one never awakes, but it is nevertheless an inept comment on McEwan, or at least on recent McEwan, for these six novels are not nightmares. They do not have the texture of nightmare, or even of dream; they do not have the heat of nightmare, or the catastrophic elation of dream; on the contrary, they are 'cool'. I mean that word in many of its senses (and indeed it is one of the few slang words to have retained a recognisable sense over at least seven recent decades, from the jazz age to the age of instant mobile communication), some of them to be admired, some to be deprecated. But all of those senses have to do not only with emotion itself but with how one can handle emotion, or how emotion can handle our selves; to do with how we may be trapped by the past, or by our own or others' misrepresentations of the past, or with how we might struggle to liberate our selves from previous selves, previous lives, possibilities that might have been, roads not travelled – Elizabeth Bowen, it seems to me, is the surest avatar here.[2]

In *Atonement*, Briony Tallis misconstrues a situation. She may do so by mistake; she may do so from a version of sibling rivalry; she may do so out of a sense of melodramatic self-aggrandisement; she may do so because of her self-perceived requirements as a budding writer of fiction. Her misconstrual of the scene she sees enacted between her sister and the young man Robbie has terrible consequences. I do not intend to rehearse the plot here, which is well known both from the book and from the film version, but instead will focus, as I will do in the other novels, on a single brief scene. Robbie, the victim of Briony's error, is struggling back from the war towards the debacle of Dunkirk; horrors are happening all around him, as the retreating forces do everything in their power to stop a potent supply of materiel from falling into the hands of the opposing forces – trucks and guns are blown up, horses are shot, roads and bridges are destroyed. He and the others

> had been going for an hour when they heard behind them a rhythmic thudding, like the ticking of a gigantic clock. They turned to look back. At first sight it seemed that an enormous horizontal door was flying up the road towards them. It was a platoon of Welsh Guards in good order, rifles at the slope, led by a second-lieutenant. They came by at a forced march, their gaze fixed forwards, their arms swinging high. The stragglers stood aside to let them through. These were cynical times, but no one risked a catcall. The show of discipline and cohesion was shaming. It was a relief when the Guards had pounded out of sight and the rest could resume their introspective trudging.[3]

A tiny moment, but in it a host of oppositions are called up. Opposition between order and chaos; between time which is measurable and time which seems only to trail off into an unthinkable distance; between the holding together of an organised self and a version of introspection which can put no shape around disparate experiences; therefore between that history which might be a version of the narrator's art (even if that narrative of the body is held together by an officer as lowly as a sub-lieutenant) and the other history which comprises mud, dirt, blood and incompetence. The clock, the door, the forced march: these are the signifiers of control, yet they pass by as though, indeed, in a kind of dream: they momentarily challenge and perhaps illumine the sludge of quotidian life, but once they have gone they come to represent – in memory – a kind of ideal which at no point truly touches upon the brutal necessities of accommodation to pointless conflict.

We, as opposed to these 'guards' but like many of the protagonists of McEwan's novels, are mere 'stragglers'; we glimpse the plot of history, but we are then swept away again, we cannot grasp the order needed. Similarly, we cannot grasp the art of narrative; or rather, we can never be sure who the narrator actually is. We learn towards the end of *Atonement* that much of the book has in fact – whatever 'in fact' might mean in this slipping, sliding terrain – been the version told by Briony herself; that the consoling fiction which appears to provide some kind of resolution to the disastrous misconceptions which she has herself engendered has merely been the result of her continuing attempt to shape the story. This might be an attempt at self-forgiveness; it might be an attempt at restitution towards those whom she has injured; since Briony herself is suffering by the end from dementia, from the ongoing illness of old age – the illness brought on by old age, or the illness which *is* old age – it might be an illusion, a distorted hope not only that all will become well but that all has already been well, in an alternative world, one where we can offend yet find ourselves with our slates, our writing paraphernalia, cleansed of guilt.

Curious moments, moments when history might be rewritten, for McEwan continue to make waves, to cause reverberations. Although his next novel *Saturday* takes place on the day of the major London protest against the Iraq war, and although the novel has a great deal to say, much of it acute, painful, full of intimate detail, about the relations between politics and the emotions, nevertheless it is possible to argue that much of the novel follows from a single moment when the protagonist, Henry Perowne, is driving. His driving, both in general and on this specific occasion, is described with an enormous wealth of detail, but the focus comes to be on a single moment – perhaps an inadvertent moment, but then, as McEwan repeatedly reminds us, the very concept of an 'accident', whether it be one with no particular consequences, one which occasions a major family or marital rift, or one which starts, or continues, a world war, is itself a question of judgement. Parapraxis would be the name of the game (the game, in this case, being squash, where the most minute of high-speed errors can have the most cataclysmic of consequences, although only – or so we suppose – within the confines of the 'court'). Here is the moment:

> He's driving with unconscious expertise into the narrow column of space framed on the right by a kerb-flanked cycle path, and on the left by a line of parked cars. It's from this line that the thought springs, and with it, the snap of a wing mirror cleanly sheared and the whine of sheet-steel surfaces sliding under pressure as two cars pour into a gap wide enough for one. Perowne's instant decision at the moment of impact is to accelerate as he swerves right. There are other sounds – the staccato rattle of the red car on his left side

raking a half-dozen stationary vehicles, and the thwack of concrete against rubber, like an amplified single handclap as the Mercedes mounts the cycle-path kerb. His back wheel hits the kerb too. Then he's ahead of the intruder and braking. The slewed cars stop thirty yards apart, engines cut, and for a moment there's silence, and no one gets out.[4]

I have not elsewhere come across such a detailed account of a minor traffic accident (apart from in legal situations, to which we shall return in The Children Act), but then such incidents have gained a specifically twenty-first-century inflection with the rise of that peculiar form of property-based violence we choose to call 'road rage'. But this is not the point: the point is again the threat, even if here temporarily withheld, of the clash between order and chaos; for the consequences which flow from this event include the closing scenes where Perowne performs an operation on the other driver, Baxter, who, he can tell, is suffering from the symptoms of Huntington's disease. These consequences also include a continuing series of reflections on the interpretations of the incident for relations within Perowne's family, all of whom view the matter in different ways, much as Perowne's own view of it varies and develops during the course of the day. When Perowne tells his wife Rosalind what has happened, she responds by saying, '"Of course it wasn't an abuse of authority. They could have killed you."'[5] This is not the conclusion he wanted her to reach – he arranged the details to prompt her in another direction, which underlines the shifting nature of perceptions of the past. Are there lies being told here, or is it more that no one version of history, even of immediate history, is stable?

Yet it is, of course, more complex even than this: the shearing of the wing mirror is 'clean', it is, after all, only an offence against an outlying part, and in its way a 'measure' of distance: if the wing is cleanly sheared, then the body can suffer no damage – or so it would appear until we hear (almost literally) the sounds of the 'raking' and the 'thwack'. But this hearing is then absolved, dismissed for the moment, within the moment, the 'moment under the moment', to quote Russell Hoban,[6] in the further moment of silence. What, one might ask, in McEwan *is* the 'moment of silence' – not merely the moment in terms of the minute slice of time, but the moment in terms of the import, the weight that comes to be brought to bear within silence, within that 'moment' when all is suspended, when history could go, as it always can, this way or that, when we are uncertain of outcome, swinging in the aftermath, uncertain whether what has just occurred – just occurred this immediate past moment – is, or is not, a matter of moment?

Or to put it a little less flightily: what is important and what is not? How do large, grand political events and reactions interact with those scenarios which we may prefer to construe as private (and perhaps the point can be no more clearly staged than within the confines of a 'private car')? Such grand movements, or at least such references to the larger outside world, are certainly all too present in the otherwise enclosed world of On Chesil Beach, which is sometimes considered to be the story of two young people whose hopes for intimacy – and indeed hopes for their own lives – are thwarted by their own repressions; and these are, like all repressions, not of them alone but referable back to all sorts of other causes, including hints of abuse. Here again we come across lies, deceptions, self-deceptions.

For *On Chesil Beach*, often considered by virtue of its brevity and perhaps of its single-minded attention to an ongoing scenario to be a lesser work of McEwan's, has its own highly developed dynamic in terms of narrative; in terms of history and who tells it; and in terms of what is said, what is lied about deliberately or inadvertently. It is a pain-filled book, and yet a gentle book, where we as readers are allowed, or encouraged, to look back on wasted lives and to contemplate what might have been different. Indeed, in the service of this perspective, this *longue durée*, McEwan has on occasion a seemingly cavalier disregard for past and present, as in this emblematic passage which positions us as readers in a totally different timespace from the protagonists:

> Their courtship had been a pavane, a stately unfolding, bound by protocols never agreed or voiced, but generally observed. Nothing was ever discussed – nor did they feel the lack of intimate talk. These were matters beyond words, beyond definition. The language and practice of therapy, the currency of feelings diligently shared, mutually analysed, were not yet in general circulation. While one heard of wealthier people going in for psychoanalysis, it was not yet customary to regard oneself in everyday terms as an enigma, as an exercise in narrative history, or as a problem waiting to be solved.[7]

We are here in the 'presence' of a voice from the 'present', looking back at a previous era with a wealth of hindsight, and yet the voice trembles and wavers. Where, for example, does the word 'diligently' come from? Is this a word of the present, applied by those with a slight scorn for the 'culture of self-exposure'; or does it also refer to a certain 'diligence' which we might expect to be a 'property' of these all too 'proper' lives, as being lived in 1962, at the outset of a historical period when so many things were about to change? It might be taken that Edward and Florence are attempting, each in a different but related way, to be 'diligent' about their lives, their behaviours, their emotions, while all the while they are on the brink of a precipice, the stones and pebbles on which they are standing are about to undergo a seismic shift, one which cannot be prevented by diligence but will leave at least Edward, at the end of the book, as a creature of total diligence and routine, 'a large, stout man with receding white hair and a pink, healthy face',[8] regulating his life with long walks and a banishing of painful introspection. 'On Chesil Beach he could have called out to Florence, he could have gone after her'; but instead he 'stood in cold and righteous silence',[9] a silence which reflects the burden of lost lives down the ages. A silence in which so many things might have been said as we stand, at a loss, in the 'garden of forking paths'.[10]

To return to my key passage, it is worth also dwelling for a moment on the phrase 'going in for', as though a resort to therapy or analysis might be a hobby, an indulgence. The voice here is surely one of the early 1960s, or perhaps even of Edward's and Florence's formative years in the previous decade. But perhaps it is also the voice or register of the later Edward, a man apparently 'wholly encrusted by convention',[11] who has been traumatically 'stopped' by the events on Chesil Beach and prefers to reside in a set of past attitudes rather than attempt to deal with change.

Perhaps one of the more interesting aspects of McEwan's next novel, *Solar*, is that it was awarded the Bollinger Everyman Wodehouse Prize for comic writing; it may or may not be a comic novel, but it would certainly conform to P. G. Wodehouse's exacting standards in terms of complexity of plotting as well as in the extraordinary tour de force of the gathering of narrative threads at the conclusion. Like much of McEwan's fiction, it is set across a number of timescales; it is also a novel which is deeply concerned with the processes of writing and reading, especially as these intersect with questions of lies and deceit. The protagonist, Michael Beard, is a much-travelled academic and scientist who appears to be a champion of solar energy, although he has in fact stolen much of the research for which he is acclaimed. His private life is stormy; he is currently married to his fifth wife, to whom he is unfaithful. Here we find him en route from a farewell party:

> For all the hours he spent on journeys, he was not a well-adapted traveller, not because he was chaotic or fearful, but because long journeys always brought him up against a certain mental deficiency, an emptiness, a restless boredom that was, he thought ... the expression of his true state, habitually obscured by the daily round or by sleep. He was not able to read seriously on an airplane. Even on firm ground he never read full-length books all the way through. ... At best he read popular science magazines like the *Scientific American* ... But even then his concentration was marred, for a lifetime's habit made him inconveniently watchful for his own name. He saw it as if in bold. It could leap out at him from an unread double page of small print, and sometimes he could sense it coming before the page-turn.[12]

No doubt Beard's inability to read to the end of a full-length book is connected to his five marriages; and no doubt this is further connected to his all too obvious narcissism. But perhaps what is more interesting, and indeed distressing, here is the 'emptiness'; where McEwan's previous protagonists have been, at least in certain senses, all too 'full' – full of ambition, full of the rich life of the *haute bourgeoisie*, or more disastrously full of unexpressed inhibition, full, at any event, of narratives they tell about themselves – Beard reflexively senses in himself a void.

It might be going too far to suggest this as a diagnosis of the specific condition of the twenty-first century, although it is no doubt significant that the dates of the various sections are expressed with precision (2000, 2005, 2009). But what is implied here about short concentration span is presumably as true of the general readership of the *Scientific American* as it is of Beard himself. At all events, there is a certain circularity here: Beard can only read popular accounts of science; these popular accounts are where his own name might figure; he thus becomes a 'popular' figure, not least to himself, a creature of the surface – a trope which is regulated and underlined by the ongoing revelation that he is in fact a plagiarist, who continues to sustain his reputation through the promulgation of a web of lies.

This behaviour is, of course, not without its penalties: in particular, at the end of the novel it is unclear whether Beard is suffering, or about to suffer, a heart attack which might prove fatal. And if this is the case, then it is equally unclear as to which of his vices or sins this might be due to: prime suspect, by the end, is gluttony, although sloth, lust and avarice are also well in the picture. Yet Beard is not lacking in self-awareness, and even, on occasion, in a certain kind of irony; the problem lies in the transition from perception to practice, and consequently – and inevitably – in the avoidance of repetition.

And as the title suggests, something far more serious than the plight of a fatally stuck ageing professor is at stake here, namely the very possibility of 'progress', as signified by solar power. Can any 'true' development be immune to the pressures of a far different story, which would focus on the baser motivations of profit, chicanery and the search for 'power', in a different but related sense? How, again, do we write and read the history of such developments? Would we prefer a narrative of purity – pure science engaged in by pure people for pure ends – or is it better to experience the demolition of the illusion (as here in the destruction of Beard's solar panels) so that we can have a better sense of the complexity of history, an enhanced awareness of the accidental ways in which change is permitted or blocked?

On Chesil Beach is set largely in the 1960s; *Solar* in the 2000s; *Sweet Tooth* returns us to the 1970s. And it takes us, from a different angle, into a world already inhabited by ghosts: Graham Greene, perhaps, certainly the increasingly incisive John le Carré – in, for example, *Absolute Friends* (2003). But the characteristic McEwan twist is also here, in the sense that there remains with us an enduring question as to who has written this complex account of a cultural 'sting' operation which, apparently, goes badly wrong – Serena, the protagonist, herself, or Thomas Haley, the writer whom she is supposed to manipulate and exploit in the continuing Cold War.

One way of identifying the key to this lies in Haley's closing letter to Serena, which both turns the 'plot' on its head and brings into sharp focus the network of deceits and impersonations which may, as McEwan so often reminds us, constitute the essence of the writerly, the heart of narrative. 'To recreate you on the page', Haley says,

> I had to become you and understand you (this is what novels demand), and in doing that, well, the inevitable happened. When I poured myself into your skin I should have guessed at the consequences. I still love you. No, that's not it. I love you more. You may think we're too mired in deceit, that we've told each other enough lies to outlast a lifetime, that our deception and humiliation have doubled the reasons for going our separate ways. I prefer to think they've cancelled out and that we're too entwined in mutual surveillance to let each other go.[13]

'To let each other go'; the phrase encompasses what we might reasonably call 'enduring love',[14] but it also encompasses the plight of characters locked together in an impossible dance, where each has formed the other according to their own image, where to separate would involve a total deconstruction and reconstruction of the individual. How, the novel asks – and McEwan has asked this before, in different ways and in different discourses – can parting ever be truly possible? Or, indeed, at a moment of parting, how can we ever be sure that the stories we have told, and are going to continue to tell, about this or that relationship are true; is such truth ever possible, especially when it would need to be shared among so many 'interested' parties?

The metaphor of the 'sweet tooth' has a number of referents. Among them are an addiction to fiction, itself in several different senses – the sense at the 'end' of a novel that all one might wish is that it might carry on; the corresponding sense at the end of a stage in life that it might be possible to recreate the savour of that which is past; the sense that whatever it is that has given pleasure might also be the source of decay, of a rotting in the mouth, of a corruption of speech, of language – how will it ever be possible to speak the truth when one has been (collaboratively) 'mired in deceit'?

But the 'sweet tooth' is also the tooth which bites, and which, vampirically, gives pleasure in the biting: as Dracula's victims become enmeshed in a search for pleasure, so too do we become enmeshed in pain and in the repetition, the recapitulation of pain. Indeed, we dwell on that pain as we might suck on a painful tooth, seeking to numb but also to extract the last twinge. 'Face it, Serena,' Haley says, 'the sun is setting on this decaying affair, and the moon and stars are too,' yet it is also true that 'you lied to me, I spied on you. It was delicious . . .'[15] Nothing so sweet as lies, nothing so sweet as subterfuge; nothing, we might add, so urgent as the avoidance of the publicisation of humiliation.

Does McEwan's latest novel, *The Children Act*, pursue this set of themes? In one way at least, it seems even darker than those which preceded it, namely in that it outlines in desperate detail the potentially – and in one case actually – fatal consequences of telling the truth, whether that be legal or emotional. Fiona Maye is a High Court judge; her husband has announced to her – in a singular effort at apparent truth which is nonetheless inflictive of a wound of the most serious kind – that he is about to embark on an affair. At the same time she is professionally involved in a case concerning a family where the son, the appropriately named Adam, is being denied blood transfusions because of his parents' religious beliefs: Fiona steps outside the box, goes to visit the young man, and ends up in a position where he 'adopts' her as a mother-figure and, when she is unable or unwilling to reciprocate, kills himself. What is happening here is, at least in part, a fracturing of Fiona's self, and of her responsibilities – on the one hand to the law, as evidenced in her careful writing of legal judgements, and on the other to other people, reflected in the difficulties in her communication with her husband and in her inappropriate actions in relation to Adam.

The children, it might be said, certainly act, or at least one of them does; and as a consequence Fiona's duty to guard the perimeters is fatally compromised. But what perimeters, what boundaries, is she guarding? Her childlessness, at least in part as a consequence of her commitment to her judicial work (although there are issues here also to do with her own sense of an 'entitled' career), could be seen to spark both her husband's defection and also her vulnerability to Adam's needs, as well as her inability to respond fully to those needs.

But it perhaps goes without saying, in a writer so alert to cultural and social conditions as McEwan, that it would be foolish – as well as blameworthy – to rest these matters with Fiona Maye's career choices – or even, indeed, with the way in which her own story might be written, by herself or by others. Yet she herself, of course, is a writer, in this case a writer of legal judgements, and perhaps it is here that one might look:

> The draft of Fiona's judgement was twenty-one pages long, spread in a wide fan face down on the floor, waiting for her to take it up, a sheet at a time, to mark with soft pencil. . . . Among fellow judges, Fiona Maye was praised, even in her absence, for crisp prose, almost ironic, almost warm, and for the compact terms in which she laid out a dispute. . . . Her own view was that with each passing year she inclined a little more to an exactitude some might have called pedantry, to the unassailable definition that might pass one day into frequent citation . . .[16]

One of the striking things about this passage is to do with materiality of the word, the materiality of *these* words: for the law is, above all, the word as enactment, as performative. Yet there is room within these words, within these careful phrasings, for style, and a style that would surely be the envy of many a novelist: 'almost ironic, almost warm' – we might interpret these words to signify, or even effect, a bridge between human feeling and the necessarily impartial distance of the law. But perhaps most commanding of all is this 'soft pencil': judgement is difficult, discrimination among views of affairs all of which may have some observable right on their side even more so, but in the end all that might separate one life-changing outcome from another is the set of marks made by a 'soft pencil', something so easy to erase and yet so compelling in its direction of the flow of the final document which will ensue.

And so again we have, as so often in McEwan, a series of questions about writing and the nature of the writer. And here in particular, the question is posed in terms of the writer, Fiona Maye, in the midst of a collapse of the relationship in life she held to be most stable, most firm: if that can demonstrate itself as undermined, then perhaps writing itself is also always in danger of being undermined, despite the extreme efforts made to ensure its veracity, its responsibility, its complex expression of complex human situations.

In McEwan's recent novels, then, there is a constantly recurring tension between writing as authoritative and writing at the mercy of wider flows of lies, deceptions, rewritings of history. Unlike many postmodernists, however, there is little relativism here: it is not at all that one account of the past is as good – or bad – as any other. It is true that McEwan shares with the postmodernists a sense that in the end writing is intricately bound up with power; but nonetheless there may be a truth to be found – or, to put it more accurately, a need to adhere to that possibility, to suggest that there might be – out there somewhere, and perhaps perennially unavailable – a truth that can somehow remedy the ills of the present, those ills of the social condition which continually inhabit McEwan's writings, and those other ills of the body and the mind which will always precede and colour our attempts to produce the truth.

From Briony Tallis's distortions of the world, occasioned by her conception of herself as a writer, through Michael Beard's uncomfortable and never fully convincing attempts to rewrite history, to Fiona Maye's endeavours to maintain a 'cool', clear line of argument against the destabilising force of breakdown, the struggle with what truth means and what value and power we can, or should, attach to it remains the driving force in these novels. Words may be writ on water, or on the sliding stones of Chesil Beach, or in the cases and almanacs of the law, but the question remains as to whether, in the end, it is we who have power over them or whether the words, the narratives, the versions of events that survive or fail to survive under the pressure of all manner of distributions of power, exert their sombre, sometimes feeble yet sometimes adamantine power over us, at the mercy, as perhaps we are, of our social history; our family history; in the end, whatever it might mean, our 'case history', which will always be fraught, or freighted, with the distortions we seem to need in order to maintain our selves.

NOTES

1. Zoe Heller, review of Ian McEwan's *Saturday*, *New York Times*, 20 March 2005.
2. See, for example, Elizabeth Bowen, *The House in Paris* (London: Gollancz, 1935).
3. Ian McEwan, *Atonement* (London: Jonathan Cape, 2001), pp. 240–1.
4. Ian McEwan, *Saturday* (London: Jonathan Cape, 2005), p. 81.
5. Ibid., p. 268.
6. See Russell Hoban, *The Moment under the Moment* (London: Jonathan Cape, 1992).
7. Ian McEwan, *On Chesil Beach* (London: Jonathan Cape, 2007), p. 21.
8. Ibid., p. 164.
9. Ibid., p. 166.
10. The reference is to Jorge Luis Borges, 'The Garden of Forking Paths' (1941), in *Ficciones*, ed. Anthony Kerrigan (New York: Grove Press, 1962).
11. See my 'Philip Larkin: Humiliation and Survival', in C. C. Barfoot (ed.), *In Black and Gold* (Amsterdam: Rodopi, 1994), p. 131.
12. Ian McEwan, *Solar* (London: Jonathan Cape, 2010), p. 49.
13. Ian McEwan, *Sweet Tooth* (London: Jonathan Cape, 2012), p. 369.
14. See Ian McEwan, *Enduring Love* (London: Jonathan Cape, 1997).
15. McEwan, *Sweet Tooth*, pp. 366, 368.
16. Ian McEwan, *The Children Act* (London: Jonathan Cape, 2014), p. 14.

FURTHER READING

For an up-to-date list of Ian McEwan's novels, see the British Council website: <https://literature.britishcouncil.org/writer/ian-mcewan> (last accessed 10 June 2016).

Byrnes, Christina, *The Work of Ian McEwan: A Psychodynamic Approach* (London: Paupers' Press, 2002).
Head, Dominic, *Ian McEwan* (Manchester: Manchester University Press, 2007).
Roberts, Ryan, *Conversations with Ian McEwan* (Jackson: University Press of Mississippi, 2010).
Ryan, Kiernan, *Ian McEwan: Writers and their Work* (Tavistock: Northcote House, 1994).
Wells, Lynn, *Ian McEwan* (Basingstoke: Palgrave Macmillan, 2010).

CHAPTER 2

David Mitchell: Global Novelist of the Twenty-First Century

Brian Finney

David Mitchell's fiction has become synonymous with a new brand of narrative, one that combines the popular with the avant-garde, the local with the global, and individual with generic forms of subjectivity. His first novel, *Ghostwritten*, which appeared the year before the new century, with its nine chapters and a coda circling the globe from east to west, immediately identified him as a writer responding to a world transformed by globalisation and climate change. It won the *Mail on Sunday* John Llewellyn Rhys Prize for a book by a writer under thirty-five. In 2003, with *Ghostwritten* and *number9dream* (2001) behind him, Mitchell was selected as one of *Granta*'s Best of Young British Novelists. With the publication of his third novel, *Cloud Atlas* (2004), he was being acclaimed as 'clearly, a genius' (*New York Times*) and the book as 'an exciting, almost overwhelming masterpiece' (*Washington Times*).[1] *Cloud Atlas* sold a million hardback copies in North America and half a million in the UK. After the appearance of his fourth novel, *Black Swan Green* (2006), *Time* magazine listed him as sixteenth on its list of the hundred men and women 'whose talent, power, and moral example is transforming the world', and credited him with having 'created the twenty-first-century novel'.[2] Since then reviewers have continued to call him 'the greatest novelist of his generation', 'one of the most electric minds alive' and 'the best thing to happen to narrative since Daniel Defoe'.[3] Two of his seven novels have been short-listed for the Man Booker Prize and a further three long-listed. He is clearly an important, trend-setting twenty-first-century novelist.

Mitchell had an early childhood stammer, which he has said made him begin to 'live inside myself' and turn to books.[4] Eventually he studied English and American literature at the University of Kent, and stayed on to write an MA thesis on the postmodern novel. For the next eight years he lived in Japan, teaching English as a second language, and while there took six months off to travel to Europe from east to west, writing the stories he would combine to form his first novel, *Ghostwritten*. In

2002 he and his Japanese wife settled in Clonakilty, a small coastal town in County Cork, where they continue to live.

'Home', Mitchell has remarked, 'is more an emotional concept than a geographical one.'[5] *Ghostwritten*'s nine chapters are set in nine different places, successively in Okinawa, Tokyo, Hong Kong, China, Mongolia, St Petersburg, London, Ireland and New York. Mitchell has said that he 'wanted the book to travel east to west because it reverses the usual direction of Orientalism'.[6] Each chapter has a different first-person narrator and uses a different voice; no unifying narrative voice is privileged over the others. Nor does English predominate over Mitchell's transcriptions of other languages: the world is seen as disparate and yet connected in seemingly random ways. Major characters from one chapter turn up as minor players in another and have chance molecular collisions with its protagonists. Objects such as green pens, music recordings and book titles turn up in more than one chapter. Even phrases uttered by one character are repeated by a different one in another chapter. For instance, Quasar, the Japanese terrorist who narrates the first chapter, observes that '[h]igh streets are becoming the same all over the world, I suppose', which is reiterated word for word by Margarita, an attendant at the Hermitage Museum who is also an art thief, in chapter six.[7] Mitchell's depiction of 'distinctive spaces that share identical characteristics and functions throughout the world' are instances of what Claire Larsonneur calls 'globalia', locations which focus on their interchangeability.[8]

In *The Consequences of Modernity* (1990) Anthony Giddens offers a classic definition of globalisation: 'the intensification of worldwide social relations which link distant localities in such a way that local happenings are shaped by events occurring many miles away and vice versa'.[9] *Ghostwritten* reflects the way that power is dispersed in the modern world, how individual lives are no longer seen as within the individual's control. As the publisher Tim Cavendish, a character in chapter eight, remarks, 'We all think we're in control of our own lives, but really they're pre-ghostwritten by forces around us' (G, 287). Pieter Vermeulen points out that *Ghostwritten* is a novel *of*, not about, globalisation because 'it *embodies* the mode of decentered relatedness in its formal organisation'.[10] Nowhere is this more apparent than in the coda, 'Underground', that reverts to Okinawa, the setting for the opening chapter. It ends where the opening begins, with Quasar on the platform after the doors have shut on the train in which he has left a poison gas device primed to go off. In the course of three pages the narrative makes indirect reference to every one of the nine chapters preceding it, reiterating their order. Chronology is simultaneously reinforced and made circular, underscoring the indeterminable nature of all the connections established in the course of the novel.

Berthold Schoene has used *Ghostwritten* to exemplify what he has called the new cosmopolitan novel, one that offers a representation of what it is like to live in a globalised civilisation rather than in a national one: 'In the twenty-first century the [novelist's] task is to venture beyond our nationally demarcated horizons into the world at large and understand the domestic and the global as interweaving one mutually pervasive pattern of contemporary human circumstance and experience.'[11] Viewing the novel as both fragmented and cohesive, he argues that it 'charts human existence both transterritorially and as always determined by locally specific conditions'.[12] Schoene further claims that Mitchell's construction of subjectivity is equally indebted to a globalised interconnectivity: 'Everybody's life relates to everybody else's, even that of perfect strangers whom they will never meet. All individuality amounts to is the production of different variations on one and the same theme of contemporary human existence.'[13] Elements in one chapter bleed into those of another. In the final analysis *Ghostwritten* offers a set of stories that tell themselves, just as contemporary lives are ghostwritten by globalised forces. In the final chapter Luisa Rey, a journalist, asserts, 'The human world is made of stories' (G, 378). We are all ghostwritten by the global forces that we create and that simultaneously create us.

Mitchell's second novel, *number9dream* (2001), is set in a Tokyo that constitutes a parallel universe. It takes its title from a 1974 John Lennon song of the same name, which describes having a dream of indecipherable meaning that Lennon had. In one of many dreams that Eiji, the Japanese protagonist, has, he asks 'John-san' what the dream means. Lennon answers, 'The meaning of the ninth dream begins after all meanings appear to be dead and gone.'[14] Ostensibly the novel shows Eiji's search for his father, yet when he finally comes face to face with him, Eiji chooses not to acknowledge who he is. Eiji is actually in search of a meaning in his life, but as Ai, his girlfriend, remarks, 'You look for your meaning. You find it, and at that moment, your meaning changes, and you have to start all over again' (n9d, 291). This explains why the novel employs what Mitchell has called 'multiple reality frames'.[15] In each of its nine chapters Eiji constructs a different meaning of what constitutes his life and identity. In each case he constructs a different narrative for himself, drawing on a series of genres from crime novels to war memoirs, and from children's stories to dreams. 'Dreams', an old woman tells him, 'are shores where the ocean of spirit meets the land of matter' (n9d, 375). Frequently readers cannot tell whether they are hearing about one of Eiji's dreams or one of his actual experiences. Eiji's quest ends once he accepts the permeability of the worlds of matter and spirit; the final ninth chapter is left blank, perhaps suggesting that full meaning is inaccessible both to Eiji and to the reader. *number9dream* is as much about the nature of narrative as about the narratives we construct from our lives. Not only does the novel make use of a range of narrative genres but it shows an acute self-consciousness about its differing uses of language. Mitchell has described how he gets 'a little throb of pleasure from a bloody perfect sentence', adding that 'words operate like musical notes that the eyeball hears'.[16] One of the novel's characters, a writer, is pursued by his own words, despite trying to hide from them in mixed metaphors. The fun Mitchell has here relates to his thematic concern with the way we narratise our lives. Generally speaking, Mitchell crafts his language not for its isolated effect but to reinforce his narration.

Cloud Atlas (2004) is Mitchell's most complex and acclaimed work to date. Inspired by Italo Calvino's *If on a Winter's Night a Traveler*, Mitchell not only interrupts each of his six narratives with another, as Calvino does; he picks each up again and completes it in reverse order, so that the second half of the novel mirrors the first half in reverse order. Each first-person narrative becomes a text read by the narrator of the next one. Ewing, the narrator of the first section who is a nineteenth-century notary, writes a journal about his travels; the first half of this journal is found by Frobisher, an early-twentieth-century musician, who narrates the second section in the form of letters to a former lover. The first batch of letters is read by Luisa Rey, a California journalist who narrates the third section. Her story turns out to be an airport thriller submitted to Cavendish, a London editor, who recounts the fourth. Cavendish's memoir is made into a 'disney' (a film) watched many years later by Somni-451, the cloned narrator of the fifth section situated in the near future. Somni's testimony is digitally recorded by the state's archivist and is accessed on an 'orison' (video device) by Zachry, a primitive Hawaiian tribesman, who narrates the sixth, central section that takes place in a distant post-apocalyptic future. Thereafter each protagonist retrieves or continues with the second half of their predecessor's narrative. For instance, Somni-451 is watching the movie based on Cavendish's memoir when government forces interrupt as they attempt to capture her. The second half of her story ends when she makes her last request before being executed, which is to watch the second half of the film about Cavendish. The next section takes up Cavendish's story where it left off in the first half. Each transition is connected in an equally ingenious way.

Mitchell calls himself 'a structure geek'.[17] He says that he thinks in terms of straightjackets and escapology: 'The tighter the straightjacket the more singular the act of escape has to be to get out of it.'[18] And yet he insists that all his novels are built out of novellas, in which he acts 'like a kid with Lego'.[19] Mitchell considers structure 'a kind of plot in its own right, running parallel to the narrative plot'.[20] How does it do this in the case of *Cloud Atlas?* Mitchell offers a hint in an article he published in *The Guardian* the year after the book was published. After admitting how besotted he had become in 2001 with Nietzsche's theory of the will to power, he says: 'I decided to write the novel as a chain of plot-and-character studies about how individuals prey on individuals.' This has become a major theme in all his fiction. The structure of *Cloud Atlas*, he concludes, ' – in which each narrative is "eaten" by its successor and later "regurgitated" by the same – could mirror, and with luck, enhance the overarching theme'.[21]

In his book-length study of Mitchell's novels Patrick O'Donnell makes his major theme Mitchell's exploration of the 'future present'.[22] What he means by this is that in Mitchell's work 'the future is anterior to the present until realised at the other end of the chronological scale as the "real" past'.[23] *Cloud Atlas* gives narrative shape to this conception of the indeterminacy of future time. In temporal terms the book moves from the past into the future and back again, defying chronology with a circular plot that nests the future in the middle of a structure that begins and ends in the nineteenth century. In the first half we read the future in the light of the past; in the second half we read the past in the light of the future: we see where the early predation of the Maori and the West (personified by Dr Goose, who tries to poison Ewing for his money) is leading civilisation to – the state crimes of the 'corpocracy' under which Somni-451 lives, and the barbaric slaughter and enslavement of rival tribesmen by the Kona warriors in the post-apocalyptic future of the central section. Viewed chronologically, the novel traces the degeneration of human life over time.

Viewed narratively, the novel suggests that, despite the persistence of evil (Goose escapes punishment), we can still resist the tide of history, as Ewing does in pledging himself to the abolitionist cause.

For his MA thesis Mitchell chose the topic 'Levels of Reality in the Post-Modern Novel'. Does this mean he subscribes to a postmodern ethos? From the start he has adopted an ironic response to postmodern conventions. In *Ghostwritten* Luisa Rey declares, 'Lunatics are writers whose works write them' (G, 378). In *number9dream* Goatwriter jumps into the pool of death after announcing that he is 'getting too old for symbolic quests' (n9d, 241). In section four of *Cloud Atlas* Cavendish writes, 'As an experienced editor, I disapprove of flashbacks, foreshadowings, and tricksy devices; they belong in the 1980s with M.A.s on postmodern and chaos theory.'[24] Clearly Mitchell wants to distance himself from such devices while making playful use of them. As Rose Harris-Birtill suggests, his novels are all metafictional texts 'about the nature of fictional creation and the act of storytelling'.[25] On the one hand Mitchell undermines the status of the six narratives in *Cloud Atlas*: Ewing's journal may have been fabricated by his son. To Frobisher it 'seems too structured for a genuine diary' (CA, 64); similarly, Cavendish criticises the spy novel containing a crusading Luisa Rey for being 'artsily-fartsily clever' (CA, 162). On the other hand the novel seems to suggest that what survives a second Fall is not science (all those abandoned giant telescopes at the summit of Mauna Kea) but the act of narration. This kind of affirmation distinguishes Mitchell's fiction from traditional postmodern narrative. As Kathryn Simpson writes of *number9dream*, 'the narrative works with and through the postmodern towards something meaningful – repeatedly plural, ambiguous, contingent and uncertain, but nonetheless poignant and significant – for Eiji and for the reader.'[26] Mitchell positions himself, in other words, as a self-consciously post-postmodern novelist.

Black Swan Green (2006), Mitchell's fourth novel, is a form of *Künstlerroman* (a narrative about an artist's growth to maturity). By way of teasing interviewers Mitchell has said variously that it is 34.6 per cent or 50.1 per cent autobiographical.[27] It is set in Worcestershire in 1982 (reminiscent of Hanley Green, where Mitchell grew up), and each of its thirteen chapters stands on its own, yet at the same time covers a month of Jason Taylor's thirteenth year (Mitchell was thirteen in that year too). Once again the novel fuses a series of self-contained narratives. Mitchell has said that short stories 'have a background white noise that creates the illusion that the world is much bigger than the mere 10 or 15 pages'. He wanted to see if he 'could sync up the white noise' in his novels, just as when you put Jason's thirteen dinosaur postcards end-to-end 'the background is one continuous whole'.[28] Jason is given a number of personae: Hangman (his stutter), Maggot (his self-contempt) and Evil Twin (his urge to choose the immoral option). Although sounding like a post-structuralist fragmented subject, Jason retains a core identity that fights with and overcomes these subversive personae, once again appropriating while at the same time departing from postmodern practice. Like Eiji, Jason hovers on the margins between fantasy and reality, and it is not always clear to the reader which is which. This lack of clarity reinforces a major theme of the book that, especially for a child, waking life and the world of dreams have equal validity.

Like Mitchell, Jason has a stammer. Jason's need to make verbal substitutions echoes Mitchell's own experience, which proved productive for his command of dialogue in his fiction: as he remarked in an interview in 2015, 'the best character-builder is not description but voice'.[29] In *Black Swan Green* he reminds us that children speak for the most part in slang – as, for example, when Jason tells us that in a game of 'Bulldogs' his opponent 'tried a poxy rugby tackle on me but I shook him free *no* sweat'.[30] Here the use of emphasis reveals that Mitchell has a keen ear, too, for the cadences of the language children use. Although fond of him, Jason's elder sister always calls him 'Thing': ' "*Thing*," Julia muled, "is being *grotesque* while we're eating, Mum" ' (*BSG*, 13). To the complaint made by critics that his ventriloquism has robbed his work of a distinctive voice, Mitchell has replied that he 'would view the label "ventriloquist" as a profound compliment'.[31]

His fifth novel, *The Thousand Autumns of Jacob de Zoet* (2010), is set in Japan (Land of a Thousand Autumns) in the late eighteenth century. Its protagonist Jacob is a member of the Dutch trading community confined by the Japanese authorities to Dejima, an artificial island facing Nagasaki. Its first and third sections are located in Dejima and the middle, more fantastic one on the Japanese mainland. It is the first novel in which Mitchell uses the third person, but he only allows insight into the thoughts of one character in each chapter. In 'On Historical Fiction', printed at the end of the novel, Mitchell writes that what attracts him to this genre is the paradoxical way 'the "historical" half demands fidelity to the past, while the "fiction" half requires infidelity: . . . the lies of fiction must be told'.[32] He sees genre as a writer's tool to be used, 'like style, structure or a character';[33] in *Cloud Atlas* and *The Bone Clocks* he uses a different genre for each section. In *The Thousand Autumns of Jacob de Zoet* he uses the genre of historical fiction to focus on spoken and written language as demanding kinds of communication. A writer who revels in challenges and constraints, he has said that 'with historical fiction, that constraint is language'.[34]

As the Dutch are forbidden to learn Japanese and the official Japanese translators are incompetent, miscommunication becomes a major theme. The two nationalities not only look down on one another but frequently misunderstand one another or deliberately mistranslate official documents (*TA*, 401). Eventually Jacob comes to realise that Japan 'doesn't want to be understood' (*TA*, 477). To give textual substance to the problems of communication Mitchell creates what he calls 'a sort of dialect, "Bygonese" ' (*TA*, 489). So one Japanese woman never says 'I', while a Japanese translator consistently gets his subject-verb agreements wrong – 'who plot to leave is executed' (*TA*, 87). The reader is hereby made to experience the characters' difficulties in understanding each other. Texts such as Jacob's forbidden copy of *The Wealth of Nations* become part of the plot. As Louisa Thomas observes, '[a] dictionary hides a marriage proposal. A book can save a man.'[35] History is a textual construct, and Mitchell builds this fact into the fabric of his narrative.

Both Mitchell's most recent novels, *The Bone Clocks* (2014) and *Slade House* (2015), make heavier use of the supernatural than his previous ones. Both feature two kinds of immortals – Anchorites who feed off the souls of the mortals they have killed, and Horologists who keep on being reincarnated and oppose the Anchorites as forces of darkness. The Anchorites (like the twins in Slade House) are representative of mortal predators from 'feudal lords to slave-traders to oligarchs to neocons'.[36] Marinus, a leading Horologist who makes this identification, plays a major role in the last three of his novels. Just as Mitchell constructs his novels from hyperlinked novellas, so he has been constructing what he calls a macronovel from hyperlinked novels.[37] As he has said that he doubts we have souls and that he does not believe in reincarnation, why is he making heavy use of these concepts in his recent two novels?[38] Mitchell's answer (the answer of a man who is middle-aged) is that he wants to question whether you would 'be willing to amputate your conscience' and make a Faustian pact at the expense of others if you could buy yourself eternal youth.[39] He sees reincarnation 'as a kind of metaphor for a single life'. 'Horologists', he argues, 'are metaphors of mortals.'[40] As one undergraduate member of a paranormal society in Slade House remarks, 'All the supernatural yarns need a realist explanation *and* a supernatural one' (SH, 94).

A minority of reviewers hate Mitchell's use of the supernatural, and Mitchell himself has commented that 'fantasy is the easiest genre to do badly'.[41] In the *New York Times* Michiko Kakutani dismissed the fantasy in *The Bone Clocks* as 'paranormal hooey'.[42] The reviewer for *The Independent* wrote that 'the plunge into the supernatural feels as if your best friend just told you she believes in fairies'.[43] Certainly both books contain passages explicating the world of immortals that intrude into our suspension of disbelief, as for example when Marinus in *The Bone Clocks* feels compelled to promise his listener that '[the] history lesson's almost over'.[44] (It's not.) Marinus later explains that 'Magic's just normal you're *not* used to' (BC, 513). But Mitchell owes enough to postmodern practice to use a parodic tone that undercuts the fantastic material in these two novels. So, for instance, his excessive use of capitalisation and banal repetition of five 'ofs' distance and frame his description of 'the Anchorites of the Chapel of the Dusk of the Blind Cathar of the Thomasite Order of the Sidlehorn Pass' (BC, 450). The final section of *The Bone Clocks* depicts another apocalyptic vision of a world reverting to barbarism after the oil supplies have almost run dry. If the Anchorites' self-centred outlook prevails, the world is doomed in Mitchell's view. As Marinus says to the surviving evil twin in *Slade House*, after she has accused him of denying her the immortal privileges Marinus enjoys, 'What's a metalife without a mission? It's mere . . . feeding' (SH, 229).

Mitchell's talent lies in his ability to infuse the fantastic with deep feeling. He makes no apologies for his excursions into the supernatural. In fact he has announced that he is planning a third volume to complete the Marinus saga.[45] His fusion of natural and supernatural is of a piece with his fusion of the personal and the global, of the waking world and the dream world, and of the realist or historical and the fictional. Mitchell values the power and pleasure of narrative above anything else, and uses every one of its devices to create innovatory and compelling fictions. The seven novels he has published to date constitute an 'Übernovel', a complex and self-contained fictional universe paralleling the one we live in. The more he adds to it the more his characters acquire three-dimensionality, and the bolder he gets in flouting traditional narrative conventions. It is that ability to be both innovative and a page-turner that has made Mitchell a contemporary literary phenomenon, one who is likely to continue to astonish and delight (and infuriate) well into the twenty-first century.

NOTES

1. Tom Bissell, 'History Is a Nightmare', *New York Times*, 29 August 2004, <http://www.nytimes.com/2004/08/29/books/history-is-a-nightmare.html> (last accessed 10 June 2016); Amanda Kolson Hurley, 'Reveling in Serendipity', *Washington Times*, 22 August 2004, <https://www.highbeam.com/doc/1G1-121083081.html> (last accessed 10 June 2016).
2. Pico Iyer, 'David Mitchell', *Time*, 3 May 2007, <http://content.time.com/time/specials/2007/time100/article/0,28804,1595326_1595332_1616691,00.html> (last accessed 10 June 2016).
3. Scott Timberg, 'Global Touch', *LA Weekly*, 15 July 2010, <http://www.laweekly.com/arts/global-touch-2166075> (last accessed 10 June 2016); John Freeman, 'Book Review', *Boston Globe*, 30 August 2014, <https://www.bostonglobe.com/arts/books/2014/08/30/book-review-the-bone-clocks-david-mitchell/C07NKyofg1GHORQkuSPTyK/story.html> (last accessed 10 June 2016); Susan Balée, '*Slade House*: A Tricky Haunted House Story by David Mitchell', *Pittsburgh Post-Gazette*, 25 October 2015, <http://www.post-gazette.com/ae/books/2015/10/25/Slade-House-A-tricky-haunted-house-story-by-David-Mitchell/stories/201510250022> (last accessed 10 June 2016).
4. Wyatt Mason, 'David Mitchell, the Experimentalist', *New York Times Magazine*, 25 June 2010, <http://www.nytimes.com/2010/06/27/magazine/27mitchell-t.html?_r=0> (last accessed 10 June 2016).
5. Leigh Wilson, 'David Mitchell', in Philip Tew, Leigh Wilson and Fiona Tolan (eds), *Writers Talk: Interviews with Contemporary British Novelists* (London: Continuum, 2008), p. 98.
6. Catherine McWeeney, 'An Interview with David Mitchell', *BookBrowse*, 2001, <https://www.bookbrowse.com/author_interviews/full/index.cfm/author_number/480/david-mitchell#interview> (last accessed 10 June 2016).
7. David Mitchell, *Ghostwritten* (1999; New York: Vintage International, 2001), pp. 11, 211. All quotations are from this edition; hereafter, page numbers will be given in the text, preceded by G.
8. Claire C. Larsonneur, 'Location, location, location', *Études britanniques contemporaines*, 37 (December 2009), 142.
9. Anthony Giddens, *The Consequences of Modernity* (Cambridge: Polity, 1990), p. 64.
10. Pieter Vermeulen, 'David Mitchell's *Ghostwritten* and the "Novel of Globalisation": Biopower and the Secret History of the Novel', *Critique*, 53 (2012), 383.
11. Berthold Schoene, '*Tour du Monde*: David Mitchell's *Ghostwritten* and the Contemporary Imagination', *College Literature*, 37 (Fall 2010), 46.
12. Ibid., p. 50.
13. Ibid., p. 52.
14. David Mitchell, *number9dream* (2001; New York: Random House, 2003), p. 380. All quotations are from this edition; hereafter, page numbers will be given in the text, preceded by n9d.
15. Toh Hsien Min, 'The Illusionist's Dream', *Quarterly Literary Review Singapore*, 1.2 (January 2002), <http://www.qlrs.com/interview.asp?id=173> (last accessed 10 June 2016).
16. Mark Greaves, 'Interview with a Writer: David Mitchell', *The Spectator*, 25 January 2013, <http://blogs.spectator.co.uk/2013/01/interview-with-a-writer-david-mitchell> (last accessed 10 June 2016); Carolyn Kellogg, 'An Interview with David Mitchell', *Los Angeles Times*, 26 October 2012, <http://articles.latimes.com/2012/oct/26/entertainment/la-et-jc-david-mitchell-q-a-20121026> (last accessed 10 June 2016).

17. Ellen Kanner, 'Interview: David Mitchell, Author of "The Bone Clocks" and "Slade House"', *Miami Herald*, 31 October 2015, <http://www.miamiherald.com/entertainment/books/article41956173.html#storylink=cpy> (last accessed 10 June 2016).
18. Kyle Northover, 'David Mitchell', *The Age* (Melbourne, Australia), 4 April 2015, p. 30.
19. Jenny Arch, 'BookCon 2014: When They Were Last Seen', 17 June 2014, <http://jenny-arch.com/tag/david-mitchell> (last accessed 10 June 2016).
20. David Mitchell, 'Get Writing: Playing with Structure', BBC, 1 March 2008, <http://web.archive.org/web/20080301101136/http://www.bbc.co.uk/dna/getwriting/module15p> (accessed 10 June 2016).
21. David Mitchell, 'Genesis', *The Guardian*, 16 April 2005, <http://www.guardian.co.uk/books/2005/apr/16/featuresreviews.guardianreview23> (last accessed 10 June 2016).
22. Patrick O'Donnell, *A Temporary Future: The Novels of David Mitchell* (London: Bloomsbury, 2015), p. 16.
23. Ibid., p. 17.
24. David Mitchell, *Cloud Atlas* (New York: Random House, 2004), p. 150. All quotations are from this edition; hereafter, page numbers will be given in the text, preceded by CA.
25. Rose Harris-Birtill, '"A row of screaming Russian dolls": Escaping the Panopticon in David Mitchell's *number9dream*', *SubStance*, 44.1 (2015), 61.
26. Kathryn Simpson, 'Coming of Age in *number9dream*', in Sarah Dillon (ed.), *David Mitchell: Critical Essays* (Canterbury: Gylphi, 2011), p. 51.
27. Shane Barry, 'Silver Daggers and Russian Dolls – David Mitchell, Author of *Cloud Atlas*, in Interview', *TMO Magazine*, 1 March 2005, <http://www.threemonkeysonline.com/silver-daggers-and-russian-dolls-david-mitchell-author-of-cloud-atlas-in-interview> (last accessed 10 June 2016); Steve Finbow, 'Q&A: David Mitchell', *Stop Smiling Magazine*, 29 June 2007, <http://www.stopsmilingonline.com/story_detail.php?id=841> (last accessed 10 June 2016).
28. Robert Birnbaum, 'David Mitchell', *The Morning News*, 11 May 2006, <http://www.themorningnews.org/article/david-mitchell> (last accessed 10 June 2016).
29. Tim Martin, 'David Mitchell on his Ghost Story *Slade House*', *Daily Telegraph*, 17 October 2015, p. 9.
30. David Mitchell, *Black Swan Green* (2006; New York: Random House, 2007), p. 8. All quotations are from this edition; hereafter, page numbers will be given in the text, preceded by BSG.
31. Timberg, 'Global Touch'.
32. David Mitchell, *The Thousand Autumns of Jacob de Zoet* (2010; New York: Random House, 2011), p. 489. All quotations are from this edition; hereafter, page numbers will be given in the text, preceded by TA.
33. Michael MacLeod, 'David Mitchell: "I Have Created My Own Middle Earth"', *The Guardian*, 17 August 2015, <http://www.theguardian.com/books/2015/aug/17/david-mitchell-i-have-created-my-own-middle-earth> (last accessed 10 June 2016).
34. David Robinson, 'Reviews: *Cloud Atlas*: It Must Be the Links Effect', *The Scotsman*, 21 February 2004, p. 9.
35. Louisa Thomas, 'David Mitchell's Brilliant Misstep', *Newsweek*, 156.3 (19 July 2010).
36. David Mitchell, *Slade House* (New York: Random House, 2015), p. 230. All quotations are from this edition; hereafter, page numbers will be given in the text, preceded by SH.
37. Alexander Alter, 'A Master of Many Universes', *New York Times*, 25 August 2014, C1.
38. Kathryn Schulz, 'Boundaries Are Conventions. And *The Bone Clocks* Author David Mitchell Transcends Them All', *New York Magazine: Vulture*, 25 August 2014, <http://www.vulture.com/2014/08/david-mitchell-interview-bone-clocks-cloud-atlas.html> (last accessed 10 June 2016); Adam Begley, 'David Mitchell, The Art of Fiction No. 204', *The Paris Review*, 193 (Summer 2010), <http://www.theparisreview.org/interviews/6034/the-art-of-fiction-no-204-david-mitchell> (last accessed 10 June 2016).

39. Glyn Morgan, 'War in Pieces: Violence and Conflict in David Mitchell's "The Bone Clocks"', *Los Angeles Review of Books*, 30 October 2015, <https://lareviewofbooks.org/review/war-in-pieces-violence-and-conflict-in-david-mitchells-the-bone-clocks> (accessed 10 June 2016).
40. Paul A. Harris, 'David Mitchell in the Laboratory of Time: An Interview with the Author', *SubStance*, 44.1 (2015), 13.
41. MacLeod, 'David Mitchell: "I Have Created My Own Middle Earth"'.
42. Michiko Kakutani, 'A Lifetime Watching the World Devolve', *New York Times*, 27 August 2014, C1.
43. Leyla Sanai, 'David Mitchell, *The Bone Clocks*, Book Review: Another Fantastic Epic with One Fantastical Flaw', *The Independent*, 5 September 2014, <http://www.independent.co.uk/arts-entertainment/books/reviews/david-mitchell-the-bone-clocks-book-review-another-fantastic-epic-with-one-fantastical-flaw-9715499.html> (last accessed 10 June 2016).
44. David Mitchell, *The Bone Clocks* (New York: Random House, 2014), p. 451. All quotations are from this edition; hereafter, page numbers will be given in the text, preceded by BC.
45. Stuart Kelly, 'Book Review: *Slade House* by David Mitchell', *The Scotsman*, 25 October 2015, <http://www.scotsman.com/lifestyle/culture/books/book-review-slade-house-by-david-mitchell-1-3927204> (accessed 10 June 2016).

FURTHER READING

For an up-to-date list of David Mitchell's novels, see the British Council website: <https://literature.britishcouncil.org/writer/david-mitchell> (last accessed 10 June 2016).

Dillon, Sarah, *David Mitchell: Critical Essays* (Canterbury: Gylphi, 2011).
O'Donnell, Patrick, *A Temporary Future: The Fiction of David Mitchell* (London: Bloomsbury, 2015).

CHAPTER 3

Hilary Mantel: Raising the Dead, Speaking the Truth

Lisa Fletcher

In 2012, Hilary Mantel became only the third author to win the Man Booker Prize twice, joining Peter Carey and J. M. Coetzee. Her winning novel, *Bring up the Bodies*, is a sequel to *Wolf Hall*, winner of the Man Booker in 2009. No sequel had ever won before and no author had gained the prestigious prize so soon after winning it for the first time. Mantel shot to fame in 2009, and at the time described her nine previous novels as something of a long apprenticeship for *Wolf Hall*, a 650-page work of historical fiction about the court of Henry VIII.[1]

Her first novel, *Every Day Is Mother's Day*, was published in 1985 to positive reviews, but she is careful to point out in interviews that she wrote this short novel about contemporary England only because she failed to find a publisher for her first work of fiction, an extremely long historical novel about the French Revolution. This longer work, *A Place of Greater Safety*, was eventually released as Mantel's fifth novel in 1992. She explains, 'I only became a novelist because I thought I had missed my chance to become a historian.'[2] If *A Place of Greater Safety* had appeared first, Mantel's career would probably have played out very differently, and the Tudor novels would almost certainly have come as less of a surprise to readers. In a review of *Bring up the Bodies* for the *New York Times*, Charles McGrath writes that Mantel 'belongs to the same generation, roughly, as her compatriots Martin Amis, Julian Barnes and Ian McEwan, and is every bit their equal', but is not as well known.[3] This is no longer the case: sales of her back catalogue reportedly rose by 900 per cent after the *Wolf Hall* Man Booker Prize 2009, and then rose further when the Chair of the judges for the Man Booker Prize 2012 proclaimed her the 'greatest modern English prose writer working today'; sales increased again when the Royal Shakespeare Company adapted *Wolf Hall* and *Bring up the Bodies* for sell-out stage productions in January 2014, then skyrocketed a year later with the BBC television adaptation of the two novels. *The Independent* speculates that Mantel's Tudor series 'has almost become an industry of its own',[4] and, with the publication of the third novel, *The Mirror and the Light*, on the near horizon, the 'Mantel brand' seems secure.[5] Nevertheless, Mantel remains an 'under-researched author'.[6] Very few scholars have offered close analyses of her work, and there is as yet no book-length study.

This chapter examines Mantel's three novels since 2000, *Beyond Black* (2005), *Wolf Hall* (2009) and *Bring up the Bodies* (2012). In an interview with Eileen Pollard, Mantel described *Beyond Black* as 'nothing but a vast preparatory exercise for writing the Tudor novels'.[7] *Beyond Black* was Mantel's second book to be published in the twenty-first century; the first was her 2003 memoir, *Giving up the Ghost*, and it is surprising that no one has considered *Beyond Black* and *Giving up the Ghost* together, since both are concerned with séances and messages from the dead. Mantel, who has said that if her life had turned out differently 'she might well have become a medium', frequently describes the work of writing a novel as a type of congress with 'ghosts': 'You talk to the dead one way or another, and you make it pay.'[8] As its title suggests, ghosts are at the heart of her memoir, both in the literal sense and as her preferred figure for glimpses of other lives she might have lived or created. To offer two examples: on the memoir's first page she recalls that she was 'not perturbed' when her dead stepfather appeared on her staircase – 'I am used to seeing things that "aren't there"'; later, the daughter she never had will 'always be a ghost of possibility, a paper baby, a person who slipped between the lines'.[9] Mantel explains that she wrote the memoir 'in order to locate myself, if not within a body, then in the narrow space between one letter and the next, between the lines where the ghosts of meaning are' (GG, 222). There are strong connections between the actual and metaphoric hauntings in *Giving up the Ghost* and her depiction of the encounters with the dead made by Alison Hart, the main character of *Beyond Black*. These invite a reading of the latter as another effort by Mantel to locate herself in relation to the meanings she unearths and those she produces as a writer of historical novels.

The multivalent figure of the 'medium' is central to *Beyond Black* and its vision of a world in which past and present are coexistent and inextricable. In this profoundly metafictional novel, 'medium' refers partly to Alison's inescapable everyday life as an intermediary between the living and the dead, partly to her profession as a conjuror of spirits for paying clients, and partly to the means by which she expresses or stores information. As is apparent when this novel is read alongside the memoir, Alison, as the conduit for voices from the past to speak to audiences in the present, embodies the fraught work of authorship in the borderland between fact and fiction. She is an 'arena of combat' in which histories that seem to have closed are re-opened and re-energised.[10] Like Mantel herself, who writes openly in her memoir and elsewhere about her rapid weight gain following treatment for long-term chronic pain, Alison is 'of an unfeasible size' (BB, 3). But if Alison is a fictional version of Mantel – and this seems indisputable – she is only half of the portrait. Alison's manager/companion Colette is characterised throughout as an insubstantial, spectral presence; she is a 'straight, flat creature' with a 'patchy, wispy' aura that recalls the pale, thin young woman Mantel remembers when she looks in the mirror and sees a 'steroid moon-face' (BB, 81, 272).[11] Mirrors and other reflective surfaces are everywhere in *Beyond Black*, and, indeed, throughout her oeuvre.

Alison and Colette are linked as analogues for the writer's life Mantel portrays in *Giving up the Ghost* by the recurring phrase 'make a living'. Alison's deeply traumatic upbringing on the outskirts of Aldershot, Hampshire, is revealed in non-chronological fragments across the course of the novel. Her 'spirit guide' Morris is a foul-mouthed and foul-smelling remainder from her childhood, one of the 'fiends from Aldershot' who gathered around her prostitute mother and now linger in the 'place beyond black' (*BB*, 129, 194). In the argot of the novel's community of psychics and palm readers, the various spirits Alison encounters – from Morris and other characters from her childhood to Shakespeare ('Bill Wagstaffe') and Diana, Princess of Wales – have moved from 'earthside' to 'airside'. Alison insists that she is a 'professional psychic, not some sort of magic act', but also regrets her 'abnormality', a consequence of the horrific childhood that left her 'brain all cross-wired so [she's] forced to know the biographies of strangers' (*BB*, 9, 305, 297). Alison's mother responds to her daughter's resistance to prostitution by asking, 'How else are you going to make a living?' (*BB*, 120). This question echoes in subtle and darkly comic ways throughout the novel: Alison asks Colette how she would make a living if she were to give up touring as a psychic, and the question undergirds Colette's project to write a book about Alison's life to sell at the 'psychic fayres' (*BB*, 50). Colette's naïve effort to write a book by recording and transcribing interviews with Alison fails not just because the tape recordings are corrupted by the cacophony of voices and sounds from 'airside', but also because Colette is unable to translate the tangled complex of past voices into a coherent narrative.

Mantel's reflection on the question of 'ghosts' in her memoir and the self-conscious metaphorics of mediumism in *Beyond Black* provide tools and concepts for analysing the complex, third-person, present-tense narration of the first two volumes of Mantel's Tudor trilogy. Stephen Greenblatt commends Mantel's 'ability to summon up ghosts'. The historical novel, he argues, 'is always an act of conjuring'.[12] Rosario Arias similarly contends that 'Mantel acts as a resurrectionist, or a medium, because she channels communication between the Tudor world and today'.[13] In other words, the narrator of *Wolf Hall* and *Bring up the Bodies* is both a 'medium' who recounts past events as they unfold and a charismatic persona who invites readers to participate in the challenge of recovering history. Mantel's own commentary on the Tudor novels and her writing process encourages the view that she is like a 'medium' who 'negotiates with the dead and lets them speak'.[14] Her 'method', she explains, is grounded in the 'ideal of fidelity to history' and a sense of 'responsibility' to the historical figures she depicts.[15]

Mantel's account of her approach to writing historical fiction informs also the emerging critical consensus that her most recent work has shifted the goalposts for writers of historical fiction away from the self-consciousness and experimentation of 'postmodern' approaches to the genre associated with authors including John Fowles, A. S. Byatt, Sarah Waters, Peter Ackroyd and David Mitchell.[16] Reviewers almost never compare *Wolf Hall* or *Bring up the Bodies* to other recent literary historical novels, despite the critical agreement that the genre is 'in robust health, critically, formally and economically'.[17] Peter Childs, for instance, contends that Mantel's Booker win for *Wolf Hall* 'cement[ed] the historical novel's position as the most prized literary genre in the twenty-first century'.[18] Mantel, however, argues that the 'boundaries of the term "historical fiction" are now so wide that it's almost meaningless, so that use of the term is beginning to look like an accusation, a stick to beat writers with'.[19] Her anxiety here may be linked to her choice of period: the novelist most often named alongside Mantel in journalism about appearances of the Tudors on page and screen is Philippa Gregory, best known for her 2002 *The Other Boleyn Girl*. The comparison invariably favours Mantel and casts Gregory not only as representative of the kind of commercial British historical fiction that would never be in the running for the Man Booker, but as a too-easy target for the view that, until Mantel, Henry VIII's reign was a 'worn-out story'.[20]

Mantel is careful to distinguish her approach to the genre from that of authors who she agrees are ducking the 'tough issues' of the present 'in favour of writing about frocks', a distinction that recalls Georg Lukács's disinterest in novels in which the past is treated as 'mere costumery'.[21] Lukács, in his seminal 1937 study of the genre, classified the true historical novel as one that achieves 'an artistically faithful image of a concrete historical epoch'.[22] It is now a critical commonplace to say that the value of the historical novel lies not in its potential to enhance our understanding of past people and events, but in its capacity to shed new light on the present: novels about the past are always also about the contemporary context in which they are written. Tamsin Spargo explains, 'The past is, in a sense, over but in another sense it is only available to us, knowable, as part of the present. The past may be real but it is, by definition, irrecoverable in its pastness.'[23] Mantel is only partially sympathetic to this view. The frequent traces of her engagement with the archives in *Wolf Hall* and *Bring up the Bodies* are not there to suggest that history is irrecoverable. Rather, the picture of the past offered by these weighty novels is one of plenitude rather than absence or lack. The Tudor novels are much closer to 'classic' historical fiction than the late twentieth- and early twenty-first-century trends critics have labelled as postmodern historical fiction, or, more recently, neo-historical fiction.

The Cromwell novels are emphatically not postmodern fiction; they are not, that is, examples of 'historiographic metafiction'. Linda Hutcheon coined this somewhat inelegant term in her highly influential book *A Poetics of Postmodernism*, first published in 1988, to classify a body of novels that 'characterise postmodernism in fiction'.[24] In brief, 'historiographic metafiction' is fiction that reflects on its treatment of history and the fictionalisation of history in general, but paradoxically sustains a belief in the validity and value of historical narratives. For Alan Robinson, Hutcheon's claims are 'now outdated'.[25] The key to understanding Mantel's approach to, and passion for, writing historical novels is her commitment to the search for accuracy: 'I cannot describe to you what revulsion it inspires in me when people play around with the facts.'[26] She explains that every named character but one in the Tudor novels comes from the historical records; even the exception, the boy Christophe in *Bring up the Bodies*, is an extrapolation of a person mentioned but not named in the primary sources. When explaining her approach to *Wolf Hall* and *Bring up the Bodies*, Mantel often recalls the experience of writing her first historical novel, *A Place of Greater Safety* (1992): 'I used to think when I set out that doing the research was enough, but then the gaps would emerge that could only be filled by imagination.'[27] Indeed, the professional values Mantel has espoused across numerous interviews – and which are implicit in the novels themselves – suggest a writer closer in spirit to historians than novelists, at least as they are characterised by critics of the historical novel.

Mantel's guiding principle is that the people of the past she portrays on the page existed in space and time:

> I aim to make the fiction flexible so that it bends itself around the facts as we have them. Otherwise I don't see the point. Nobody seems to understand that. Nobody seems to share my approach to historical fiction. I suppose if I have a maxim, it is that there isn't any necessary conflict between good history and good drama. I know that history is not shapely, and I know the truth is often inconvenient and incoherent. It contains all sorts of superfluities. You could cut a much better shape if you were God, but as it is, I think the whole fascination and the skill is in working with those incoherencies.[28]

For numerous reviewers, the most 'surprising' thing about *Wolf Hall* and *Bring up the Bodies* is Mantel's choice of an 'unlikely hero', Thomas Cromwell.[29] Before Mantel, Tudor fictions on page, stage and screen, most notably Robert Bolt's play *A Man for All Seasons* and its 1966 film adaptation, had portrayed Cromwell as the villain in Henry VIII's court and Thomas More as the saintly hero. Mantel, whose admiration of Cromwell's 'brilliant mind' comes through on every page of the novels, professes little interest in the history or drama of 'people who start off possessing power'.[30] The clearest statement of the view of history undergirding these novels comes midway through *Wolf Hall* when Cromwell ponders how to tell Harry Percy, the Earl of Northumberland, that his claims to have been betrothed to Anne Boleyn are pointless because the 'world is not run from where he thinks': 'Not from castle walls, but from counting houses, not from the call of the bugle but by the click of the abacus.'[31] The penultimate chapter of *Bring up the Bodies* – at over 150 pages nearly a novel in itself – is titled 'Master of Phantoms, April–May 1536' and presents Cromwell as a man at the height of his powers: Anne Boleyn and the five men executed with her are like characters in a narrative of Cromwell's construction. In Mantel's version of this famous episode, Cromwell is as much motivated by a desire to serve his king – whose impatience to be rid of Anne and marry Jane Seymour cannot be denied – as he is to avenge the treatment of his dead master and mentor, Thomas Wolsey; Cromwell's relationship with Wolsey is at the heart of *Wolf Hall*. Anne's five co-accused were each players in a vulgar play performed after Wolsey's death, but it takes time and patience for Cromwell to seal their fates. In the final pages of *Wolf Hall* Mantel, the narrator, and Cromwell – their voices are deliberately blurred – reflect on the relationship between the living and the dead. Cromwell recalls his boyhood fear of ghosts, but now knows differently: 'It's the living that turn and chase the dead. The long bones and skulls are tumbled from their shrouds, and words like stones thrust into their rattling mouths: we edit their writings, we rewrite their lives' (*WH*, 649). It is in moments like this that the 'intermingling' of author and character, which Mantel says she 'cannot stop', is most apparent.[32] By the end of *Bring up the Bodies* this 'master of phantoms' is aware that he too will become a ghost to be chased through the archives. The novel's final page invites further reflection on Mantel's project: 'those who come after me . . . will sift through what remains and remark, here is an old deed, an old draft, an old letter from Thomas Cromwell's time: they will turn the page over, and write on me.'[33]

After writing the first two paragraphs of *Wolf Hall*, Mantel says that she realised she would write Cromwell's story from 'behind his eyes' and that all decisions about 'how to tell the story' would flow from this perspective.[34] The novels are written almost entirely in the present tense and the third person, closely focalised on Cromwell. This 'grammatical intimacy' brings the author, narrator, protagonist and readers into a tight circuit of exchange, with the author/narrator holding the position of greatest authority in the making of meaning, but always from a perspective which privileges fidelity to the historical record.[35] The first chapter of *Wolf Hall*, like that of other Mantel novels, eschews exposition. Instead the novel opens in Putney in 1500 with an unattributed snippet of dialogue, 'So now get up' (*WH*, 3). The next paragraph launches readers into the close third-person viewpoint used for much – but, importantly, not all – of this novel and its sequel: 'Felled, dazed, silent, he has fallen; knocked full length on the cobbles of the yard' (*WH*, 3). The person speaking is Walter Cromwell, who is in the middle of beating his son, Thomas; Walter's next kick 'knocks the last breath out of him; he thinks it may be his last' (*WH*, 3). The novel's first page thus introduces one of its most remarked upon stylistic devices: with rare exceptions, Cromwell is referred to throughout the novel, which concludes in July 1535, by the unqualified pronoun 'he'. Mantel amended this device for *Bring up the Bodies*, so that her protagonist becomes 'he, Cromwell'.

As indicated above, the second novel takes up where *Wolf Hall* left off and ends with an event that Cromwell orchestrates on behalf of his king: the execution of Anne Boleyn and her five co-accused. Reviewers tended to read 'he, Cromwell' and its variants as a gesture of generosity to readers who were disoriented by the idiosyncratic grammar of *Wolf Hall*, but Mantel is too clever and too confident a writer to adjust her prose for enhanced readability. Instead the foregrounding of Cromwell's name in *Bring up the Bodies* is an invitation to readers to share Cromwell's (and Mantel's) incredulity that the bloodied blacksmith's son we met at the beginning of *Wolf Hall* would rise to become the king's 'right hand' (*BUB*, 237). '[W]ho', the narrator asks early in *Bring up the Bodies*, 'would have thought that Thomas Cromwell would be anything at all?' (*BUB*, 34–5). The implied audience for this question consists of readers who conceive of historical fiction as a conversation between the past and the present by passages in the second person, and, crucially for Mantel, who recognise the value of looking anew at a history which many assumed to be over-examined.

There are numerous instances of second-person narration in both novels, designed to invite the reader closer still to Cromwell than the limited third-person perspective allows. The day on which his wife, Liz, dies from sweating sickness is mostly 'nothing to remember', but there is 'something wrong when you arrive home' (*WH*, 101). 'You' here is clearly Cromwell, but the effect of the second-person pronoun is to ask readers to imagine themselves being part of this sixteenth-century scene. Twenty-first-century readers need not have experienced the illness to empathise with the shock and pain of Cromwell's loss: 'Then you see the dismayed faces; they turn away at the sight of you' (WH, 101). When his young daughters die of the same disease a year later, Cromwell's first-person thoughts are reported by the narrator, a technique that Mantel reserves for moments when Cromwell is most impassioned: 'I never knew her, he thinks; I never knew I had her' (WH, 152). Heightened emotion also accounts for the very rare moments when the narration slips more fully into the first person, as though the narrator has got too close to Cromwell. A key example follows a pivotal scene in which Cromwell cries for his lost family: 'Very well. I dry my tears, those tears from All Hallows Day' (WH, 162). Mantel offers her treatment of this episode as an example of the value novelists can add to the work of historians: before *Wolf Hall* historians had interpreted Cromwell's tears in relation to Wolsey's downfall and his fear for his own career, but Mantel notices that the event clearly took place on the day of the dead, and that Cromwell, who had lost his wife and two children over the course of the previous three years, may well have been crying tears of grief. 'This appears', she insists, 'to be the kind of thing that a novelist notices and that historians manage to ignore, generation after generation.' Recreating the private life of historical protagonists is 'part of the bargain. Otherwise you're just a pseudo-historian.'[36]

The novelist Margaret Atwood sees Mantel's use of present-tense narration as a strategy to avoid one of the 'pitfalls' of historical fiction, the exaggeration of the strangeness of the past so that readers feel alienated; in the Tudor novels we are 'right there with Cromwell'.[37] The immediacy of the events portrayed in the novel and the implied propinquity of Cromwell to the reader is intensified by Mantel's adept use of deictic words. Deixis (meaning 'pointing') refers to those elements of language that anchor meaning to particular contexts: pronouns and temporal and spatial indicators such as here, there, now and then. In fact, a close reading of the Tudor novels shows that 'here' and 'now' are key words in both. Early in *Wolf Hall*, the narrator remarks, 'Nowhere else but here he is still a runaway, still a little, beaten boy' (WH, 42). In the opening chapter of *Bring up the Bodies*, 'Thomas Cromwell is now about fifty years old' (BUB, 6). Unusually for historical fiction, the narrator almost never intervenes to anticipate events in Cromwell's future of which he could not be aware in the narrative's present: in *Wolf Hall*, when his mother-in-law decides not to send the girls to the country during sweating sickness season, 'It's the wrong decision';[38] and in *Bring up the Bodies*, before Cromwell receives the (false) news that the king has died, the narrator forecasts, 'Later that day ... he will be on his way to Greenwich, shocked, apprehensive.'[39] Mantel makes the past present by positioning readers at Cromwell's shoulder to watch events unfold without the benefit of hindsight so often granted us by historical novelists.

Mantel's approach to the genre of the historical novel is close to the view Robinson espouses in his recent book, *Narrating the Past: Historiography, Memory and the Contemporary Novel*: 'I approach historical fiction as a form of history in its own right, which confronts similar cognitive and imaginative challenges to those faced by historians.'[40] For Robinson, both historians and novelists 'project an anachronistic narrative world'.[41] The author's interpretation of historical sources creates what he terms the *'present past'*: a virtual past reality from the point of view of the writer's present. The present past is 'only provisionally valid and open to constant revision', but Robinson stresses that this provisionality is a source of creative energy and possibility rather than a belief in the 'unknowability or sublime unrepresentability of the past'.[42]

Arias regards *Wolf Hall* and *Bring up the Bodies* as examples of 'neo-historical fiction'.[43] Definitions of 'neo-historical fiction' emphasise the subgenre's 'self-analytic drive';[44] however, as Jerome de Groot argues, historical fiction is almost always self-analytical: 'The form is obsessed with pointing out its own partiality, with introducing other voices and undermining its authority.'[45] Mantel's 'authorial proximity' to both her protagonist and implied readers in the Tudor novels has the opposite effect.[46]

Like Mantel, Cromwell communes with ghosts to reflect on the meaning of his life and create his plots: first his wife and daughters; then his beloved master, Thomas Wolsey; and later Thomas More, amongst others. The 'cast of characters' at the beginning of *Bring up the Bodies* includes a list of the dead. The closeness of Mantel to Cromwell is essential to one of the main messages about historical fiction that this book seeks to deliver: the past is no more defined by competing and contradictory versions of the truth than the present is. Cromwell's life was a tissue of fact and fiction even as it unfolded: 'why is it that his life as a child doesn't seem to fit one bit with the next?' (*WH*, 357). A short paragraph in *Bring up the Bodies* – a rare moment of narratorial intervention – does away with the notion that past truths are any more contingent and contradictory than those still in the making:

> What is the nature of the border between truth and lies? It is permeable and blurred because it is planted thick with rumour, confabulation, misunderstandings and twisted tales. Truth can break the gates down, truth can howl in the street; unless truth is pleasing, personable and easy to like, she is condemned to stay whimpering at the back door. (*BUB*, 159)

Mantel offers Thomas Cromwell – organised and rational, but with a gift for imagining the dead – as her vehicle to the distant past. Like his twenty-first-century creator, Cromwell is a rare person in that he likes 'everything squared up and precise' *and* 'will allow some drift at the margins' (*WH*, 228).

At the time of writing, the date of publication for the third Tudor novel remains uncertain and, if internet chatter is anything to go by, readers are becoming impatient. In February 2015 Mantel said on Australian national radio, 'I hear on the one hand that it will be out next week, on the other hand that it will be at least ten years, [but] neither of these [is] true.'[47] It remains to be seen whether Geraldine Brooks is right that the Tudor novels are 'surely destined for the literary canon',[48] but there is no doubt that Mantel has shaken our assumptions about the definition and purpose of the contemporary historical novel.

NOTES

1. Christopher Tayler, 'Wolf Hall by Hilary Mantel – Review', *The Guardian*, 2 May 2009, <http://www.theguardian.com/books/2009/may/02/wolf-hall-hilary-mantel> (last accessed 10 June 2016).
2. Mona Simpson, 'Hilary Mantel: Art of Fiction No. 226', *The Paris Review*, 212 (Spring 2015), <http://www.theparisreview.org/interviews/6360/art-of-fiction-no-226-hilary-mantel> (last accessed 10 June 2016).
3. Charles McGrath, 'A Bloody Season', *New York Times*, 25 May 2012, <http://www.nytimes.com/2012/05/27/books/review/bring-up-the-bodies-by-hilary-mantel.html?_r=0> (last accessed 10 June 2016).
4. Nick Clark, 'Wolf Hall: Hilary Mantel's Tudor Tales Spawn a Lucrative Industry with Stage and TV Adaptations', *The Independent*, 11 January 2014, <http://www.independent.co.uk/arts-entertainment/theatre-dance/news/wolf-hall-hilary-mantel-s-tudor-tales-spawn-a-lucrative-industry-with-stage-and-tv-adaptations-9052643.html> (last accessed 10 June 2016).
5. Stuart Jeffries, 'Hilary Mantel: "If I'm Suffering, I Can Make That Pay"', *The Guardian*, 17 October 2012, <http://www.theguardian.com/books/2012/oct/17/hilary-mantel-if-suffering-can-make-pay> (last accessed 10 June 2016).
6. Eileen J. Pollard, '"Mind What Gap?": An Interview with Hilary Mantel', *Textual Practice*, 29.6 (2015), 1,035–44; 1,036.
7. Ibid.
8. Jeffries, 'Hilary Mantel'.
9. Hilary Mantel, *Giving up the Ghost: A Memoir* (2003; London: Fourth Estate, 2013), pp. 1, 158. All quotations are from this edition; hereafter, page numbers will be given in the text, preceded by GG.
10. Hilary Mantel, *Beyond Black* (2005; London: Fourth Estate, 2013), p. 2. All quotations are from this edition; hereafter, page numbers will be given in the text, preceded by BB.
11. See also *Giving up the Ghost*, p. 217.
12. Stephen Greenblatt, 'How It Must Have Been', *New York Review of Books*, 5 November 2009, <http://www.nybooks.com/articles/2009/11/05/how-it-must-have-been> (last accessed 10 June 2016).
13. Rosario Arias, 'Exoticising the Tudors: Hilary Mantel's Re-Appropriation of the Past in *Wolf Hall* and *Bring up the Bodies*', in Elodie Rousselot (ed.), *Exoticising the Past in Contemporary Neo-Historical Fiction* (Basingstoke: Palgrave Macmillan, 2014), pp. 19–36; p. 19.
14. Ibid., p. 22.
15. Simpson, 'Hilary Mantel'.
16. Arias, 'Exoticising the Tudors', p. 22.
17. Jerome de Groot, *The Historical Novel*, The New Critical Idiom Series (London: Routledge, 2010), p. 1.
18. Peter Childs, *Contemporary Novelists: British Fiction since 1970* (Basingstoke: Palgrave Macmillan, 2012), p. 299.
19. Hilary Mantel, 'Booker Winner Hilary Mantel on Dealing with History in Fiction', *The Guardian*, 17 October 2009, <http://www.guardian.co.uk/books/2009/oct/17/hilary-mantel-author-booker> (last accessed 13 June 2016).
20. Christopher Benfey, 'Renaissance Men', *New York Times*, 29 October 2009, <http://www.nytimes.com/2009/11/01/books/review/Benfey-t.html?pagewanted=all&_r=0> (last accessed 13 June 2016); McGrath, 'A Bloody Season'.
21. Georg Lukács, *The Historical Novel*, trans. Hannah and Stanley Mitchell (London: Merlin, 1974), p. 19.
22. Ibid.

23. Tamsin Spargo, *Reading the Past* (Basingstoke: Palgrave Macmillan, 2000), p. 1.
24. Linda Hutcheon, *A Poetics of Postmodernism: History, Theory, Fiction* (London: Routledge, 1988), p. ix.
25. Alan Robinson, *Narrating the Past: Historiography, Memory and the Contemporary Novel* (Basingstoke: Palgrave Macmillan, 2011), p. xiii.
26. Larissa MacFarquhar, 'The Dead Are Real: Hilary Mantel's Imagination', *The New Yorker*, 15 October 2012, <http://www.newyorker.com/magazine/2012/10/15/the-dead-are-real> (last accessed 13 June 2016).
27. Jeffries, 'Hilary Mantel'.
28. Simpson, 'Hilary Mantel'.
29. Frances Wilson, '*Bring up the Bodies* by Hilary Mantel – Review', *The Guardian*, 13 May 2012, <http://www.theguardian.com/books/2012/may/13/bring-up-bodies-hilary-mantel-review> (last accessed 13 June 2016). See also Tayler, '*Wolf Hall*'; Greenblatt, 'How It Must Have Been'; Marianne Brace, '*Wolf Hall*, by Hilary Mantel', *The Independent*, 7 May 2009, <http://www.independent.co.uk/arts-entertainment/books/reviews/wolf-hall-by-hilary-mantel-1680694.html> (last accessed 13 June 2016); Wendy Smith, 'Book Review: Booker Prize-Winner *Wolf Hall* by Hilary Mantel', *The Washington Post*, 6 October 2009, <http://www.washingtonpost.com/wp-dyn/content/article/2009/10/06/AR2009100602905.html> (last accessed 13 June 2016).
30. Simpson, 'Hilary Mantel'.
31. Hilary Mantel, *Wolf Hall* (London: Fourth Estate, 2009), p. 378. All quotations are from this edition; hereafter, page numbers will be given in the text, preceded by *WH*.
32. Tim Adams, 'Hilary Mantel Interview: "My Problem Is Never Ideas. My Problem Is Time"', *The Guardian*, 26 April 2014, <http://www.theguardian.com/books/2014/apr/27/hilary-mantel-interview-wolf-hall-novelist-margaret-thatcher-assassin> (last accessed 13 June 2016).
33. Hilary Mantel, *Bring up the Bodies* (London: Fourth Estate, 2012), p. 407. All quotations are from this edition; hereafter, page numbers will be given in the text, preceded by *BUB*.
34. Simpson, 'Hilary Mantel'.
35. Michael Caines, '*Wolf Hall*: Hilary Mantel's Henrician Hero', *The Times Literary Supplement*, 13 May 2009, <http://www.the-tls.co.uk/articles/public/wolf-hall-hilary-mantels-henrician-hero> (last accessed 13 June 2016).
36. Simpson, 'Hilary Mantel'.
37. Margaret Atwood, '*Bring up the Bodies* by Hilary Mantel – Review', *The Guardian*, 4 May 2012, <http://www.theguardian.com/books/2012/may/04/bring-up-the-bodies-hilary-mantel-review> (last accessed 13 June 2016).
38. Mantel, *Wolf Hall*, p. 150.
39. Mantel, *Bring up the Bodies*, p. 180.
40. Robinson, *Narrating the Past*, p. x.
41. Ibid.
42. Ibid, pp. x, xiii.
43. See Arias, 'Exoticising the Tudors'.
44. Elodie Rousselot, 'Introduction', in Rousselot (ed.), *Exoticising the Past*, pp. 1–16; p. 1.
45. De Groot, *The Historical Novel*, p. 8.
46. James Wood, 'Invitation to a Beheading: The Thomas Cromwell Novels of Hilary Mantel', *The New Yorker*, 7 May 2012, <http://www.newyorker.com/magazine/2012/05/07/invitation-to-a-beheading> (last accessed 13 June 2016).
47. Gillian O'Shaughnessy, 'Hilary Mantel reveals timing of her next book and what's after Thomas Cromwell', *Afternoons*, ABC Perth, 15 February 2015, <http://blogs.abc.net.au/wa/2015/02/hilary-mantel-reveals-timing-of-her-next-book-and-whats-next-after-thomas-cromwell.html> (last accessed 13 June 2016).

48. Geraldine Brooks, 'Cromwell Gets Ahead', *Sydney Morning Herald*, 12 May 2012, <http://www.smh.com.au/entertainment/books/cromwell-gets-ahead-20120510-1ydms.html> (last accessed 13 June 2016).

FURTHER READING

For an up-to-date list of Hilary Mantel's novels, see the British Council website: <https://literature.britishcouncil.org/writer/hilary-mantel> (last accessed 13 June 2016).

Arias, Rosario, 'Exoticising the Tudors: Hilary Mantel's Re-Appropriation of the Past in *Wolf Hall* and *Bring up the Bodies*', in Elodie Rousselot (ed.), *Exoticising the Past in Contemporary Neo-Historical Fiction* (Basingstoke: Palgrave Macmillan, 2014), pp. 19–36.

Pollard, Eileen J., '"Mind What Gap?": An Interview with Hilary Mantel', *Textual Practice*, 29.6 (2015), 1,035–44.

Rennison, Nick, 'Hilary Mantel', *Contemporary British Novelists*, Routledge Key Guides Series (London: Routledge, 2004), pp. 98–100.

CHAPTER 4

Zadie Smith: The Geographies of Marriage

Gretchen Gerzina

The publication of Zadie Smith's *White Teeth* in 2000 had an enormous impact on the turn-of-the-century literary scene. With its assemblage of cultures, argots, races and classes, it spoke to a contemporary audience of a London that had been irrevocably altered by immigration and multiculturalism. That it had been written by a twenty-four-year-old from northwest London, who began it as a student at Cambridge University, made it a *cause célèbre*, heralding a new kind of writer in a new kind of London. Following in the footsteps of Pepys and Dickens, Smith made it clear that this new polyglot way of expressing the experience of being a Londoner was shaped by geography, experiences and voices. As she said in a lecture delivered at the New York Public Library eight years after the novel appeared, 'Recently my double voice has deserted me for a single one, reflecting the smaller world into which my work has led me. Willesden was a big, colourful, working-class sea; Cambridge was a smaller, posher pond, and almost univocal; the literary world is a puddle.'[1] The book, however, made huge ripples in this otherwise tiny literary world.

If globalisation seems now to be supplanting the British novelist's traditional preoccupation with regional and national identity, an examination of Zadie Smith's work to date – consisting at this point of four novels, some short stories and a considerable number of essays – shows that the global can comfortably sit inside the local, sharing language and relationships. In Smith's work, it is the local, in all its geographic clarity, that is the metonym standing for much more than mere location. In her first and fourth novels, *White Teeth* and *NW* respectively, the world consists of a very particular part of London: the 'North-West London of Cricklewood, Willesden, Harlesden, Kilburn and Hampstead'.[2] In these places, 'You have no choice but to cross borders and speak in tongues. That's how you get from your mother to your father, from talking to one set of folks who think you're not black enough to another who figure you insufficiently white. It's the kind of town where the wise man says "I" cautiously, because "I" feels like too straight and singular a phoneme to represent the true multiplicity of his experience.'[3]

Although much of the scholarship on Zadie Smith's work looks at it (incorrectly, in my opinion) through a postcolonial lens, this chapter instead views it in terms of the geography of marriage. Especially in the novels *On Beauty* (2005) and *NW* (2012), it examines the family within a spatial setting in which one of the partners is an outsider to that particular location, and the other partner is intrinsic to it. In both novels, one of the partners is an actual foreigner, and one of the partners is the bearer of a secret. In both novels there is an analogical epic journey through that geography. In *NW*, Keisha/Natalie's story of social advance is paralleled and undermined by her journey through the underworld of her council estate past in the company of a drug addict as she deserts her mixed-race, Italian-born husband and family; in *On Beauty*, the property-owning and generationally grounded African-American Kiki visits the London background of her adulterous husband Howard, and their children navigate urban and suburban Boston. While interracial relationships figure in all these marriages, race is not the crucial factor, nor is it ever truly the point. Indeed, in *NW*, Smith deliberately only describes the race of the white character, subverting the way that race is normally portrayed in fiction. Both novels take place within very specific geographies in which movement and transgression test whether the centre can hold.

Although *White Teeth*, Smith's debut novel, takes place primarily in north London neighbourhoods, it was border crossings of race, religion, class and generations that made it so compelling to readers. Through a mixture of wit and a perfect ear for speech, Smith seemed to wrench the English novel fully into the twenty-first century. Opening with the thwarted suicide attempt of Archie Jones, a World War II veteran whose Italian wife has deserted their loveless marriage, it swerves into his rebirth as the husband of a Jamaican teenager and the best friend of a Bengali Muslim from Bangladesh, whom he had known in the war. Both men have undistinguished careers. Archie designs folds in a paper-printing factory, and Samad, obsessed by his great-grandfather's dubious historical importance, is a waiter in a curry house, and both become parents. Samad is in an arranged marriage and struggles with secular desires. Archie and Clara's daughter struggles with body image and self-worth, while Samad's twins move into religious and political positions that differ from his attempts to direct them. The children are therefore thorough Londoners, despite only one of the parents being English by birth. To this ethnic stew Smith adds the Jewish and Catholic Chalfens, Hampstead intellectuals of liberal but questionable leanings.

The book was abundantly, and for the most part favourably, reviewed on both sides of the Atlantic, spurred on by the appearance of a young, mixed-race writer who had reportedly received an advance of £250,000 for a first novel begun while a university student. The notoriously hard to please Michiko Kakutani heralded it in the *New York Times* as 'a novel that announces the debut of a preternaturally gifted new writer – a writer who at the age of 24 demonstrates both an instinctive storytelling talent and a fully fashioned voice that's street-smart and learned, sassy and philosophical all at the same time. This, "White Teeth" announces, is someone who can do comedy, drama and satire, and do them all with exceptional confidence and brio.'[4] It won the *Guardian* First Book Prize, the James Tait Black Memorial Prize, the Whitbread First Novel Award and the Commonwealth Writers' First Book Prize, and was short-listed for the Orange Prize, in 2000. It went on to be a television mini-series in 2002, airing in both Britain and America.

British reviewers are not always kind to successful writers, and James Wood denounced *White Teeth* (along with other postmodern works by Salman Rushdie, David Foster Wallace and Don DeLillo), making use of a term he coined for the occasion, 'hysterical realism'. Hysterical realism, he argued, is to be found in 'faux-Dickensian' works – works that avoid the nuances of character by 'forever seeing connections and links and plots, and paranoid parallels', and by creating characters who are 'fully alive'. Echoing in some ways Virginia Woolf's denunciation of writers like Arnold Bennett and H. G. Wells, Wood wrote that 'These novelists proceed like street-planners of old in South London: they can never name a street Ruskin Street without linking a whole block, and filling it with Carlyle Street, and Turner Street, and Morris Street, and so on.' The very things that drew new readers to these novels were the things he rued in the frantic pace and whirlwind, conceptual relationships, and 'a fervid intensity of connectedness', rather than a leisurely development of character.[5] Yet by the use of this street-mapping analogy, he recognised the importance of local geography in Smith's work.

The young Smith, rather surprisingly, wrote a response in *The Guardian* that largely agreed with him about her work, even if she was taken aback by being lumped in with other more established and celebrated novelists.[6] As a young writer just learning her craft, she was surprised by the relentless attention paid to her novel. The main question she asked herself, she said, was 'But how does it work? I want to dismantle it as if it were a clock, as if it had parts, mechanisms. I wonder if Wood will take that question, then, as a replacement for my earlier one. Not: how does this world work? But: how is this book made? How can I do this?'[7]

These are the very questions that she has continued to ask herself with each subsequent novel. Despite her conciliatory response to Wood, who despaired of calculated and cold inhuman protagonists, she created in 2002's *The Autograph Man* Alex-Li Tandem, a seemingly hollow young Chinese-Jewish man in suburbia, obsessed with the celebrity culture of movie star photographs and autographs. Told in a deliberately schematic way that opens with a chart called 'The Kabbalah of Alex-Li Tandem', followed by a page of Lenny Bruce's delineations of Jewishness and 'goyishness', and chapter headings that are definitions or outlines of the events to come, it is as though she was seeing how far she could carry the conceit. Perhaps this is what led to the subtitle, 'A Novel'.

If readers expected the sophomore effort to be another book about multi-vocal identities in northwest London, they instead found themselves in an unnamed location near Heathrow, with a person whose drugged blackout leaves him without recent memories and apparently without a conscience or soul. He discovers that he owns the autograph of his favourite faded star, Kitty Alexander; he is convinced that it is a mysterious gift, but his friends believe he created it himself. When he suddenly realises that he is booked on a flight to New York to attend a convention, he abandons his black girlfriend on the eve of her cardiac surgery, and ends up searching for – and finding – the lost star Kitty, and bringing her back with him to London.

The underlying existential question in the novel is 'what is real?'. As Urszula Terentowicz-Fotyga puts it, 'If *The Autograph Man* offers a vision of reality in which place is not a clear support of identity, it is not because of migration and displacement but because of a problematic sense of "the Real".'[8] The geography shifts between London and New York and back to London, yet Alex always seems to be nowhere. His lack of true inner mobility is signified by his wrecked car, ruined in an accident that he cannot recall. Instead of a marriage, the younger black woman and the older white woman form a friendship, and Alex must make peace with them, with his father's long-ago death, and with himself. He must, in the truest sense of the phrase, find out where he is.

Because Smith never wants to write the same book twice, she approaches each new novel as an opportunity for reinvention. With the exuberant but rather chaotic opening salvo of *White Teeth*, critics struggled to find a literary category in which to place her. If her Cambridge education, her knowledge of life on the streets of London, and her 'cheerful multiculturalism opens her writing to charges of playing to the masses', writes Maeve Tynan, 'her explicit literariness leaves her vulnerable to accusations of elitism'.[9] This helps to clarify her earlier statement on originally being 'double-voiced', since the London voices of Willesden and the 'posher' voices of Cambridge originally seemed to be unbridgeable. This could be the reason she pushed *The Autograph Man* into the realm of categories, grids, quotations and lost memory.

With *On Beauty*, Smith found herself relaxed and self-assured enough to tackle what she had wanted to do from the start: 'With a brazen ahistoricism I can't intellectually defend, around February 2003 I indulged myself and sat down to write the big, "realist" (better to say in the style of Realism), slightly Edwardian novel that I had dreamt of writing as a child. It was the book I couldn't quite manage when I was 20, sitting down to write *White Teeth*.'[10] 'Can I do that?' she asked herself. Eschewing the pyrotechnics of her younger self, she viewed writing a realist novel as 'brazen' and self-indulgent, something that led critics to compare her rewriting of E. M. Forster's Edwardian novel to Jean Rhys's retelling of *Jane Eyre* in *Wide Sargasso Sea*. For Smith, however, the question was not whether she could retell Forster's story as an outsider, but instead whether she could transplant a similar one to a new geographical location, with different political and societal issues and problems. The London and its suburbs of *Howards End* are not the Boston and its suburbs of her third novel. With this geographical shift comes a look at a different kind of mixed family, in which the marriage is less about race than about aesthetics and family and political values.

In *Howards End* these oppositions are between two families, the Schlegels and the Wilcoxes, representing culture on one side and business on the other. The binaries and oppositions in both *Howards End* and *On Beauty* have been well discussed, with the Belseys and the Kippses forming the poles in Smith's novel. As a campus novel, the familiar formulation of university intrigues and arguments allows her to stay within two known outlines yet delve into issues that work even better within an American context. Kiki Belsey's background, documented by the hanging portraits of her African-American foremothers as freed slave, maid and nurse, allows the family to be middle class in a desirable house close to a desirable university. She is comfortable with her history, and even presumably with the body that has grown drastically since she first met Howard. It is Howard, despite his whiteness, who brings little other than his working-class Englishness to the couple; it is Kiki's house, history and country. With a family originally from Florida, she has gone so far as to name her daughter after the Harlem Renaissance writer Zora Neale Hurston, whose book *Their Eyes Were Watching God* Smith originally resisted reading when her own mother recommended it to her.

Even so, Howard needs to be schooled about his own white privilege. Smith's London, discussed below in *NW*, is a geography carefully inscribed by streets, council estates, terraced houses, shops and bus routes. *On Beauty*'s Wellington is demarcated by town and gown. The campus and its environs, including cafés and libraries, are a foreign country to those in the surrounding inner city areas. As a black hospital administrator married to a white professor, Kiki is different in colour, size and profession from nearly everyone in Howard's world. Although the house that she brings into this marriage qualifies her to be an insider, Kiki finds herself performing blackness when among them. As she tells her oblivious husband, 'you *never* notice. You think it's normal. Everywhere we go, I'm along in this ... this *sea* of white. I don't see any black folk unless they be cleaning under my feet in the fucking café in your *fucking* college. Or pushing a fucking hospital bed through a corridor. I *staked my whole life* on you. And I have no idea any more why I did that.'[11]

The differences between Wellington and London are political as well as personal. When visiting professor and Trinidadian Rembrandt scholar Monty Kipps arrives from London, he brings to this third country his ultraconservative views on race, affirmative action and religion. The British practice of 'positive discrimination' is not at all as ensconced in law and institutional policy as it is in many American locations, and on American campuses, as in Wellington, it causes deep divisions. Viewing himself as an academic insider who became prominent through his own merits, Kipps finds the American system as practised in universities repugnant.

His lovely Marylebone house, seemingly peaceful and religious, is an island of calm and order, especially compared to the chaos of the Belsey home, where the children struggle with their identities and place in the world. Adolescent son Levi adopts a Brooklyn patois and hip hop persona as representing 'true' blackness, while Jerome, on an internship in London, falls for the Kipps aesthetic, and for their daughter, with the quintessentially British name of Victoria. According to Susan Alice Fischer, 'the entrenched positions that the characters take on in their intimate and public lives have a destructive effect, which halts progress in both arenas'.[12] In this sea of adopted identities, only Kiki remains her true self. Although Tracey Walters views many of the black women Smith creates as stereotypes, she finds that with Kiki, who stands up to her wayward husband, 'Smith manages to create female characters that transcend their stereotypical image'.[13] Kiki's growth from wife and mother, to friend of Carla Kipps, the wife of Howard's nemesis, to independent woman transcends place. Even when she deserts the house, leaving behind her philandering husband to care for it and the children, and moves into an unnamed place where he cannot find her, her missing presence in the house is palpable.

Many critics and scholars found Smith's use of Forster's novel overdetermined and too full of literary allusions ('We feel here the heavy hand of authorial intrusion; Smith's predilection for scholarly reference taking precedence over believable representations of her characters').[14] However, it is exactly the imposition of a modern American location and perspective upon an English Edwardian antecedent that allows the novel to explore marriage and identity in a fresh and culturally relevant context. Writing about Forster in her book of essays, *Changing My Mind*, Smith says, 'Here's the thing about literary criticism: it hates its own times, only realising their worth later. And then, twenty years after that, it wildly sentimentalises them, out of nostalgia for a collective youth.'[15] Smith displays no nostalgia for the novels of her youth, and admires Forster for being 'an Edwardian among modernists, and yet – in matters of pacifism, class, education and race – a progressive among conservatives'.[16] It might be said that with *On Beauty*, she was a realist among post-postmodernists.

It was a deliberate choice for the English publisher of *NW* to present the author's name and the book's title in letters cut out of the map of London, against a multi-coloured background of expanding rhombuses. Like the map of London, a city sewn together by interlocking villages that grew together over centuries, Smith's novel *NW* is stitched together by literary styles, classes, races and voices. This seeming inconsistency of form eluded some critics, who saw it as a failed experiment in postmodernism instead of a careful and meaningful design, but Smith herself, who took seven years to write the book, declared herself 'much prouder of this book than any book I've ever written'.[17] Even James Wood, so often quoted for his panning of *White Teeth* in 2000, was effusive in his praise for this novel twelve years later:

> Smith has a restless, continuous relation with the novelistic tradition, and appears to be trying out different styles and forms in this new, Joycean / Woolfian / Dos Passos-ish work—first and third person, stream of consciousness, free, indirect style, dialogue written out like a screenplay, numbered vignettes, and so on. This seems to me pretty brave, because it risks alienating former readers who have just gotten comfy with her last work.

He appreciates that readers struggle with a work that is so unfamiliar, and so difficult to categorise:

> The decentered and interrupted form feels right here, because this novel is trying to bring home a whale of a city, and to number the days of people who do not necessarily feel that they themselves possess an ordered internal calendar—who may feel, like Natalie, one of the protagonists, that they lack a continuous sense of self. . . . But, in fact, there *is* a marvelous, implied center to this novel's style—or perhaps current would be a better word than centre: underneath the formal experimentation runs a steady, clear, realistic genius.

The former sceptic ended by naming *NW* one of the best books of the year.[18]

NW links four characters, some of whom are intimately involved, and some who never meet except when they hear about the other in the news. Three of them grew up in the housing estates of Willesden, whose tower blocks were ironically named for philosophers (the buildings which Smith models them on were ironically named for writers), and the three still live nearby, in areas demarcated by class. Leah Hanwell's parents are Irish and English, and Leah, now married to an African hairdresser, works in social services among Afro-Caribbean women who resent her marriage. They live in a council flat with their beloved dog, where Leah hides her contraceptives and abortions from her husband. Her former best friend Keisha has moved aggressively through the education ranks to become a barrister, and along the way changed her name to the less black-sounding Natalie; she marries a handsome, wealthy man who was conceived in a single encounter between a Trinidadian man and an Italian woman. They have two children and live in a large house in gentrifying Kilburn, not that far from where Keisha grew up. As a child, Leah had a tremendous crush on Nathan Bogle, who also lived in the estates, but whose beauty as a boy disintegrated into drugs and crime when life failed to offer him better options. All these characters come together in a long, realistic and hopeful section of the novel, told about the last day in the life of a man called Felix – happiness – who seems to be moving toward a gratifying future but who dies tragically and unexpectedly at the end of the section.

The novel clearly defines what I call the geography of marriage. As with *On Beauty*, the husbands in *NW* are strangers in a strange land, married to women whose home territory they now inhabit. However, in this novel, it is the husbands who are centred and focused, and the wives, Leah and Natalie, who are lost. Smith's use of form in the women's sections reflects their inner chaos. Leah's sections are mainly Joycean stream of consciousness, and Keisha/Natalie's disjointed 185 segments, some only a sentence long, reflect her inability to accept fully the life she has so determinedly crafted for herself. As she descends into a split life as successful wife and mother versus near prostitute, and ultimately into an underworld journey through northwest London with Nathan Bogle, she, like Leah, travels with the aid of drugs through a dark night of the soul.

With *NW* set against the backdrop of the Caribbean carnival in Notting Hill Gate, two other works inform these two women's descents. In Leah's case, Smith's short story 'Hanwell in Hell', published in *The New Yorker* in 2004, is the antecedent. In this story, an anonymous Melvillian man recounts a strange night-time encounter in Bristol with a Mr Hanwell; he is now writing to Hanwell's daughter to try to explain what he learned that night. Like the narrator, Hanwell turns out to be a war veteran. He now washes dishes in a restaurant, but was once a chef in a Soho restaurant, on Dean Street in London, after learning to cook in France while in the military. After several drinks, the two men end up in Hanwell's miserable flat, where Hanwell reveals that his daughters are in London, and that his wife hanged herself. Colour blind, he is painting the walls a 'violent, hellish deep red' that he mistakes for a sunny yellow, hoping that someday his daughters will join him.[19] We know that they will not, and that they will not understand why they are not all together. In life, and perhaps in death, Hanwell is truly in hell. In NW Smith does not make explicit the link between Leah Hanwell, and her refusal to become a parent, and this Hanwell, but they are definitely connected; as Smith says of the two stories, 'the world is linked'.[20] Hanwell's marriage is lost, and Leah is well on the way to losing hers through a refusal to tell her husband the truth.

The second referent falls in Keisha/Natalie's night-time odyssey with Nathan Bogle. When her husband discovers her barely concealed online presence on a website that links people looking for sex with people willing to provide it, she leaves her house without proper clothing, shoes, wallet or transport pass. Disorientated, and her marriage and life in tatters, she walks the streets where she encounters the equally dishevelled, and probably drugged, Nathan. Together they walk and walk, smoke weed, hide in the shadows, and sit on the side of the road. With carnival lurking in the London wings, their wandering is reminiscent of the 1959 film *Black Orpheus*, Marcel Camus's retelling of the Orpheus myth set in Rio, with Eurydice dead in the underworld. Instead of the Brazilian *favela*, or slum, the episode in NW takes place in the seedier parts of Willesden and Kilburn. And as Eurydice's guide at the beginning of the film says, 'No one can resist the madness.'[21]

Keisha/Natalie's period of madness ends when she and Leah, also deeply disturbed and nearly catatonic after her secret about not wanting children is revealed to her husband Michel, join forces and call a hotline to suggest that Nathan is Felix's killer. Whether or not this is true is unclear; Smith herself says that it is meant to be ambiguous.[22] Leah's marriage survives, and the women bond again over the murder of someone they never met. Yet the reconciliations only occur with the loss of Felix, or 'happiness'. As Anne Enright writes, 'Though it remains absolutely rooted, stuck to the map, contexts change and narrative styles shift. This is a book in which you never know how things will come together or what will happen next.' And, since the traditional forms and language cannot express the self, 'None of these things make sense on the streets of northwest London.'[23]

It would initially appear that the insider status of the two women, as well as that of Nathan, would make them far more at home in their setting than their foreign-born husbands. Instead, their husbands settle comfortably into this area of London, but Leah and Natalie, who have returned from educational and sexual experimentation over the years, find themselves spiritually and even morally depleted. The part of London that sustained them as children, and where they returned as wives, now seems a foreign and frightening territory to them.

Citing the failure of an 'overdetermined and ossified London' in Smith's first three novels, Laurent Mellet sees London as a 'mere geographical and cultural grid-mapped city' in which characters wander in oblique ways through their past and present.[24] In the progression of Smith's novels, location becomes increasingly focused, while form and approach experiment to accommodate the many possibilities of using fiction to express reality. As she has said, paraphrasing Susan Sontag, 'style is a way of expressing truth'.[25] The truths that these experiments in style approach are rooted in place, but also with the search for self and connection with others that is inextricably linked to the past and to location.

NOTES

1. Zadie Smith, 'Speaking in Tongues', *New York Review of Books*, 26 February 2009, <http://www.nybooks.com/articles/2009/02/26/speaking-in-tongues-2> (last accessed 13 June 2016). Based on a lecture given at the New York Public Library, December 2008.
2. Laurent Mellet, '"Just keep on walking in a straight line": Allowing for Chance in Zadie Smith's Overdetermined London (*White Teeth*, *The Autograph Man* and *On Beauty*)', in Vanessa Guignery and François Gallix (eds), *(Re-)Mapping London: Visions of the Metropolis in the Contemporary Novel in English* (Paris: Publibook, 2008), p. 187.
3. Smith, 'Speaking in Tongues'.
4. Michiko Kakutani, 'Quirky, Sassy and Wise in a London of Exiles', *New York Times*, 25 April 2000, <http://www.nytimes.com/2000/04/25/books/books-of-the-times-quirky-sassy-and-wise-in-a-london-of-exiles.html> (last accessed 13 June 2016).
5. See James Wood, <https://newrepublic.com/article/61361/human-all-too-inhuman> (last accessed 13 June 2016).
6. Zadie Smith, 'This Is How It Feels to Be Me', *The Guardian*, 13 October 2001, <http://www.theguardian.com/books/2001/oct/13/fiction.afghanistan> (last accessed 13 June 2016).
7. Ibid.
8. Urszula Terentowicz-Fotyga, 'The Impossible Self and the Poetics of the Urban Hyperreal in Zadie Smith's *The Autograph Man*', in Tracey L. Walters (ed.), *Zadie Smith: Critical Essays* (New York: Peter Lang, 2008), p. 59.
9. Maeve Tynan, '"Only Connect": Intertextuality and Identity in Zadie Smith's *On Beauty*', in Walters (ed.), *Zadie Smith: Critical Essays*, p. 73.
10. Quoted in Philip Tew, *Zadie Smith* (Basingstoke: Palgrave Macmillan, 2010), p. 93.
11. Zadie Smith, *On Beauty* (New York: Penguin Press, 2005), p. 206.
12. Susan Alice Fischer, '"Temporal Layers": Personal and Political History in Zadie Smith's *On Beauty*', in Philip Tew, *Reading Zadie Smith: The First Decade and Beyond* (London: Bloomsbury, 2013), p. 82.
13. Tracey L. Walters, 'Still Mammies and Hos: Stereotypical Images of Black Women in Zadie Smith's Novels', in Walters (ed.), *Zadie Smith: Critical Essays*, p. 126.
14. Tynan, '"Only Connect"', p. 79.
15. Zadie Smith, 'E. M. Forster, Middle Manager', in *Changing My Mind* (Kindle edition, n.p.).
16. Ibid.
17. Gaby Wood, 'The Return of Zadie Smith', *The Telegraph*, 25 August 2012, <http://www.telegraph.co.uk/culture/books/9495181/The-return-of-Zadie-Smith.html> (last accessed 13 June 2016).
18. James Wood, 'Books of the Year', *The New Yorker*, 17 December 2012, <http://www.newyorker.com/books/page-turner/books-of-the-year> (last accessed 13 June 2016).
19. Zadie Smith, 'Hanwell in Hell', *The New Yorker*, 27 September 2004, <http://www.newyorker.com/magazine/2004/09/27/hanwell-in-hell> (last accessed 13 June 2016).
20. Zadie Smith, conversation with Gretchen Gerzina, 2 February 2016.
21. Marcel Camus, *Black Orpheus* (*Orfeu negro*) [film made in Brazil, 1959].
22. Smith, conversation with Gerzina, 2 February 2016.
23. Anne Enright, 'Mind the Gap', Sunday Book Review, *New York Times*, 21 September 2012, <http://www.nytimes.com/2012/09/23/books/review/nw-by-zadie-smith.html> (last accessed 13 June 2016).
24. Mellet, '"Just keep on walking in a straight line"', p. 188.
25. Zadie Smith, Lecture, Dartmouth College, 2 February 2016.

FURTHER READING

For an up-to-date list of Zadie Smith's novels, see the British Council website: <https://literature.britishcouncil.org/writer/zadie-smith> (last accessed 13 June 2016).

Guignery, Vanessa, and François Gallix (eds), (Re-)Mapping London: Visions of the Metropolis in the Contemporary Novel in English (Paris: Publibook, 2008).
Tew, Philip, Reading Zadie Smith: The First Decade and Beyond (London: Bloomsbury, 2013).
—— Zadie Smith (Basingstoke: Palgrave Macmillan, 2010).
Walters, Tracey L. (ed.), Zadie Smith: Critical Essays (New York: Peter Lang, 2008).

PART II

Realism and Beyond

CHAPTER 5

Maggie O'Farrell: Discoveries at the Edge

Susan Strehle

If the twenty-first-century British novel follows Maggie O'Farrell's lead, it will include family dramas of psychological depth and feminist interest. Far removed from post-postmodernist reflexivity and historical revisionism, O'Farrell's six novels bring an updated psychological realism to bear on the tangled lives of contemporary British characters. The novels function as mysteries in which a present event sends the protagonist on a quest, often interior and reflective; the answer lies in the past, where a hidden or frustrated passion has thwarted the protagonist's (sometimes an entire family's) self-knowledge and acceptance. Feminist in their focus on women, the novels take a psychological rather than programmatic approach to women's issues and therefore approach gender with complex understanding. They suggest that twenty-first-century feminist fiction may present a subtle sympathy for men and women limited by outdated but powerful traditions. Realist rather than post-modernist in their assurance that secret histories can be uncovered, understood and survived, the novels sometimes reference national history, but their interest lies in personal histories of love, lust, courage and betrayal. O'Farrell's record of positive reviews, literary prizes and healthy sales suggests that twenty-first-century readers remain interested in realist human narratives.

In the six novels she has published since 2000, O'Farrell focuses on protagonists caught between past and present, plunged into extreme states where secret histories emerge, and struggling against the obscure residue of a repressed past. The novels explore secrets kept through decades in troubled families, warping relationships and turning unconventional protagonists into detectives ransacking the familial and cultural past. The novels often focus on female characters, but they also develop complex and interesting male characters. Sophisticated literary mysteries invoking tradition with an innovational edge, the novels update fictional conventions in complex, layered plots that, as one reviewer put it, 'appeal to a broad audience, but they're also smart and provocative'.[1] O'Farrell's transformative twenty-first-century sensibility explores contemporary characters' efforts to develop creative responses to histories that isolate them and to legacies of family secrecy and shame.

O'Farrell's biography suggests some reasons for her fascination with outsiders, rebels and protagonists on the edge. Her early life crosses a series of British outskirts, places bearing a somewhat uneasy, outsider status within the United Kingdom. She was born, the second of three girls, in Coleraine, Northern Ireland, but moved when she was two to Wales and ten years later to Scotland. 'My sisters and I', she told an interviewer, 'can't really get away from the idea we don't really know where we belong. It's very hard.'[2] When another interviewer asked her which of these places define her, she commented, 'All of them and none', and added that her husband, writer William Sutcliffe, 'had to drag me kicking and screaming' back to London, where they now live with three children.[3] Earlier in her life she spent a year working in Hong Kong, realising she 'had no idea what I was going to do with my life'.[4] She wrote poetry and worked as a journalist before her first novel, appearing in 2000, inaugurated her career as a writer of fiction. O'Farrell's novels have sold well and won prizes: *After You'd Gone* won a Betty Trask Award (2001), *The Distance Between Us* a Somerset Maugham Award (2005), and *The Hand that First Held Mine* the Costa Novel Award (2010). In 2007, Waterstone's bookshops selected O'Farrell for inclusion in *25 Authors for the Future*.[5] Although her novels have been widely and positively reviewed, critical analysis of her fiction has been limited.

O'Farrell's novels turn on sudden disappearances and reappearances that trigger major changes for the characters. In one interview, she comments that 'I suppose I'm drawn to the romance of things that have vanished. That's what fascinates me about living in cities. Everywhere you go, you're constantly bumping into the past.'[6] With a focus on women's romantic lives, her fiction explores psychological catastrophes that change the course of love and send her protagonists into extreme states. Catastrophic events call up memories of the sometimes-damaging familial bonds that have shaped the characters and defined their values. Aiming for compelling characters, psychological depth and near-Gothic mystery and suspense, O'Farrell interweaves past and present, realistic accounts of present events and impressionistic evocations of psychic landscapes, plausible dialogues and tour-de-force poetic reflections of memory and feeling.

O'Farrell's first novel, *After You'd Gone* (2000), develops mystery and suspense around protagonist Alice Raike's extreme state: she lies in a coma, drifting in and out of murky semi-consciousness. She has travelled by train to Edinburgh, visited her sisters, seen something shocking in the train station, and then returned to London – where she steps into traffic and is hit by a car. The novel alternates its focus between Alice's history, narrated in the third person, and her present state, narrated in the first person, as she becomes aware of her family gathered beside her hospital bed. Her relationships to family members are complicated; she feels alien, dark and tall between sisters who are fair and short, uneasy in her relationship to an over-critical mother. She has chosen lovers who reflect her outsider status and then married John, a British Jew whose widowed father insisted that he must marry within his faith and who has subsequently refused to have any contact with the couple, once they have married. A few years of happiness with John end when he dies suddenly, a random victim in the London bombings.

The title of this first novel emphasises the power of that catastrophic disappearance to change everything for Alice; but her own disappearance into unconsciousness also triggers changes within her family and uncovers long-buried secrets. The novel asks a question at the beginning that it answers only at the end: what did Alice see in Edinburgh that led her to step into traffic? Eventually we learn that she saw clear evidence of her mother's long-standing extramarital affair with a man whose physical appearance makes him her father; she witnesses, in short, the roots and branches of her own outsider status. In her hospital bed, the novel suggests, Alice must decide whether to return to life and consciousness or not. As she remembers John's funeral and the sudden disappearance of his coffin into a crematorium, she recalls covering her eyes. Appropriately, sound rather than sight pulls Alice back to life; when John's father arrives to apologise and to connect with her, she feels herself rising toward consciousness. This transformative choice arrives 'after you'd gone' for Alice and for Mr Friedmann. More ambiguously, Alice's parents exchange knowledge that will certainly change their lives, perhaps for the better.

After You'd Gone establishes successful artistic patterns for O'Farrell's fiction: the present crisis not only creates suspense and interest but also places the focus on character and motivation. The narrative develops complex portraits of major and minor characters; probing psychological states, it functions as realistic fiction and employs traditional third-person omniscience to build a large set of characters around Alice. O'Farrell also uses Alice's suspension in the coma, which precludes action or development in the present, as an invitation to explore the tangled past in non-linear order and to represent her reflections and memories in impressionistic prose: 'There are times when I am there and times when I am not – when I am elsewhere, blocked off, blocked in.'[7] She creates an appropriate symbol for the unconscious Alice, who experiences the coma as a kind of submersion, in John's pet axolotl, a lizard-like creature that hangs suspended in a tank of water, melancholy and absolutely motionless. This image prepares effectively for the suggestive end of the novel, when Alice wonders whether to 'tread water or swim back down against this force' but experiences the awakening of consciousness as a 'rushing towards some surface'.[8]

In her second novel, *My Lover's Lover* (2002), O'Farrell braids together three stories of anxious love, each of them frustrated by the beloved's former lovers. Lily is strongly attracted to Marcus and accepts his invitation to move into his loft apartment, but as they become lovers she discovers the haunting presence of his former lover, Sinead. In an opening section that evokes Daphne du Maurier's famous novel *Rebecca*, O'Farrell represents Lily's growing unease as she discovers the ominous signs of a too-sudden departure: a single dress hanging in the wardrobe, a ghostly presence and a lingering scent, and a distracted lover who will not tell her anything. A second section of the novel develops Sinead's story, told to Lily in alternating first- and third-person sections that juxtapose the start and the end of her affair with Marcus; her discovery of his infidelity triggers a painful decision to end the relationship. A third narrative adds an important male perspective on love, as Marcus's long-time friend and occasional roommate Aidan discovers that he carries a long-suppressed tenderness and sympathy for the now-desolate Sinead; his growing attachment is, like the others', held in check by the ongoing presence of his lover's lover.

The narrative hinges on Marcus's inability or refusal to tell the truth. Mysterious, charming, apparently attentive and devoted, he exerts a magnetic attraction for Lily. At first, his unwillingness to explain Sinead's departure appears to be a plot device, characterising him as a man bereft, and compelling Lily to look for answers from Sinead. At deeper levels, however, O'Farrell reveals a fundamental dishonesty in his character, a compulsion to lie to himself as well as his lovers, and a profound self-absorption. In a deftly understated sequence completing the reference to du Maurier's *Rebecca*, Lily appears before Marcus in the dress Sinead has left behind – but he fails to recognise it or to connect it with his lost love, entirely absorbed in ordering takeaway food for himself. While du Maurier's seemingly mysterious lover, de Winter, reveals himself in the 'dress scene' as a loyal husband victimised by a faithless wife, Marcus demonstrates instead an exclusive focus on his own appetites.

The women in *My Lover's Lover* survive their encounter with Marcus and pass through extreme states to understanding; their journeys reflect O'Farrell's faith in the healing power of an intelligent acceptance of the past. Sinead's crisis occurs in a single day and night, when Marcus returns from a six-month absence and confesses his infidelity. Narrated to Lily in Part 2 of the novel, Sinead's account emphasises her shock and grief as she understands what Marcus has revealed about himself and decides to leave him. Her assessment of his character at this end point emerges in her detailed recollections of the start of their affair, when he invited her to rural China but failed to appear for four days. Lily's passage through an extreme state has occupied Part 1 of the novel; even more dramatic, her experience of the start of an affair with Marcus is literally haunted by the ghost of her predecessor. Sinead's ghost ignores Marcus, who cannot see her, but watches and warns Lily. Although Lily and Sinead do not become friends, they benefit from shared knowledge of parallel experiences. The novel ends with a chance crossing of their paths in Australia, where the two women and Aidan have all reached more fulfilling stages in their journeys.

O'Farrell's third novel, *The Distance Between Us* (2004), draws on the author's passage through a form of encephalitis as a young child (O'Farrell had a viral infection at eight and missed two years of school) and her later experience as a journalist in Hong Kong. In this novel, protagonist Stella Gilmore has lived her adult life in an extreme state and, as a result, she has developed a habit of disappearing when anyone gets too close. Like the protagonists from O'Farrell's novels that precede and follow, Stella has encountered a brutal, violent male; but Anthony Cusk is a school bully rather than a full-grown man, and his aggressive acts, foreshadowing but not including rape, are directed against both Stella and her older sister Nina. Close since their early years, the sisters develop an exclusive bond in their early teens after Nina nearly dies of a rare viral infection and returns to school a year later to be mocked and shunned. Through a series of flashbacks in random order, the novel gradually unfolds the story, told near the end as external circumstances force Stella to recall it. When she returns to school, other students avoid Nina, who is plagued by uncontrollable shaking and memory loss. From her first day back at school, Anthony acts out the other students' dislike of Nina, now a special needs child. He bullies and torments with increasing aggressiveness as the school year goes on, until he catches the two sisters alone near a precipice during a field trip to Scotland. When he raises his fist and threatens her sister, Stella pushes him and he falls to his death.

Haunted by the knowledge that she was responsible for this young bully's death, Stella lives at an edge like O'Farrell's other protagonists. She and Nina hide their involvement in Anthony's death and become each other's only confidantes, even into a young adulthood where both have lovers and Nina has an erratic and uneven marriage. Stella buries the traumatic past, evades commitment, and disappears whenever events threaten to expose the guilt she has never resolved. As the novel begins, she flees London after encountering a large man who reminds her of Anthony. This flight has one crucial difference: Stella goes back to northern Scotland, to the small town where Anthony died, to uncover and possibly resolve the past.

The Distance Between Us compounds the mysteries of Stella's detachments and disappearances with a second narrative, seemingly unrelated to Stella's story. Like O'Farrell's other novels, *Distance* creates suspense and mystery from the juxtaposition of two apparently disconnected stories: the first of four parts of the novel alternates between Stella in London and Jake in Hong Kong, where he is caught in a Chinese New Year's crush that kills a friend and seriously injures the girl he has been dating – who begs Jake to marry her before she dies. Jake acquiesces; his kindness to Mel as she gradually recovers parallels Stella's protection of her sister. The brief glimpses of Jake and Stella in the first thirty pages of the novel establish their suitability as a pair, while emphasising an apparent impossibility: half a planet away, Jake marries a woman he does not love, while Stella returns to northern Scotland.

The novel develops another satisfying parallel between the two characters in the way it brings them together: Jake's quest for his own roots takes him to the same place in northern Scotland where Stella goes for resolution. Both professionals in related media fields, both take menial jobs at the same hotel, and both suffer in related ways from traumatic violence. Jake's arm, fractured and dislocated in the Hong Kong crush, has healed, but in accepting responsibility for the street violence that nearly killed Mel, he has made an empty and damaging marriage. In burying her accidental killing of Anthony, Stella sees his presence everywhere, and her repeated flight from intimacy leads her to an empty and damaging isolation. Misunderstandings and misreadings of each other create appropriate barriers and deferrals of the growing attachment between Jake and Stella, and in typical O'Farrell fashion both characters find no simple resolution to the historical burdens they carry: Jake finds an empty structure where his father lived but no trace or understanding of the man, and Stella gains no meaningful acceptance of Anthony's death. Subtly reminiscent of Jane Austen, the novel arrives at the union it has promised from the beginning by resolving not the pain these characters have experienced, but instead the isolation that has clouded their perceptions of each other.

Considered by reviewers to be among her best, O'Farrell's fourth novel, *The Vanishing Act of Esme Lennox* (2006), contrasts two sisters who are both suspended in extreme states. Older sister Kitty sinks into Alzheimer's amid confused memories and self-justifications. Younger sister Esme has been institutionalised in a mental hospital for sixty-one years. Their granddaughter Iris receives news that Esme, of whose existence she is unaware, is to be released, and Iris must take responsibility for the odd but entirely sane seventy-something woman. Like other O'Farrell families, this one has deeply buried secrets that emerge in fragments with Esme's release from the asylum. While this novel did not win prizes, it sold well, earned O'Farrell good reviews on both sides of the Atlantic, and was highly praised.

The narrative contains three strands: in the first, narrated in the present tense and the third person, Iris makes present-day efforts to understand Esme and to resolve her own troubled affairs with a married man and with her stepbrother; in the second, narrated in the past tense and the third person, Esme remembers her youth in colonial India and later Scotland as the second daughter of wealthy parents who disapprove of her; in the third, narrated in the past tense and the first person, Kitty caroms through fragmented and jumbled memories, alternating between self-justification and guilt refracted through the fog of dementia. Cloaked in the trappings of a socially advantageous marriage, Kitty has achieved everything her parents wanted; but her husband does not consummate the marriage, and Kitty feels empty and isolated. At the age of sixteen, Esme is raped by an aggressive Scot who claims to admire her spirit and independence just before he tries to destroy them. She is sent to Cauldstone Hospital by her parents, at sixteen, for rebelliousness and what they take to be wicked sensuality; she has been caught dancing, dressed in her mother's silk gown, before a mirror. When Esme turns out to be pregnant, Kitty finds a way to fulfil her wish for a family: she takes Esme's baby to raise as her own son, and she arranges to have Esme institutionalised for the rest of her life. The fog of Kitty's memory loss enables O'Farrell to reveal her selfishness and cruelty even in the ways she denies responsibility.

A strongly feminist novel, *The Vanishing Act of Esme Lennox* shows the shallow and dissatisfied lives of women within Edwardian social constraints. Esme and Kitty's mother and grandmother appear narrow, querulous and unhappy; the mother in particular ignores her children and increasingly dislikes Esme for failing to be obedient, decorative and passive. The novel exposes the punishments inflicted on women to keep them in line – in particular, their incarceration in psychiatric institutions like Cauldstone. O'Farrell writes in the acknowledgements section of the novel that she consulted Elaine Showalter and R. D. Laing to develop the portrait of Cauldstone and the women incarcerated there. For Iris, the reminder of the constraints on women of her grandmother's generation triggers admiration and wonderment that Esme remains vital and astute, despite a lifetime of discipline and punishment. While she is a product of women's liberation, Iris realises that her own life raises some questions worthy of feminist analysis. The novel emphasises Iris's decision to accept responsibility, first for taking whatever steps are needed to free Esme, then for ending her affair with a married man. These decisions appear in immediate contrast to Kitty's denials of responsibility for the theft of Esme's baby and freedom.

A stolen child recurs in O'Farrell's fifth novel, *The Hand that First Held Mine*

(2010); but where the earlier novel focuses on Esme's loss of her son, *Hand* dramatises the son's loss of a mother. As in other O'Farrell titles, two plots appear in this novel, generating narrative suspense around the question of their relationship: in 1955, Lexie Sinclair leaves Devon for London, joins the bohemian Soho scene, becomes a journalist, and lives for a time with the charismatic Innes Kent. In present-day London, Elina and Ted struggle with new parenthood; Elina has gone through an emergency C-section, and she drifts through a fog of weakness and pain as she adjusts to her baby son's needs. The extreme state in this novel appears to belong to Elina, baffled and groggy in the haze of new motherhood. As time passes, however, Ted also enters a traumatised state as parenthood calls up repressed memories of his own early childhood that eventually expose a massive and damaging family lie.

In O'Farrell's fiction, the answers to narrative mysteries coincide with answers to family mysteries; recovering what has been hidden out of shame (Alice's mother's long affair, Marcus's multiple liaisons, Stella's accidental/intentional killing of Anthony, Esme's rape and Kitty's theft of her baby) enables the protagonist to face and understand the past in the present. Many of the shameful secrets that paralyse families are related to sex. Setting *Hand* apart, the Lexie Sinclair narrative depicts an unmarried woman who chooses and enjoys lovers without shame in the 1950s and 1960s. After Innes's sudden death, she focuses on her career as an art critic and, some ten years later, has an affair with Felix; she gets pregnant and has a son, Theo, but refuses to marry Felix. She ends the relationship, not because he has other lovers, but because he chooses as one of them Innes's damaged and vindictive daughter Margot, whom she has warned him to avoid. A few years later she has a satisfying affair with an art critic; when they vacation in Lyme Regis, she drowns in the sea. A self-assured woman, Lexie models the kind of parenting that refuses to hide and repress.

Theo, however, becomes Ted when Lexie dies and he is turned over to Felix and Margot to raise. Avaricious, petty and exploitative, Margot's mother Gloria has raised Margot to deliver vengeance, while Felix is an indifferent and absent father. They tell the three-year-old Ted that he is their son, effectively erasing the mother who loved him. Theft turns out to be the shameful secret in the novel: Gloria has stolen Innes's house, removed valuable paintings he gave Lexie and, like Dickens's Miss Havisham, raised a cruel young woman to steal hearts and ruin those around her. The victim of multiple thefts, Ted grows up sad, cowed and isolated; when his own son is born, he has an increasing awareness of the lies forming his past. These losses are partially restored as the novel ends: Theodore recovers memories of his mother Lexie, and Felix finally tells him the truth, confronts Margot, and delivers a genuine apology as well as a pledge to return the paintings. Elina restores his mother's 'hand' when she returns from the newspaper archives with the articles Lexie wrote, including some that focus on the son whom she called Theo. While Margot has tried to erase Lexie's life, Elina recovers her written words, evidence of her intelligence and strength, and also of her love for her son. Fit partner for Theo and appropriate channel for Lexie's final contact with her son, Elina promises to follow Lexie's model of independence and honesty. Beside these signs of recovery and restoration, however, O'Farrell invests some of her most powerful writing in the poignant depiction of Lexie's last thoughts as she drowns, signalling disappearances from which there is no consoling recovery and losses that cannot be redeemed.

O'Farrell's sixth novel, *Instructions for a Heatwave* (2013), begins, like many of her other novels, with a sudden disappearance: Robert Riordan walks out of his London home to buy a newspaper and does not return. His wife Gretta calls their three children home to London in the midst of a record-breaking heatwave; the family gathering in these circumstances triggers extreme states for everyone as it evokes long-held secrets that have divided family members and limited their lives. In many ways O'Farrell's most complex novel to date, *Heatwave* develops the anxieties, failures and secrets that amplify misunderstandings across the twenty different relationships among the five characters in this family, as well as their partners. The extended family members in *Heatwave* converse, remember, resent, forgive, confide, interpret, challenge, encourage and confront each other. The result is a densely woven study of several characters engaged in complex family dynamics.

Secrets withheld and exposed play a role in *Heatwave*, as they do in every O'Farrell novel. A sympathetic omniscient narrator attends all of the characters as they reveal levels of pained estrangement from people they love and recall past actions and conversations that created distances. Michael Francis, for example, tells Aoife about the infidelity that threatens his marriage. Her mother's favourite and a woman adept at superficial appearances, Monica believes incorrectly that Aoife revealed a secret abortion that ended her marriage. Aoife's secret is a dyslexia so severe that she has never learned to read. Revealed last, Gretta's secret is the most significant: an Irish Catholic, she never married their father, because Robert had married another woman in Ireland. With her secret, Robert's emerges too: his brother fled with his bride on their wedding day, and Robert has for years paid for his brother's care in Ireland. This last revelation sends the family to Ireland, where the novel ends with Robert's return to a family much improved by new understandings.

O'Farrell's latest novel demonstrates the qualities that have led readers and reviewers to admire her fiction: the narrator brings a warmly sympathetic understanding to complex, believable characters who grapple with contemporary problems in a vividly detailed world. An initial suspense amplifies outward as other characters' dramas and fears emerge in relation to the novel's primary mystery, moving both action and relationships forward together. O'Farrell's wise, insightful omniscience represents characters of both genders and many different ages with more tender sympathy and greater understanding than they bring to each other; this narrative stance models the acceptance of failings and flaws that some of the characters achieve as the novels end. Powerful writing contributes to the success of these novels, which engage feelings without sentimentality. A poet before she was a novelist, O'Farrell uses metaphors and similes to develop the emotional resonance of her characters' perceptions. A highly skilled writer with great gifts of observant wit and human warmth, she demonstrates that readers still value complex psychological portraits, updated realism, and excellent writing.

NOTES

1. Stacey D'Erasmo, 'Bubbling to the Surface: Maggie O'Farrell's *Instructions for a Heatwave*', Sunday Book Review, *New York Times*, 26 July 2013, <http://www.nytimes.com/2013/07/28/books/review/maggie-ofarrells-instructions-for-a-heatwave.html?pagewanted=all&_r=0> (last accessed 13 June 2016).
2. Sarah Broughton, 'The Lingering Influence of Childhood Migrations', *New Welsh Review: Wales's Literary Magazine in English*, 59 (Spring 2003), 20–4.
3. Rachel Hore, 'A Life Less Ordinary: Maggie O'Farrell's Diaries Have Provided the Author with Plenty of Inspiration', *The Independent*, 24 April 2010, <http://www.independent.co.uk/arts-entertainment/books/features/a-life-less-ordinary-maggie-ofarrells-diaries-have-provided-the-author-with-plenty-of-inspiration-1950408.html> (last accessed 13 June 2016).
4. Carl Wilkinson, 'Hong Kong for Beginners', *The Observer*, 6 February 2005, <http://www.theguardian.com/travel/2005/feb/06/observerescapesection2> (last accessed 13 June 2016).
5. See <http://www.thebookseller.com/news/waterstones-tips-25-top> (last accessed 13 June 2016).
6. Alastair Sooke, 'Maggie O'Farrell Interview', *The Telegraph*, 17 April 2010, <http://www.telegraph.co.uk/culture/books/7597512/Maggie-OFarrell-interview.html> (last accessed 13 June 2016).
7. Maggie O'Farrell, *After You'd Gone* (2000; New York: Penguin, 2002), p. 167.
8. Ibid., p. 372.

FURTHER READING

For an up-to-date list of Maggie O'Farrell's novels, see the British Council website: <https://literature.britishcouncil.org/writer/maggie-ofarrell> (last accessed 13 June 2016).

Showalter, Elaine, *The Female Malady: Women, Madness, and English Culture 1830–1980* (New York: Pantheon, 1985).

Wilentz, Gay Alden, *Healing Narratives: Women Writers Curing Cultural Dis-ease* (New Brunswick, NJ: Rutgers University Press, 2000).

CHAPTER 6

Sarah Hall: A New Kind of Storytelling

Sue Vice

Sarah Hall's prize-winning fiction is unusual for the wide-ranging nature of its concerns. These include region and ecology, aesthetics and gender, as well as such topics as the flooding of a Lakeland valley to build a reservoir, the artistry of tattooing, a futuristic vision of a British dictatorship, and the planned reintroduction of wolves into Cumbria. Yet although critics praise Hall's fiction for its distinctive imagery and style, several have noted in it an absence of the tension, suspense and jeopardy of conventional narrative.[1] An exploration of her novels shows that, in place of these plot-related elements, a new kind of fiction is evident, drawing on poetic and imagistic features in place of either a postmodern self-consciousness or the overt politics of realism in order to tell a story.

Hall's first novel, *Haweswater* (2002), was inspired by the real-life flooding of the Cumbrian Mardale Valley in 1935 to create a reservoir designed to serve the population of Manchester. This entailed the destruction of the valley's farms and villages, though we find in the acknowledgements, as a means of emphasising its imagined form, that the story the novel tells 'is fictional and is not intended to depict actual individuals, companies or situations, nor are the dates historically accurate'.[2] *Haweswater* focuses on the love affair between two fictional characters, Janet Lightburn, the daughter of a Mardale farmer, and Jack Liggett, the emissary of Manchester Waterworks. As their shared initials suggest, the lovers are drawn together precisely because of the 'electric energy' (H, 114) of their intensely opposed perspectives: Janet takes legal advice against the construction of the dam, but for Jack the flooding of the valley paradoxically honours a childhood spent visiting the Lakelands. The positional antipathy between the two is acted out in the detail of their relationship: we learn that Janet 'still needed to attack [Jack] before she could love' (H, 120), and that after his public declaration of their bond 'her anger converts itself' into passion (H, 180). In anticipation of *The Wolf Border* (2015), where we learn that the wolves' only predator, the golden eagle, is 'long gone from the county',[3] it is Jack's re-engagement with the landscape and its wildlife that causes his death. He seeks to return to its nest in the hills the body of an eagle, killed at his behest by a poacher, but dies in the attempt. Since Janet can neither live without Jack nor leave the land where he is buried, she chooses to end her life by blowing herself up in the walls of the newly constructed dam.

As its title suggests, water is the governing element of *Haweswater*, and is one that appears throughout Hall's work. It is a welcome regional feature in *The Wolf Border* but a sign of ecological disaster in *The Carhullan Army* (2007). In *Haweswater* it represents both the beauty and the danger of the Lakeland landscape; Mardale has its own lake, but its destruction is ensured by the creation of an even greater one, as Janet's brother Isaac puts it to Jack: 'Yor t'fella that's gunna mek t'lake bigga' (H, 81). To Jack, the destruction of people's homes is justified by the fact that the valley is 'designed to hold water. That's what it was meant for' (H, 99). Isaac is the personification of the water's duality, living as he does 'between two worlds' (H, 75): he is as much at home in the water as he is on the land. His father Samuel protests, in what Jack thinks of as the 'bitten-at language of the area' (H, 91), about the planned reservoir by invoking his son's propensity: 'Our children cannot swim t'class and t'church. Well, maybe except young Isaac' (H, 53). The discourse of biblical sacrifice is apparent both in Isaac's name and in what his mother Ella considers to be the blasphemous notion that he should have been born a fish (H, 77). Yet Isaac is not as 'waterproof' (H, 135) as everyone believes him to be. In adult life, he becomes a diver who accepts a commission for an archaeological dive in Haweswater to examine the remains of a village, from which he never resurfaces. Like Janet, Isaac dies in, and as a consequence of, the reservoir. The narrator's conclusion, and the novel's final words, are 'He was home', referring at once to Isaac's preferred element and to the submerged village where he was born.

Like all of Hall's novels, *Haweswater* exhibits a creative contradiction between its fictive and its political significance. The 'tension between progress and tradition' is evident throughout her fiction,[4] but, as Hall herself has argued, *Haweswater* is not intended to possess a straightforward moral meaning, since, as she puts it, 'It was never meant to be a political book. . . . The flooding of Mardale was an inevitable industrial change.'[5] In *Haweswater* social transformation, and the abrupt encounter with modernity that the reservoir represents, are conveyed in personal terms. The 'inevitability' of such change alongside its human cost is implicit in the novel's retrospective viewpoint, which avoids blame or nostalgia, while those of Hall's novels characterised by historical flashforwards, particularly *The Carhullan Army* and *The Wolf Border*, imply the need for ecological vigilance.

The voices of Hall's narrators vary throughout her work, ranging from the omniscient narrators in *Haweswater* and *The Electric Michelangelo* (2004) to the alternation between different perspectives in *How to Paint a Dead Man* (2009) and the short stories of *The Beautiful Indifference* (2011), where first-person narration and third-person omniscience exist alongside free indirect discourse and, more unusually, second-person narrative. *The Carhullan Army* is Hall's only novel narrated entirely in the first person. This is not simply a literary device, but part of the novel's documentary appearance. The narrator, known simply as Sister, has been arrested after an attempted rebellion by an army of women against 'the Authority', the tyrannical rulers of a Britain of the near future. The novel's paratexts emphasise its status as found material. We learn from the prefatory epigraph that the text is a 'statement' from a 'female prisoner': 'English Authority Penal System archive ... Transcript recovered from site of Lancaster holding dock.'[6] Yet the blurring of futuristic realism with symbolism is also apparent, as the first chapter's heading shows: 'File One: Complete Recovery.' The notion of 'recovery' is twofold. While Sister's words have been retrieved by the state, her psyche had earlier been repaired by her decision to flee from the home in Rith she had shared with her husband Andrew. Sister's flight took her to the farm at Carhullan run by the 'Unofficials' in what, as she puts it, 'my father's generation had called the Lake District' (CA, 10).

Just as in *Haweswater*, the question of land ownership underlies the plot of *The Carhullan Army*. As Jack Liggett argues in the former novel, no appeal by local people is possible against the construction of the Haweswater reservoir, because there is 'no higher authority' than parliament's authorisation of Manchester City Waterworks (H, 50). In *The Carhullan Army*, a similar act of compulsory purchase has taken place by the government, this time of Crown land. By this means the Authority are able to 'move people into those rat holes they call quarters' (CA, 104), as Jackie Nixon, Carhullan's leading spirit, claims. A confluence of market crashes and relentless rain has produced a country fully dependent on the USA for its warlike foreign policy and its imported food. Hall's dystopia follows Margaret Atwood's *The Handmaid's Tale* (1985) rather than George Orwell's *Nineteen Eighty-Four* (1949) in representing gender division and reproductive control as crucial to the power of the new ruling dispensation, who have decreed that the right to bear children is to be won by lottery. Thus the removal of Sister's contraceptive coil, which she describes as like an ear-tag inserted by a 'farmer' to control his herd (CA, 28), is one of the first reparative events to take place on her arrival at Carhullan.

First-person narrative in this novel has a literary function even beyond the testimonial and documentary: that of unreliability. The possibility of misdirection is harder than usual to perceive, since Sister is the reader's only guide to the new reality of Authority-run Britain and the alternative life at Carhullan. The omission of any account of her role in the novel's climactic armed conflict between the women and the Authority, a cause for regret to some critics, could be ascribed to Sister's partial view and her reluctance or inability to describe it. Yet the literality of its absence, accounted for as 'Data Lost' in the chapter's heading, makes this omission appear as an authorial decision, motivated perhaps by a reluctance to 'overwhelm', as Benedicte Page has it, a cerebral novel with action.[7] Sister's account of the charismatic Jackie Nixon is the most subtly rendered site of unreliability. Hall has said, 'I didn't want [Jackie] to go over the Colonel Kurtz edge of complete madness ... I wanted her to remain fairly level.'[8] However, Sister's partial viewpoint transforms her into a figure akin to Marlow, the narrator of Kurtz's story in Joseph Conrad's *Heart of Darkness* (1899), making the reader work hard to decipher a moral meaning in what she relates. In Conrad's novella Marlow is blind to the collaboration with colonial murder that he describes.[9] Similarly, in *The Carhullan Army* Jackie is initially described by Sister as if she is a natural and 'indigenous'

(CA, 82) embodiment of the landscape, her eyes 'the colour of slate riverbeds', and thus, 'I knew that the territory had somehow gone into the making of her' (CA, 78). Both the claim to 'know' and the establishment of a link between Jackie and the threatened landscape are devices that appear to legitimise this subjective viewpoint. Among the events that Sister presents uncritically is Jackie's insistence that women's customary disinclination to engage in armed combat is simply the product of social conditioning. Sister implies that, under Jackie's leadership, gender binaries are subverted, but in fact they are simply reversed.[10] Sister is at her most morally unreliable in relating an episode in which Jackie insists that her followers murder Chloe, a reluctant Carhullan member who, with her husband Martyn, tries to opt out of the military attack on Rith. Sister claims that 'I knew I was complicit in their deaths ... I did not feel remorse. I knew that it had needed doing' (CA, 203), and concludes ominously by repeating the real-life euphemism, used by British and American forces, for civilian killings during the first Gulf War of 1991: 'There was no other collateral damage at Carhullan' (CA, 203).

While Rachel Hore regrets *The Carhullan Army*'s focus on dystopian detail at the expense of elaborating on the 'tantalising' hints at the 'big picture' of its historical context,[11] other critics have discerned in it a more specific political allegory than this would suggest. In a 2007 review, written at the time of the 'credit crunch' and just after the wettest British summer on record, Michael Arditti claimed that *The Carhullan Army* 'could not be more timely', and it was the flooding of her Cumbrian home that inspired Hall to begin the novel.[12] Johan Kisro reads the detail of the Authority's reliance on the USA even more specifically as a deliberately low-key reference to Britain's following America into the Iraq War in 2003.[13] In this sense Hall's novel resembles Pat Barker's novel *Regeneration* (1991), which is about the First World War but prompted by the first Gulf War. It is the figure of Jackie, and the inevitable failure of the women's rebellion, which makes *The Carhullan Army* profoundly dystopian in a way different from, for instance, Cormac McCarthy's *The Road* (2006) with its redemptive ending. Even such an 'unofficial' grouping as that of the women of Carhullan, exterior to the monolithic centre of power, is eventually co-opted and vanquished.

The Electric Michelangelo equally approaches an imagined world by means of intricately presented detail. For some critics, this has constituted a liability: Alex Clark claims that Hall has a preference for commentary over drama, which runs the risk of 'muffling' character and plot.[14] While this might be true of *The Carhullan Army* and *Wolf Border*, in part because of the subjective narrative viewpoints in each case, it is less so in Hall's fictional recreations of past eras. As she has argued of *The Electric Michelangelo*, such scenarios are constructed not as the pretext for realist dramatisation, but for the sake of aesthetic experimentation: 'I threw everything at it: language, rhyming sentences, non-existent plot.'[15] However, any claim that the plot of *The Electric Michelangelo* is non-existent might seem exaggerated, since it does have a clear narrative arc. This concerns the apprenticeship of Cyril Parks, known as Cy, in the early years of the twentieth century, to the irascible and drunken master tattooist Eliot Riley, who works on the seafront at Morecambe. After Riley's death, Cy travels to the USA to ply his trade as a fully fledged 'electric Michelangelo' in

Coney Island, Morecambe's 'richer, zany American relative'.[16] After a traumatic love affair, Cy returns home to the Cumbrian coast, since, in a term that links him with the region's geology, he is profoundly 'Morecambrian' (*EM*, 326). Yet Hall's comment about the novel's plotlessness does acknowledge the narrative's progression by means of description and spectacle rather than action,[17] as we see for instance in such sustained imagery as the burning of Morecambe Pier in a snowstorm, and the appearance of the aurora borealis over the Morecambe sands.

The novel's opening, in which we encounter the young Cy living in his mother's establishment for consumptives, which doubles up as an abortionist's, introduces a notion of the body as the terrain for art. Cy has 'eyes for the grotesque things of life' (*EM*, 10), as if in preparation for his avocation as tattooist. The hybridity of human bodily existence which Mikhail Bakhtin celebrates in his analysis of the literary grotesque is present to the extent that Cy forgets 'to feel disgusted' (*EM*, 20) by the bodily disintegration around him.[18] Rather, he sees mutable shapes and 'stories' even in the bowls of tubercular fluids that he is charged with cleaning: 'The boat became a seagull with crooked wings, which then became a blooming flower, which then became the turret of a castle' (*EM*, 19). These images, physically born of the body, prefigure the 'dreamscapes' (*EM*, 89) that Cy will etch on to his clients' skin. As he discovers, the very act of tattooing releases or 'lances' people's stories, so that they '[bleed] their history', which is then 'recorded like a photograph album or a diary of pictures on their bodies' (*EM*, 260). Jem Poster comments on 'the conflict between [Cy's] priestly sense of his artistic calling and the claims of the flesh he routinely handles',[19] and such a conflict in Hall's novel implies a levelling out of these high and low registers. For Riley, tattooing itself is a 'personal socialism' (*EM*, 149). Thus, in refutation of the apparent clash in the novel's title between Renaissance artistry and the mechanisation of modernity, Riley insists that there is little difference between Michelangelo's concerns and those of the 'scraper', or tattooist: 'Now the thing to remember about Michelangelo is this; he'd a bugger of a time getting blue paint. Just like us' (*EM*, 109).

Cy's greatest American challenge is a commission from Grace, a young circus performer of uncertain European origin, who wants her whole body to be tattooed with images of black-rimmed green eyes. As Ashley Orr has observed, the commission is an overtly symbolic 'act of resistance',[20] since Grace hopes that the tattoos will enable her to return the spectator's gaze in her circus act: 'They will pay to see me looking back at them . . . It will be funny, like being the invisible woman' (*EM*, 272). Similarly, the reader's gaze is disrupted by uncertainty when Cy and Grace have an argument, since the narrator's comment that 'Her eyes were passionate actors playing their part' (*EM*, 275) blurs the distinction between the tattooed signifiers and the bodily signifieds. A more shocking blurring occurs when Grace's efforts to resist the male gaze are violently rejected in an acid attack on her by her neighbour Malcolm Sedak. As is the case in some of the examples from Rabelais quoted by Bakhtin as exemplifying the revivifying notion of the bodily grotesque, pain coexists with linguistic bravura in the description of the attack's effects: 'Green from the largest ruptured iris on her abdomen had collected above her appendix, and it seemed in comparison a beautiful emerald seam against the strip-mined earth of the rest of her' (EM, 306). In a return to the presiding imagery of Michelangelo's art, Grace seems to Cy to resemble 'a fresco with a jar of paint stripper knocked over her' (EM, 306). The personalising of the fresco as 'her' emphasises anew the bodily nature of the tattooist's art.

Like *The Electric Michelangelo*, *How to Paint a Dead Man* focuses on artistry, the body and death: that is, the disjunction between aesthetic permanence and human fragility. The visual and imagistic nature of much of Hall's fiction is apparent here in a novelistic equivalent of painting. The text is composed of four stories about artists: the first two are set in Italy in the 1960s and tell of a famous painter named Giorgio and his former pupil, Annette, who is gradually losing her sight; the second two stories take place in contemporary Britain and are concerned with a young woman named Susan and her father Pete. Each story is the novelistic equivalent of a self-portrait, presented in its own terms and without any overall explanatory narration. This effect is polyphonic as well as painterly, or 'pointillist', in Sarah Dunant's phrase,[21] since each voice is allowed to speak for itself, leaving the reader to work out what is reliable and what is not. The title of Pete's sections, 'The Fool on the Hill', in the second pair of stories, tells us something not only about his self-ironising voice, but also about his experience of being trapped overnight on a Cumbrian hillside. By contrast, the title of Annette's sections, 'The Divine Vision of Annette Tambroni', appears to be imposed by an external commentator, and the title of Giorgio's, 'Translated from the Bottle Journals', by an outside editor. Susan's sections are enigmatically entitled 'The Mirror Crisis', a phrase which arises from her conception of losing her twin brother Danny's fraternal reflection, while also referring to the self-address of her second-person narrative: 'You haven't been feeling like yourself for a while now, since the accident.'[22] Although Sarah Dunant expresses frustration with the meditative tone of the novel, preferring the sections that are instead full of 'tension', her perception that Hall is using a new kind of narrative strategy, to convey an existential or philosophical meaning, can aptly be applied to the whole of her body of writing.[23]

The plot of Hall's most recent novel, *The Wolf Border*, centres on the reintroduction of wolves to Britain, over five hundred years after their extinction, as part of an initiative by the Earl of Pennington on his Annerdale estate in Cumbria. The character through whose eyes we see almost all the action is Rachel Caine, a Cumbrian native who returns from a wolf reserve in Idaho to be a consultant on the Earl's personal project. This is despite the fact that Rachel finds her new location uncongenial at first: 'The tree, the pink house, the dense, deciduous woods – she is the wrong woman for such a story' (WB, 82). Her homecoming is not freely chosen but provoked by the death of her mother, and by her own accidental pregnancy.

While these events continue Hall's commitment to representing the varieties of female and bodily experience, including childbirth, they also offer uncanny parallels to the wolf plot. Rachel's surname echoes that of Adam and Eve's fratricidal son, who was a farmer to his brother Abel's shepherd. Yet this is an ironic echo, one that functions to remind us of the iconographic role of the wolf in literary and cultural history rather than to offer a direct biblical parallel. Rachel is not viewed kindly by locals who are either shepherds or farmers, and, far from murdering her brother

Lawrence, she eventually saves his life. It is the reintroduced wolves to which her life is linked. Even linguistically, in *The Wolf Border* it is often hard to distinguish a human from a lupine referent, and this effect intensifies into overt comparison, one often made by the characters themselves. After a meeting with Thomas Pennington, Rachel thinks, ostensibly of wolves but also obliquely of the aristocracy, 'they are never without enemies, they are too successful a creature, too good at what they do' (WB, 83). The varieties of crossover increase in their overtness, despite Rachel's sense that 'analogies are not helpful' (WB, 221), as she later reflects on the hostility of the Earl's estate manager by linking herself with the animals: 'She, and they, represent dire competition, beyond his experience' (WB, 117).

The comparisons reach a startling conclusion when the midwife attending the birth of Rachel's son tries to put her at ease by asking, 'So you breed wolves then, Rachel. Are you having a wolf today?' This moment offers an echo of Hall's magic-realist short story 'Mrs Fox' (2014), in which a litter of fox cubs really are the offspring of a human father and vulpine mother.[24] *The Wolf Border* repeats the concern shown in 'Mrs Fox' with disrupting the distinction between wild and tame, here in realist form. This is clear in relation to the wolves in their fenced-in Annerdale 'utopia' (WB, 259), where a sense of wilderness is carefully created; it is also implicitly present in relation to Rachel herself. As the wolves are paradoxically nurtured to be wild, Rachel's own 'wild', independent life is tamed. She experiences her return to Britain from the USA as a diminution, just as the wolves are in 'captivity'.

The novel's title itself conveys a hybrid political and poetic meaning. The 'border' is that between Scotland and England, against which Cumbria defines itself – indeed, Rachel has to remind journalists that the region is not Scottish. It is also a metaphor for the politics of land ownership, since the reintroduction of wolves at Annerdale can only take place due to the Earl's ability to fence off large tracts of his estate, signifying the boundary between real and artificial wilderness. Both the notion of reintroducing wolves and that of a successful campaign for Scottish independence, in contrast to the real-life vote against it which took place in 2014, are gentler examples of *The Carhullan Army*'s dystopian alternative history. In Hall's novel, Scottish independence is 'inextricably tied to the physical environment',[25] and while the reintroduction of the 'level 5' wolf predators promises economic and ecological benefits for Scotland, the animals are also a symbol of 'the newest nation's' political reclamations since 'great swathes of foreign-owned land are . . . recovered' for common ownership (WB, 289). The novel's ending is a variant of the homecomings we have witnessed in *Haweswater* and *The Electric Michelangelo*, only this time the beings whose arrival is celebrated are not humans but escaped wolves: as the pack crosses the border into Scotland, they are greeted in Gaelic by the pilot whose helicopter is allowing Rachel to track their movements: 'Fàilte, he'd said' (WB, 432).

While Hall's novels echo the tropes and genres of much twenty-first-century fiction in Britain, including neo-Victorian, dystopian and post-feminist writing, her work is unusual in drawing on lyrical and fantastic effects in order to construct a new kind of poetic realism. Although her writing is inevitably influenced by postmodern self-consciousness, this is not the genre into which it falls. Hall's novels are most often identified in relation to the representation of region, particularly that of her native Cumbria. The landscape is invoked within a wide variety of fictional contexts, and exists vividly on its own account and also to convey matters of symbolic and global importance, including those of climate change, class and land ownership. Alongside this central topographical element is Hall's precise yet inventive use of language, characterised by the appearance of dialect as well as specialised and neologistic vocabulary; a substratum of political concern, particularly with gender and ecology; and a generic and symbolic self-consciousness, by virtue of which critical estimates seem often to be anticipated or even included in the text's fictional world. It is by such means that the paradox of Hall's work's reputation for aesthetic success alongside an absence of conventional plotting can be resolved.

NOTES

1. See for instance Sarah Dunant's review of *How to Paint a Dead Man*, 'Umbrian Shadows', *The Guardian*, 6 June 2009, <http://www.theguardian.com/books/2009/jun/06/how-paint-dead-man-sarah-hall> (last accessed 14 June 2016); and Alex Clark's of *The Wolf Border*, 'In Search of Wilderness', *The Guardian*, 1 April 2015, <http://www.theguardian.com/books/2015/apr/01/the-wolf-border-by-sarah-hall-review> (last accessed 14 June 2016).
2. Sarah Hall, *Haweswater* (London: Faber, 2002), p. 267. All quotations are from this edition; hereafter, page numbers will be given in the text, preceded by *H*.
3. Sarah Hall, *The Wolf Border* (London: Faber, 2015), p. 348. All quotations are from this edition; hereafter, page numbers will be given in the text, preceded by *WB*.
4. Simon Richardson, 'Sarah Hall: About the Author', BBC Arts, <http://www.bbc.co.uk/programmes/articles/1voldyYk9MXlrG33m204Pqj/sarah-hall> (last accessed 14 June 2016).
5. Roger Lytollis, 'How Mardale Inspired a Novel', *News and Star*, 24 June 2006, p. 22.
6. Sarah Hall, *The Carhullan Army* (London: Faber, 2007), p. 1. All quotations are from this edition; hereafter, page numbers will be given in the text, preceded by *CA*.
7. Benedicte Page, 'Sarah Hall: *The Carhullan Army*', *The Bookseller*, 22 August 2007, <http://www.thebookseller.com/blogs/sarah-hall-carhullan-army> (last accessed 14 June 2016).
8. Sarah Hall, quoted in Helen Brown, 'Sarah Hall: Floods, Curses, Fanatics: It's Good to Be Home', *The Telegraph*, 1 December 2007, <http://www.telegraph.co.uk/culture/books/3669631/Sarah-Hall-Floods-curses-fanatics-its-good-to-be-home.html> (last accessed 14 June 2016).
9. See Robert Eaglestone, 'Reading *Heart of Darkness* after the Holocaust', in R. Clifton Spargo and Robert M. Ehrenreich (eds), *After Representation: The Holocaust, Literature, and Culture* (New Brunswick, NJ: Rutgers University Press, 2010), pp. 190–209.
10. Soo Nee Ng, '(Re)Configurations of Power and Identities in Twenty-First Century Fiction', unpublished PhD thesis, Goldsmiths College, University of London, 2010, pp. 41–2.
11. See Rachel Hore, review of *The Carhullan Army*, *The Independent*, 6 October 2007, <http://www.independent.co.uk/arts-entertainment/books/reviews/the-carhullan-army-by-sarah-hall-395975.html> (last accessed 14 June 2016).
12. Michael Arditti, 'Psychopath in the Community', *The Telegraph*, 8 September 2007, <http://www.telegraph.co.uk/culture/books/fictionreviews/3667787/Psychopath-in-the-community.html> (last accessed 14 June 2016); Hall, quoted in Brown, 'Sarah Hall: Floods, Curses, Fanatics'.
13. Johan Kisro, 'Finding Dystopia in Utopia: Gender, Power and Politics in *The Carhullan Army*', unpublished essay, University of Stockholm, 2014, p. 4.
14. Clark, 'In Search of Wilderness'.

15. Sarah Hall, quoted in Sarah Crown, 'Interview with Sarah Hall', *The Guardian*, 28 March 2015, <http://www.theguardian.com/books/2015/mar/28/sarah-hall-books-interview-the-wolf-border> (last accessed 14 June 2016).
16. Sarah Hall, *Electric Michelangelo* (London: Faber, 2004), p. 182. All quotations are from this edition; hereafter, page numbers will be given in the text, preceded by *EM*.
17. See Kerri Horine, 'The Tyranny of the Spectacle: Tattooed Bodies in Contemporary Visual Culture', unpublished PhD thesis, University of Louisville, 2008, p. 69.
18. As Bakhtin argues, 'In grotesque realism . . . the bodily element is deeply positive', since it is 'unfinished, outgrows itself, transgresses its own limits', as we see in the case here where bodily fluids inspire artistry. Mikhail Bakhtin, *Rabelais and His World*, trans. Hélène Iswolsky (Bloomington: Indiana University Press, 1984), pp. 19, 22.
19. Jem Poster, 'Written in Skin', *The Guardian*, 27 March 2004, <http://www.theguardian.com/books/2004/mar/27/featuresreviews.guardianreview24> (last accessed 14 June 2016).
20. Ashley Orr, 'Inked in: The Feminist Politics of Tattooing in Sarah Hall's *Electric Michelangelo*', talk delivered at Australian National University Literary Studies Seminar, April 2015.
21. Dunant, 'Umbrian Shadows'.
22. Sarah Hall, *How to Paint a Dead Man* (2009; London: Faber, 2010), p. 3.
23. Dunant, 'Umbrian Shadows'.
24. Sarah Hall, *Mrs Fox* (London: Faber, 2014).
25. Clark, 'In Search of Wilderness'.

FURTHER READING

For an up-to-date list of Sarah Hall's novels, see the British Council website: <https://literature.britishcouncil.org/writer/sarah-hall> (last accessed 14 June 2016).

Bakhtin, Mikhail, *Rabelais and His World*, trans. Hélène Iswolsky (1965; Bloomington: Indiana University Press, 1984).

Hall, Sarah, *The Beautiful Indifference* (London: Faber, 2011). [Short stories].

Mealing, Lotti, 'The Mermaid as Postmodern Muse in Sarah Hall's *The Electric Michelangelo*', *Contemporary Women's Writing*, 8.2 (2014), 223–40.

Robinson, Iain, '"You just know when the world is about to break apart": Utopia, Dystopia and New Global Uncertainties in Sarah Hall's *The Carhullan Army*', in Siân Adiseshiah and Rupert Hildyard (eds), *Twenty-First Century Fiction: What Happens Now* (New York: Palgrave Macmillan, 2013), pp. 197–211.

CHAPTER 7

A. L. Kennedy: Giving and Receiving

Alison Lumsden

While some critics have attempted to read A. L. Kennedy's early short stories and novels within paradigms of nationality and gender, most acknowledge that they refuse to settle into these categories. Her pre-2000 fiction has more often been read as concerning itself with isolated individuals and the limits of community and communication. David Borthwick, for example, has said that *Night Geometry and the Garscadden Trains* (1990) is like 'an early manifesto of her work' which repeatedly returns to the topic of the 'psychological vortex of its subjects' through which 'the reader must reconstruct the characters' identities according to an idiosyncratic logic'.[1] Others have commented on Kennedy's concern with 'defeated individuals' who exist 'within a void, defined by social invisibility' and who suffer from 'ontological anguish'.[2] While some have seen potentially redemptive features in her fiction,[3] on the whole it has been defined in terms of isolation and social disease in a world 'close to [the reader's] own bleaker and inadequate experiences'.[4]

Correspondingly, Kennedy's style has been linked to postmodern concerns with the limitations of language and communication, 'as though the writing was itself involved in an attempt to snag against the very thing it describes'.[5] Both in its focus on alienated individuals who cannot communicate with the world around them, and in its narrative style, which draws attention to the fractures and incoherencies of language, Kennedy's work thus has been read in broadly postmodern terms. This view has arisen in acknowledgement of its essentially self-reflexive nature and its concern with the limits of communication, both within and outwith the fictional world.[6]

In 1999, however, Kennedy published *Everything You Need*, a novel that was very different from any that she had written before.[7] At over five hundred pages, *Everything You Need* is significantly longer than her earlier work and, as its title suggests, it brings together a wealth of fictional material. For a number of critics this novel marks a move away from the template that had formed the basis of Kennedy's success, and they voiced disappointment: 'one suspects that Kennedy has failed to understand her own literary strengths and capacities,' commented Philip Tew. 'Kennedy has lost her *naïveté*.'[8] Similarly, for David Borthwick this and Kennedy's later work show marks of 'heavy-handed authorial manipulation' indicating 'a concern with the authority of the author rather than the honesty of the character'.[9] This sense of Kennedy as having lost touch with her own strengths was compounded by the publication in the same year of *On Bullfighting*, in which she offered a surprisingly candid account of the problems she was encountering with her craft: 'I'm a writer who doesn't write and that makes me no one at all. I don't look very different, but I have nothing of value inside.'[10] All in all, for some, including Helen Stoddart, it seemed as if Kennedy was suffering from an unproductive '"end of the century" anxiety about the end of writing and meaning'.[11] However, since 2000 Kennedy has been highly productive; she has not only written three books of short stories and three novels, but has also been involved in writing for film, television and radio, her most recent venture being to write for *Doctor Who*.[12] So if the turn of the century marks something of a shift in Kennedy's writing, what exactly did it entail, and is there any substantive difference between the fiction she published before 2000 and what she has published subsequently? More specifically, do her novels move away from a postmodern concern with the limits of communication towards a greater sense that communication between characters, and indeed between the text and the world beyond it, may be possible? This chapter will explore this question by considering her three twenty-first-century novels, *Paradise* (2005), *Day* (2008) and *The Blue Book* (2012).[13]

Perhaps the simplest way to open this discussion is by considering *Everything You Need* as a point of transition. While Kennedy's earlier work concerns itself with individuals who are isolated both from themselves and from those who surround them, and who often fail, or at least partially fail, in their attempts to reach out to others, *Everything You Need* is self-consciously located within a community, and is therefore a novel that concerns itself with the role of writing within it. It is the story of the writer Nathan Staples and his attempt to establish a relationship with his daughter both through his own writing and through her developing understanding of what a writer can achieve. This novel refocuses rather than rejects the questions raised by Kennedy's earlier work, and suggests that, rather than existing within a sealed self-reflexive loop, the act of writing and the resulting work of art may offer pathways towards communication beyond their own enclosed artistic spaces. As Kaye Mitchell puts it, in *Everything You Need* relationships are reimagined as being between the 'writer and the word', which together 'make for the perfect relationship', thus potentially circumventing the postmodern anxieties of twentieth-century fiction.[14]

However, there is a danger in describing Kennedy's work in overly positive (and simplistic) terms. While *Everything You Need* may gesture towards the potential for communication, there is little sign of it thematically in *Paradise*, the first of Kennedy's novels to be published in the twenty-first century. *Paradise* is the story of Hannah Luckraft, an alcoholic approaching the age of forty. In one sense the novel is located in familiar Kennedy terrain since, despite its protagonist being both

Scottish and female, questions of gender and nation are typically not foregrounded. It is the story of a woman locked into her own seemingly cyclical narrative, unable to escape the isolation that has been caused by alcohol and its inevitable problems. For Hannah, people are divided into 'groups' and 'solitaries' (P, 6), and it is clear that she wishes to belong to the latter category: 'And, thankfully, no one else is with me when the doors whump shut and seal me in the queasily rising box' (P, 13), she writes upon entering a hotel lift, adding later, 'The most reliable measure of a person lies in what they do when they're alone, when they have no need to pretend' (P, 18).

Yet Hannah does attempt to reach out to others in this novel. Some of these attempts result in farce, such as the occasion when she attempts to help a woman in a wheelchair only to tip her accidentally into the road, while others, such as her relationship with fellow alcoholic Robert, ultimately result in loss and pain. Elsewhere, communities are exposed as false or fake – Hannah's bizarre hallucinatory account of her journey across Canada by train, for example, or of the clinic where her brother sends her for rehabilitation, where belonging to a 'group' is part of the cure: '"Where do you feel you fit into the group?" . . . Obviously, no one sane would even attempt to answer that' (P, 173).

Paradise, then, seems to hold out little hope that relationships, far less communities, can actually be forged in any productive or meaningful way. Some critics have seen some hope of a tentative redemption within it, reading the possible presence of Robert in the hotel room with Hannah at the end of the novel as a sign that 'recovery *might* be possible through engagement with another human being'.[15] However, the circular nature of the narrative and the lack of clarity at the end calls any such optimism into question, rendering it simultaneously 'Kennedy's least optimistic novel', in which Hannah is trapped within the terms of her own fragmented, isolated and isolating narrative.[16]

At first sight *Day* similarly questions the possibility of meaningful community in the wake of the traumas of the twentieth century. Set shortly after the Second World War, *Day*, like so much British fiction of the early part of the twenty-first century, moves towards the genre of the historical novel. This is a new departure for Kennedy and may mark an attempt to circumvent the claustrophobic space of her earlier contemporary narratives where characters are frequently trapped within the circumstances of their own lives and the narratives in which these lives are described. *Day* is the story of Alfred Day, who has served as a tail-gunner in a Lancaster bomber. Coming from a clearly dysfunctional home, Alfred experiences his first real sense of a community in the fellowship and camaraderie of his fellow crewmen. Inevitably, however, this is destroyed when several members of the crew are killed, and later when his plane crashes. The real time of the novel finds Day cut adrift after the end of the war, unable to recreate the friendships he has experienced with his crew or as a prisoner of war, and attempting to re-enact them by volunteering as an extra in a film being made about an escape from a prisoner-of-war camp. Clearly this is in some ways the kind of 'fake' community that Kennedy has called into question in her earlier fiction, and the reader is not initially hopeful that it will offer Alfred Day any kind of solace. Moreover, he is estranged from his wartime lover, Joyce, seemingly inhabiting the isolated space of so many of Kennedy's characters where communication has lapsed or collapsed to destroy relationships. Nevertheless, *Day* ends with some glimmers of hope. We are told that Alfred returns to this dramatised version of a prison camp in order to try to make sense of his life: 'It had seemed not unlikely that he could work out his own little pantomime inside the professional pretence and tunnel right through to the place where he'd lost himself, or rather the dark, the numb gap he could tell was asleep inside him . . . So it could possibly make sense that he'd turn up here and at least work out what was missing, maybe even put it back' (*D*, 35–6).

Experienced readers of Kennedy's earlier fiction might find it unlikely that this 'professional pretence' will bring Alfred much satisfaction, yet the novel does seem to suggest that it might. Rather than offering simply the kind of circular re-enactment of trauma that we might expect in her work, revisiting the camp in the form of 'professional pretence' serves as a kind of therapy whereby Alfred's emotions are 'unlocked' in order for him to reconstitute himself and move on. Just as it is unclear how this process of revisiting actually works in modern trauma therapy, so it is also unclear how this process operates within *Day*'s narrative. Nevertheless, by the end of the novel Alfred Day is making tentative steps towards re-establishing a relationship with the world by moving in with his friend Ivor and by renewing his relationship with Joyce. In spite of the tentative future conditional tense in which this last section of the novel is told – 'You intend to kiss her with your new moustache. You intend not to bother if people see' (*D*, 279) – there is a kind of optimism at the end of *Day* suggesting that in spite of the individual and collective traumas of the twentieth century, establishing authentic relationships may yet be possible. Kennedy's foray into the historical novel thus suggests that revisiting the past may offer one mechanism by which characters can break the cycle of entrapment that her earlier characters encounter. Similarly, historical fiction may offer a method by which the novel can escape the self-enclosed loop of postmodern fiction to open up new narrative possibilities for the writer.

Kennedy's latest novel, *The Blue Book*, also offers some tentative hope that relationships can be recovered from the debris of people's lives. On the surface it again seems to operate within the landscapes so frequently found in Kennedy's fiction. Its protagonist and narrator Beth is crossing the Atlantic in the company of her boyfriend Derek. She seems to be moving towards the territory of the isolated individual who is incapable of building or sustaining a relationship; as she crosses the ocean, it is on a ship that remains on course while she becomes emotionally adrift. Beth gradually reveals that she once worked with Arthur Lockwood, a fake psychic, and that she had a relationship with him. Arthur's spurious attempts to reunite people with the dead creates once again the sense of a society where all communication is suspect, and where language is used to construct false communities. Yet in spite of this Beth and Arthur do appear to achieve some kind of honesty and intimacy, and although Beth's final act of disclosure leaves the lasting status of her relationship with Arthur in some doubt, they at least appear to have reached a form of communication where professional pretence is stripped away. Thematically these novels all explore the question of whether individuals can break free from the postmodern isolation and alienation encountered by the characters in Kennedy's earlier work, and, to a limited extent, suggest that this may be possible. However, what is perhaps more significant is that *The Blue Book* also posits the possibility of an alternative kind of relationship, that between text and reader, and it is in this, perhaps, that the greatest evidence of the transition made between Kennedy's earlier and later fiction can be seen.

In her collection *On Writing*, a book based on a series of blogs produced for *The Guardian* between 2011 and 2012, Kennedy offers an account of the writing process, public expectations of the role of the writer, and her reasons for writing. Alongside reiterating 'the positive role that the arts in general, and reading and writing in particular, can play in any life' (and she is at pains to state that this also involves a positive effect on public life and society), Kennedy repeatedly points out that writing is a form of reaching out to others.[17] Readers who genuinely engage with her work, she suggests, are an absolutely crucial element in it: 'Viciously selfish, compulsive, obsessive and odd though many writers may be, we do everything we do for other people' (OW, 76). In terms of how Kennedy's earlier work has been read as engaging with isolation, fragmentation and failure to form or sustain relationships, this is interesting, for it suggests that rather than being about the *impossibility* of communication, Kennedy sees forming a reciprocal communication between text and reader as essential to her aesthetic principles: 'I happen to believe that giving and receiving a kiss operates very much along the same lines as giving and receiving a word – it's simply that the giving and receiving are done in different rooms at different times – they are still an attempt to touch, be touched, be recognised, to exist in passion, to be human' (OW, 135). Elsewhere in the volume she voices a more overt scepticism concerning the fracturing of language, suggesting that it has a far greater communicative capacity than literary theorists (or philosophers concerned with the complexities of language) are prepared to allow: 'I do not believe that if I raced into Wittgenstein's study and yelled "Fire!" he'd just say, "What do you mean, exactly?"' (OW, 348). For the later Kennedy it is clear that language is *essentially* about communication, and the writer of fiction (or perhaps the teller of stories) occupies a unique position in communicating with those 'in different rooms and at different times', the reading audience.

These issues lie at the heart of *The Blue Book*. The novel opens with an apostrophe to the reader: 'But here this is, the book you're reading ... Your book – it's started now ... You could, if you wanted, heft it, wonder if it weighs more than a pigeon, or a plimsoll, or quite probably rather less than a wholemeal loaf. It offers you these possibilities' (BB, 1). The narratological theorist Gerald Prince has proposed the idea that fiction may have an implied narratee as well as an implied narrator, a constructed individual to whom the text is addressed.[18] However, what Kennedy is suggesting here is, arguably, something far more intimate, whereby every reader of her novel becomes a narratee, feeling as though the text is intimately – like a kiss – addressed to them, a conceit maintained throughout the novel by repeated, and increasingly personal, apostrophes.

Moreover, if a relationship is being forged here between reader and text by narrative style, the novel's questioning of the limits of communication and the role of storytelling in our lives is also intrinsic to its subject. As we read we discover that Beth and her former lover Arthur have spent their early lives operating as fake psychics, using a series of numbered and coded lists as prompts to communication so that they can successfully dupe their audience. These numbered lists recur throughout the novel and are initially used by the couple when they resume their relationship on board the ship. They are also echoed in the bizarre double numbering of the novel's pages so that the reader is prompted to try to work out the relationship between some of the random numbers that appear at the top of the pages and their meanings in relation to the lists used by Arthur and Beth.

As the novel moves towards its conclusion, however, the couple try to achieve what may be perceived as a more authentic form of communication as they abandon these codes to reach a greater intimacy: '"I don't like lists,"' Arthur says, '"Not any more"' (BB, 355). In a final twist, though, Beth decides that Arthur must now know 'the whole story' and ends the novel by handing him a blue book, 'a kind of weight in her hand, less than a pigeon, or a plimsoll, or a wholemeal loaf' (BB, 359). This is the book she has made for Arthur, the 'whole story', a disclosure that will allow them either intimacy or separation. Yet it is also the book we have been reading, the story we have been told, and we realise that the intimacy we have felt as a reader is simultaneously, if not alternatively, Beth's intimacy for Arthur, and that we as readers have been potentially tricked, just as Beth's and Arthur's audiences have been tricked by the false stories they have been told during their psychic readings.

This clearly complicates the reflections on community and communication that the novel offers and for some critics repositions Kennedy's later fiction within the template of her earlier work. Alice Bennett, for example, argues that these manoeuvres display a continuity with its belief in 'the impossibility of communication even at the most intimate of moments'. Moreover, she continues, it thus undermines the concept that fiction can be used as a medium for communication, since 'the novel shows that the mediums' apparent knowledge is achieved through linguistic tricks and techniques that built intimacy and connection, techniques that are uncomfortably close to those used in more conventional narrative fiction'.[19] As a consequence she concludes that at the very point when Kennedy has forged an apparently more intimate relationship via the Web and Twitter, 'she has written a book that does its best to arouse suspicions of the kinds of false intimacies fiction can construct'.[20] Thus Bennett reads *The Blue Book* within the broadly postmodern terms observed by critics of her earlier work, as concerning itself not with the potential for communication, but the ongoing failure of it.

To endorse this reading wholeheartedly, however, one would have to presume that everything Kennedy has written in her blogs and in the less ephemeral *On Writing* is in some ways disingenuous. While we must be wary of assuming that she is proposing in these works any real intimacy between herself as writer and her readership, she does suggest that a relationship can be established between the reader and the text. While she may alert us to the dangers of assuming false relationships with the writer she may be simultaneously validating the power of novel writing and storytelling as powerful forms of communication. Indeed, *The Blue Book* suggests that such concepts are not necessarily in opposition.

Bennett's less optimistic reading is predicated on the observation that as we read, the 'elasticity' of the 'you' that appears to have been us, the reader, 'springs back to the confines of the text and to just one character'.[21] But this is perhaps too simple an explanation of what occurs in the text. The twentieth-century philosopher John Macmurray argues that we should think of community less as an idea of shared collective identity than as a matter of interpersonal exchange (the concept of a 'you' and 'I' in mutual relation). By forging individual relationships with others, he says, we begin to form the basis by which communication and its concomitant partner community may be achieved.[22] Similarly, by establishing a relationship (even if only temporarily or provisionally) between the text and the reader as 'you', Kennedy's novel may establish a meaningful relationship and one that is of lasting value. Moreover, it is a relationship that, in spite of the revelations at the end, is not altogether destroyed or undermined. Similarly, while the fake psychic readings that take place are in some ways abhorrent, Kennedy also proposes that they may have value. In *On Writing* she states that 'the reader', after all, 'does agree he or she will be lied to' as that is part of the contract we agree to when we read fiction. However, 'honesty of approach . . . [is] vital in the writer's relationship with the reader' (*OW*, 154).

'Honesty of approach' is an interesting term and one which both Beth and Arthur interrogate. Recounting a weekend she has spent with her mother after her father's death, Beth remembers that a magpie appears at the window and that her mother takes this as a sign of her father's blessing: 'But it isn't [her father],' she says. 'It's a bird. It's a story her mother will tell and that will help her and will be special and will never be taken away' (*BB*, 264–5). In other words, it may not be true, but it is nevertheless a form of consolation. Similarly, while Arthur promises Beth he will take 'early retirement' and no longer meet with his clients, he also recognises that he has provided some of them with a comfort that he cannot easily take away from them: 'But I would have to keep . . . There would be maintenance . . . Christ, Beth. I don't want to harm them' (*BB*, 330). The stories he tells may be lies, but they are, nevertheless, not without meaning, just as the blue book that Beth hands Arthur is a story offering truth and *The Blue Book* we have been reading contains 'honesty' within its fiction.

It is this more optimistic view of the reading experience that is ultimately reinforced by the novel's narrative strategies. While the intimacy between book and reader that is established in the opening words of the novel may be unsettled, there is no doubt that the questions raised at the end of it encourage us to be active rather than passive readers of this text, thus establishing a new relationship with it. The revelations that occur at the end, along with the intriguing numbering patterns already described and the rhetorical repetitions which occur between its opening and its conclusion, only serve to invite the reader to begin the whole text again, thus increasing, rather than diminishing, the intimacy that the reader has established with this novel. Wolfgang Iser posits the idea of active readership, suggesting that some texts encourage us not simply to absorb literature but to become active in the production of the meanings within it.[23] All three of the novels Kennedy has written in the twenty-first century both invite and indeed require this kind of 'active' reading. While this may be most overt in *The Blue Book*, it is also evident in both *Paradise* and *Day*, where temporal shifts, movements from exterior to interior realities and indeterminate endings refuse to allow us to be passive readers, instead demanding our full participation in the creation of meaning in the text. For Kennedy 'really reading' is a process that demands being 'completely engrossed' (*OW*, 135). Her own work, she acknowledges, is not easy and demands this kind of reading from her audience. Her reciprocal aesthetic reaches out to us, ensuring that communication does take place and that a valuable and meaningful relationship is by necessity established between reader and text.

The fiction that Kennedy has published in the twenty-first century shares something with her earlier work in that it remains tentative about the capacity of damaged individuals to form lasting and meaningful relationships. Similarly, it refuses to be categorised in terms of either nation or gender. However, it also moves beyond that earlier work towards a confidence in the potential for words and storytelling to create valid and significant connections with the reader, the 'other'. Relationships may, she suggests, be formed by the capacity of words to 'touch, be recognised'. In his well-known essays 'The Literature of Exhaustion' and 'The Literature of Replenishment', the novelist John Barth describes his own journey from postmodern redundancy located in a fiction forged via a language that could never adequately communicate, to a belief in the capacity of a fiction that moves beyond this to recognise the transformative power of story.[24] The transition that A. L. Kennedy's fiction has made in the twenty-first century may well follow a similar trajectory, moving from an end-of-millennium angst to a reaching out through the power of words. Some critics seem to resent this development in her work, hankering after the isolation, anxiety and fragmentation that they saw in her earlier fiction. Kennedy's recent novels, however, resist this approach, inviting us, through the intimacy of their narrative struggles and strategies, to find reciprocity within them that defies their own threats of fragmentation.

NOTES

1. David Borthwick, 'A. L. Kennedy's Dysphoric Fictions', in Berthold Schoene (ed.), *The Edinburgh Companion to Contemporary Scottish Literature* (Edinburgh: Edinburgh University Press, 2007), pp. 264–71; pp. 265, 267.
2. Philip Tew, 'The Fiction of A. L. Kennedy: The Baffled, the Void and the (In)visible', in Richard J. Lane, Rod Mengham and Philip Tew (eds), *Contemporary British Fiction* (Cambridge: Polity, 2003), pp. 120–39; pp. 120–1.
3. See, for example, Sarah M. Dunnigan, 'A. L. Kennedy's Longer Fiction: Articulate Grace', in Aileen Christianson and Alison Lumsden (eds), *Contemporary Scottish Women Writers* (Edinburgh: Edinburgh University Press, 2000), pp. 144–55.
4. Tew, 'The Fiction of A. L. Kennedy', p. 128.
5. Helen Stoddart, '"Tongues of Bone": A. L. Kennedy and the Problems of Articulation', in Nick Bentley (ed.), *British Fiction of the 1990s* (London and New York: Routledge, 2005), pp. 135–49; p. 137.
6. Brian McHale identifies irony and self-reflexivity as key components of 'high postmodernism' along with a resistance to art as a form of communication. See Brian McHale, *The Cambridge Introduction to Postmodernism* (Cambridge: Cambridge University Press, 2015), p. 20.
7. A. L. Kennedy, *Everything You Need* (London: Jonathan Cape, 1999).

8. Tew, 'The Fiction of A. L. Kennedy', p. 136.
9. Borthwick, 'A. L. Kennedy's Dysphoric Fictions', p. 271.
10. A. L. Kennedy, *On Bullfighting* (London: Yellow Jersey, 1999), p. 3.
11. Stoddart, '"Tongues of Bone"', p. 137. This sentiment is echoed by Philip Tew (see 'The Fiction of A. L. Kennedy', p. 136) and by Will Self, whom Tew quotes in his essay. Borthwick suggests that 'In Kennedy's fiction this new millennial *Zeitgeist* translates into a preoccupation with the disjunction of private experience and public life as characters retreat into their privacy to avoid acknowledging their own irrelevance in the face of larger forces' ('A. L. Kennedy's Dysphoric Fictions', p. 266).
12. The three novels are *Paradise* (2005), *Day* (2008) and *The Blue Book* (2012), and the three books of short stories are *Indelible Acts* (2002), *What Becomes* (2009) and *All the Rage* (2014). Kennedy's first venture into screenwriting, *Stella Does Tricks* (1997), was followed in 2001 by *Dice*, co-written with John Burnside. The episode of *Doctor Who* she wrote is 'The Drosten's Curse' (14 July 2015).
13. A. L. Kennedy, *Paradise* (London: Vintage, 2005); *Day* (London: Vintage, 2008); *The Blue Book* (London: Vintage, 2012). All quotations are from these editions; hereafter, page numbers will be given in the text, preceded by P, D and BB respectively.
14. Kaye Mitchell, *A. L. Kennedy* (Basingstoke: Palgrave Macmillan, 2008), pp. 91–2.
15. Borthwick, 'A. L. Kennedy's Dysphoric Fictions', p. 268.
16. Ibid.
17. A. L. Kennedy, *On Writing* (London: Vintage, 2014), p. 1. All quotations are from this edition; hereafter, page numbers will be given in the text, preceded by OW.
18. See Gerald Prince, 'Introduction to the Study of the Narratee' (1973), reprinted in Jane P. Tompkins (ed.), *Reader-Response Criticism: From Formalism to Post-Structuralism* (Baltimore and London: Johns Hopkins University Press, 1980), pp. 7–25; p. 7.
19. Alice Bennett, 'Cold Reading *The Blue Book*: A. L. Kennedy's Critique of Mind Reading', *Critique: Studies in Contemporary Fiction*, 56.2 (2015), 173–89; 175. Available at <http://www.tandfonline.com/doi/abs/10.1080/00111619.2013.870878> (last accessed 14 June 2016).
20. Ibid., p. 178.
21. Ibid., p. 179.
22. John Macmurray, *Persons in Relation* (London: Faber & Faber, 1961), p. 24.
23. See Wolfgang Iser, *The Implied Reader: Patterns of Communication in Prose Fiction from Bunyan to Beckett* (Baltimore and London: Johns Hopkins University Press, 1974), p. 280.
24. John Barth, 'The Literature of Exhaustion' and 'The Literature of Replenishment', in *The Friday Book: Essays and Other Nonfiction* (New York: G. Putnam's Sons, 1984).

FURTHER READING

For an up-to-date list of A. L. Kennedy's novels, see the British Council website: <https://literature.britishcouncil.org/writer/a-l-kennedy> (last accessed 14 June 2016).

Borthwick, David, 'A. L. Kennedy's Dysphoric Fictions', in Berthold Schoene (ed.), *The Edinburgh Companion to Contemporary Scottish Literature* (Edinburgh: Edinburgh University Press, 2007), pp. 264–71.
Mitchell, Kaye, *A. L. Kennedy* (Basingstoke: Palgrave Macmillan, 2008).
Stoddart, Helen, '"Tongues of Bone": A. L. Kennedy and the Problems of Articulation', in Nick Bentley (ed.), *British Fiction of the 1990s* (London and New York: Routledge, 2005), pp. 135–49.
Tew, Philip, 'The Fiction of A. L. Kennedy: The Baffled, the Void and the (In)visible', in Richard J. Lane, Rod Mengham and Philip Tew (eds), *Contemporary British Fiction* (Cambridge: Polity, 2003), pp. 120–39.

CHAPTER 8

Alan Warner: Timeless Realities

Alan Riach

Alan Warner's first novel, Morvern Callar (1995), begins in the Scottish westcoast ferry port and rail terminus of Oban, but the town, the landscape around it and its general ethos are not immediately recognisable. Rather than make use of documentary realism, Warner imbricates his novel's references to actual time and place in a world of imagined timeless identities and relationships. The result is a sense of defamiliarisation that is also to be found in his later fiction, where the fundamentals of place, time, politics and power are contextualised to imply that all identities are in perennial relation, partial development, and a continual unresolved balance of conflict and disharmony.

The eponymous main character of Morvern Callar is a young woman who lives in Oban but is more familiar with the working-class areas, pubs, supermarkets and the day-to-day lives of people who live in the town than she is with the picturesque seafront and the ferries to the islands best known to tourists. Warner's defamiliarisation of Oban, and his non-judgemental attitude to Morvern's decision to abscond with her dead lover's book manuscript and pass it off as her own, set this novel apart from much contemporary Scottish fiction. Ultimately, though, she becomes an admirable figure, a character with whom we come to sympathise, in part because the defamiliarising setting of the novel confronts us with the need to examine our values as readers, then re-examine them later in the novel, when she moves to Spain.

Scotland is the setting for Warner's next novel, These Demented Lands (1997), and also for The Man Who Walks (2002), but not a Scotland easily recognised from historical or traditional realistic accounts. These two novels are surreal, unaccountable, visionary: dream landscapes shift into nightmares of pastoral fields and coastlines, seas and islands that are momentarily idyllic, then ragingly infernal. The bodily properties of individual characters and the geographical identities of the terrain they move through are permeable, tough, vulnerable, wounded and bleeding, pregnant and regenerative. Bodies are abused and torn in horrific and repulsive ways, yet the novels' characters show resilience and resourcefulness in ways that could not be foreseen. Nothing is inevitable, except perhaps the motivation, the almost abstract priority of the quest, a commitment to discovery and the sometimes necessary practice of concealment.

Everything in these two novels comes at a personal price, and orientation is crucial. What do the characters find to be reliable co-ordinate points? Who do they discover are duplicitous, not to be trusted? Their own memories become essential: forgetting and remembering are forced upon individuals by the urgencies of circumstance. What to remember and what to forget are things chosen by individuals, but their choices cannot be entirely relied upon. Memory and acting on remembered things form a drama, create a sense of tension in these two novels. The characters – and they include Morvern Callar, still recognisable, but now with a daughter and commitment to an unforeseen future – are often defined by their actions, where and how they are to be discovered, what they have done and are likely to do. In other words, in these novels, Warner has set out to create a world that still arises from the terrain around Oban, its hinterland, north and south, and the Western Isles of Scotland. A balance between a specific set of identifiable locations and a sense of timeless realities – eternal quests for fulfilment, regeneration, self-determination – characterises both novels.

More conventionally realist are *The Sopranos* (1998) and *The Stars in the Bright Sky* (2010). These novels follow Morvern's contemporaries, both at home and away. In *The Sopranos*, Orla, Kylah, (Ra)Chell, Manda and Fionnula (the Cooler) are on an excursion from Our Lady of Perpetual Succour School and go pub crawling, shoplifting and body-piercing, as they make their way to a singing competition in 'the city'. Boozing, adventuring, dazzling in their language, self-determination, self-confidence and actions, the Sopranos are clearly individuated but collectively a force of resistance to the dead hand of convention. The novel is in high spirits throughout, acknowledging threats to come in the future but all the more defiant for that. It ends with them all looking out brightly 'as the day's sun came silvering over the bay and the tips of the back country hills, already in full summer flush in this time of their lives'.[1]

The Stars in the Bright Sky reunites them, out of school now, meeting in Gatwick, set to go on an economy-flight holiday to celebrate themselves and the spirit of their anarchic defiance of the world's conventions. These women, now in their twenties, are Scots in England, and Finn's friend Ava, half-French and a philosophy student, complements their collective Scottish history. The novel is bristling with the accoutrements of its date: published in 2010, it is set in 2001. With mobile phones, credit cards, acrylic nails and pedicures, the international context is inescapable in Gatwick, where possible destinations beckon: Benidorm, Paris, Las Vegas. After a coruscating narrative, mainly set within the strict confines of the airport itself, but also involving a brilliantly Candide-like excursion into Kent (bright young Scots women abroad in the home counties and looking around: a certain recipe for good comedy), we return to the airport and the imminence of the future. Flights are cancelled, suddenly. The news comes over: it is 9/11. The twin towers of the World Trade Centre in New York have been brought down by suicidal terrorists flying two planes into them. The novel ends in shock and incomprehension. The Sopranos are sobered, for once: 'Why would people do that?' one of them asks. 'The six of them sat together; people were running past and sometimes talking into mobile phones. Yet others passed calm and even laughing.' And the final sentence leaves us in suspense: 'They all waited to see what would happen next.'[2]

Though also set in London, *Their Lips Talk of Mischief* (2014) takes place not in 2001 but in 1984. Date and place make a cradle for the uncertainties and reflexive wisecracks tossed out by the first-person narrator, Douglas Cunningham, and a second character, Llewellyn Smith, and a cradle, too, for the vulnerability of the central female character, Aoife McCrissican. A bloodily wounded (and thus sympathetically vulnerable) Llewellyn meets Cunningham, who is sheltering in the warmth of a hospital A & E department, and invites him home to his small, rundown flat in Acton where he lives with his fiancée, Aoife. Within seconds of seeing Aoife, Cunningham recognises ('with a bizarre distress') that he finds her 'menacingly beautiful'.[3] These characters, coming from Scotland, Wales and Ireland, are caught in the metropolitan capital of imperial legacy. Between them, flamboyant, arch and witty repartee about writing as art or commerce flourishes. Conflicts between motivations of acquisition and self-indulgence or tenderness and care become the mainstay of the narrative. The entire novel is an evocation of swithering, a Scots word for ditheringly considering different choices and not making one.

Published in the immediate aftermath of the referendum on independence in Scotland, *Their Lips Talk of Mischief* came as a surprise. Warner had been outspoken in his support for independence, but his decision to centre this novel in London, and to foreground vital choices with which the characters are confronted, is important.[4] Amongst other things, his characters choose between writing as a commercial or artistic priority, between sexual fidelity or declaration of romantic commitment, and between exploiting various situations and selflessly helping others. Deep questions about the effect of the places the characters choose to reside in, those where they had their upbringing, and the opportunities all such places might afford to develop or foreclose potential, underlie specific references. Ostensibly a comedy of manners, the novel is by quick turns both funny and moving in its restraint, with witty, knowing dialogue, grand scenes, including the depiction of the wedding and dinner party of Llewellyn and Aoife, and a sharp poignancy in the developing care that Cunningham shows for their baby. These details might suggest that *Their Lips Talk of Mischief* is simply a historical, realist novel, yet despite its setting and the psychological and physical representations of the characters, the deeper political contexts through which these move inform the work and imbue it with an implicit sense of the portentous.

Where does this skilful deployment of implication come from? To answer that, we have to go back to *The Worms Can Carry Me to Heaven* (2006). This novel too is set far from Scotland. Although Spain is never named, and the story centres closely on the account of experiences by its first-person narrator, Manolo Follana, it nevertheless manages to build a deep historical background for itself, a history of fascism and a subtle understanding of its relation to media, newspapers, radio, film and television. Manolo, an architect, is a singular character, a combination of the comically fastidious, pathetically self-centred, unpleasantly vain, and unpredictably heroic. Both the national political history of Spain and the psychological realism with which the main character is presented would suggest the novel's firm limitations, and yet, once again, the deeper political questions of power, media, sexual self-consciousness, the motivation to help others as opposed to the impulse to seek wealth and comfort, are all presented as perennially appropriate, in Scotland as much as in Spain.

We grow up with Manolo, meeting his family and their different political allegiances in Franco's Spain and the legacy of the Civil War. With patience and subtlety, nuance and sympathy, the novel shows how big words like 'fascism' or 'migrants' have particular personal meaning to the characters. Ahmed, an immigrant Manolo fears and suspects, then befriends and helps, gives an account of his life which shifts any predisposition to stigmatise. Yet just as matters of racism, sexuality and economic reality are depicted in personal contexts without any programmatic or overt explication, their relevance is implicitly much broader than their manifestations in what reads at first like a rather quirky minor comic novel.

The Worms Can Carry Me to Heaven and *Their Lips Talk of Mischief* may be read on their own terms, yet in the context of Warner's oeuvre and the historical era he has been writing in, their relevance to aspects of the British state and Scotland within that state is an essential consideration. It is not simply that 'Spain' stands for 'Scotland' or that the three main characters in *Their Lips Talk of Mischief* are allegorical figures representing their specific nationalities. Rather, the human histories, personal, familial, social, political, in both these novels carry their meanings in ways that portend affinities beyond the definitions of realism. Warner is preoccupied with the relationship and identities of Scotland and Britain but in certain novels his interest in the nature of that relationship and those identities is disclosed obliquely.

A slight reference, two sentences near the beginning of *The Worms Can Carry Me to Heaven*, is suggestive: 'The development of tourism on our coasts exploded in the sixties and seventies along with cheaper jet travel. All the apartment and hotel construction was heavily encouraged and often subsidised by the fascists.'[5] That word 'heavily' is deliberately chosen, and the word 'fascists' might be replaced by 'government'. In the same paragraph, Manolo comments: 'As far as our fellow Europeans were concerned, it was a willing exchange of democracy for suntans in those days. Our new airport was one of the main gateways to the foreign package holiday tourists flowing to and from our country. People forget this society was formed by a police state' (*TW*, 61). Manolo goes on to consider the consequences of the tourists' 'two-week visitations' on the design of new Spanish villas and holiday homes: 'our country has built a thousand-mile coast made of second- and third-rate St Tropez's where people can feel that certain ritual which comes with a sunset ... and an exotic-seeming, discount drink in the hand' (*TW*, 61). Neither dismissive scorn nor facile optimism characterises Manolo, and Warner shares this capacity to depict the liabilities as well as the virtues in his characters, and the histories of their nations.

What happened next was Warner's return to an earlier era and familiar territory. *The Deadman's Pedal* (2012) is set mainly in the 1970s and moves with its main character as he leaves school and finds work, describes childhood dens and adult homes, private worlds and public lives, motives rising from selfishness and senses of responsibility, modes of commercial transport, lorries and trains, social structures of class, the difference and relation between nature and engineering. Questions of tradition and change in the political system and the economy are implicit throughout. The cultural moment sees the rise of punk rock in the 1970s and 1980s, opposed to the unctuous friendliness of mass media and the rise of celebrity culture and mediocrity. The novel, arguably more than any other, shows Alan Warner utterly confident in his cultural moment. Yet the first sentence delivers the timeless sense all the previous novels have been evoking in different ways, but here given as a governing fact for everything that this novel will go on to detail: 'Now and for always, Simon will be moving through the night, up on those diesel locomotives – a stable of just thirty or so as familiar as his home – crossing these lone territories between stations in a blackness as complete as outer space.'[6] We have here history and time, geography and location, evoked but not yet specified, a hinterland of cultural memory ('moving through the night' suggests generic film noir and fiction, just as 'stables' and 'lone territories' suggest the genre of westerns).

The first paragraph of Warner's novel describes the moment of adolescence, the moment of approaching maturity, and we go on to read about Simon's first job, his first love, his first departure from home and from his parents. The novel is in some respects as 'counter-cultural' as punk rock, recollecting Alexander Trocchi's *Young Adam* (published in 1954, with David Mackenzie's film adaptation starring Ewan McGregor released in 2003, not long before *The Deadman's Pedal*), another story of a young man facing uncertainty and a world of adult laws. Yet in a sense it is a conventional *Bildungsroman*, a coming-of-age story, like Robert Louis Stevenson's *Kidnapped*. Mortality, loyalty and limitations are essential to it.

The deadman's pedal is a safeguard, an inbuilt mechanism to ensure continuity after death. Should the driver of a train have a heart attack and die, the deadman's pedal will effectively brake and slow down and bring the train to a safe stop, protecting all on board. It is actual, but the function of the metaphor is also deeply embedded in the book, a foresight of possible accident and protection against it. Thus the symbolism in the title relates to a mundane, factual mechanism but extends to the portentous quality that imbues events and characters throughout, without undue emphasis. To indicate this risks exaggerating the symbolism in the book and may obscure an appreciation of the ease and quickness of Warner's writing. Yet, as in Stevenson's *Kidnapped*, layers of history, geography and politics are worked into the narrative unobtrusively. Just as *Kidnapped* represents and dramatises social and political change taking place in a Scotland of post-Culloden Hanoverian succession, so in *The Deadman's Pedal* the Thatcher era of the late 1970s and 1980s is palpably approaching. The ethos of unions, workers' rights, traditional class priorities, is beginning to lose to the priorities of entrepreneurial laissez-faire capitalism. It would seem that Warner is writing about the past as a kind of social historian, but the experience of reading the novel delivers more than that. The timeless quality I have referred to is omnipresent.

This is suggested perhaps even by the dedication to Michael Moorcock, famous prolific author of science fantasy since the 1960s, creator of iconic anti-hero Jerry

Cornelius and more recently known as chronicler of quasi-dreamlike post-Blitz London (the world he grew up in). The dedication is to Moorcock and 'all the boys of the old station' (*DP*, v), suggesting a band of tranquilly defiant rebels from a world of once upon a time. Warner's writing is hypersensitive to this tone, and careful not to indulge in nostalgia. Disguises help. Oban itself is, as in earlier work, 'the Port', and just up the road, Fort William is 'the Garrison'. The harbour, the housing schemes and supermarkets, the hinterland of Oban is immediately recognisable but imagined anew. Cleverly, near the beginning, Warner has us accompany Simon and two friends up to a hilltop hideout, 'Meditation Rock', looking out over the town and its environs. Simon will return to this spot later in the novel and its childhood charm will have gone by then. Even magic places do not stay as they were forever.

The structure of *The Deadman's Pedal* is important. It can be summarised in twenty-one (unnumbered) episodes: (1) A Prelude, italicised, beginning as quoted above: *Now and for always . . .* /// (2) **1961**: Wednesday 19 April /// (3) **1973**: Friday 8 June; (4) Wednesday 4 April; (5) Monday 18 June; (6) Friday 22 June; (7) Sunday 12 August; (8) Thursday 23 August; (9) Tuesday 28 August /// (10) **1974**: Tuesday 8 January /// (11) **1973**: Thursday 15 November; (12) Saturday 1 September /// (13) **1974**: Sunday 3 February; (14) Tuesday 5 March; (15) Tuesday 19 March; (16) Sunday 31 March; (17) Thursday 11 April; (18) Wednesday 12 June; (19) Saturday 15 June; (20) Tuesday 18 June; (21) Thursday 27 June, and the ending: 'He shook his head at it all, looking out through the splayed leaves across the Port – and to the inner summer lands, going eastward, backboned by roads, veined with single tracks and passing places, the railway and all he knew' (*DP*, 376). By clearly dating the episodes, Warner endorses a kind of realism. But this is not a straightforwardly linear narrative. There are forward-dated sections and returns to earlier dates, which create suspense while endorsing historical specificity. Times are changing, but not at the same rate for everyone. In terms of the economy, the railways Simon goes to work on are nationalised, while the haulage firm which is Simon's father's business is a private enterprise in competition with rail transport. Fishing is a crucial part of the local economy (the movement of the fish is significant: they go south), as is the hospital: the whole working economy of the area is essential to the story.

Characters are tightly bound to their place and to their hierarchical locations in this place, but the connections and transport systems they need to negotiate are precarious and changing. Destiny may be found in a sense of returning (the Port is tidal, there is a shoreline landscape, and archipelagic identities), but it is shifting, subject to change. Power, money and political decision-making might happen somewhere else, but within the territory of the novel, there is no periphery in the archipelago itself, though there are backwaters and further places, islands beyond the horizon. Human beings in this world have agency but share vulnerability. One characteristic of Warner's writing is that there is neither disdain nor irony displayed at the expense of any of his characters. Even the school bully, Forth, is given his own legitimacy in a thumbnail sketch precluding any easy caricature.

And the landscape is a living entity. The place is developed as a character with extending identity, vulnerable and subject to exploitation. The shape of its terrain is humanly discerned: 'It was beginning to grow lighter . . . As if the world was just an idea, slowly being thought up by some great imagination' (*DP*, 13). How the characters discover themselves in the landscape is reminiscent of the opening of the novel by Fionn Mac Colla, *And the Cock Crew* (1945), where people are described walking through a valley as mist rises to reveal the extent and height of the mountains surrounding them.[7] There is a supernatural feeling to these moments of revelation, yet this is secured in entirely accurate and credible descriptions of places, weather conditions and aspects of human behaviour. When Simon and his girlfriend Varie make love, they are interrupted by hail rattling on the outside of their shelter at the same moment as they break the circle drawn out superstitiously in the earth upon which they are lying. The portent is clear, and we learn that in fact this is also the moment of the conception of their child. Yet nothing emphatic or ponderous occupies the writing at this point. Accidents may be miracles.

Cairns Craig, in *The Modern Scottish Novel: Narrative and the National Imagination*, refers to Morvern Callar finding herself in a place between 'distant mountains lifting up as if explosions of steam', in the place 'where the water turned angry black – wide wide ocean that goes on forever', and notes that Morvern is journeying 'between the eternal space of the mountains she was named after and the miniature narratives of an inconsequential history, at the edge of an ocean which gives her "The Rudder Feeling"'. This feeling, Craig says, 'occurs when the direction of history is undone by the limitless space in which its journey takes place'.[8] This is to say that, however specific the historical and geographical referents may be, the sense of the illimitable and the immaterial – the timeless – is embedded in the characters and stories presented here.

The same year *The Deadman's Pedal* appeared, Ali Smith published her book *Artful* (2012).[9] Its four separate sections are: 'On time', 'On form', 'On edge' and 'On offer and on reflection'. It is salutary to read *Artful* alongside Warner's novel. Smith is ostensibly writing a series of meditative essays on art of different kinds: Dickens's *Oliver Twist*, poems by Edwin Morgan, Stevie Smith, Boris Pasternak, William Carlos Williams, Sylvia Plath and others, visual art by Michelangelo, films with the actress Aliki Vougiouklaki, and so on. However, as you read the essays you become aware that they are contextualised within a story, a novel, so to speak, where the main characters are the author and an unnamed 'you' – who, it seems, is dead and gone. All the arts are long conversations, usually with the dead, but the timeless qualities they embody deliver a living dialogue. Warner's fiction, like Smith's, bristles with such lively matter.

Does this suggest something beyond whatever might have been described as postmodernism? Perhaps no labels are needed to see that there is a moving on from the mere rejection or abandonment of 'grand narratives' as unquestionably reliable. After the contest of old socialism and new capitalism (in British terms, the decline of the triumph of Blair, known so well now as the child of Thatcher), there is, it would appear, a return to fundamental realities. In fiction, this requires more than realism and something less defined or easily categorised as allegory or symbolism. With regard to evolving aspects of feminism, Warner's work is clearly of central importance. His women and men are equally in the world, their points of view are understood equally to provoke timeless questions of power and empowerment, recognition of the relation between functions of identity, position and authority.

And in the immediate political arena, matters of region and nation, history and class, are central in Warner's fiction, but not always in the foreground. His novels take as their given context social and political qualities of colonial dominance, whether in British or Spanish contexts. Oban and its hinterland, the Western Isles, Scotland, England, London and a specific coastal town in Spain are focal locations, but the context of the British state, or, in *The Worms Can Carry Me to Heaven*, Spain with its history of Civil War and fascism, contextualise everything. At the end of *The Stars in the Bright Sky*, 2001 is the gateway year and 9/11 is the key to open it into the twenty-first century.

In all Warner's novels, though, there is a heightened sense of the value of the potential of the vulnerable individual for effective intervention. What seems final is always only partial. Agency applies to locations as much as to characters. The self-conscious, unobtrusively politicised ethos of Warner's fiction is more about the relations and enactments of hierarchical political and social power, and the lives of individual persons, than the virtues of regional experience or explicit aspiration to national self-determination, even though that aspiration is undimmed in its author. It needs to be, because there are still and always will be folk out there wanting to rule over you. Imperialism has not gone away.

NOTES

1. Alan Warner, *The Sopranos* (London: Jonathan Cape, 1998), p. 324.
2. Alan Warner, *The Stars in the Bright Sky* (London: Jonathan Cape, 2010), p. 394.
3. Alan Warner, *Their Lips Talk of Mischief* (London: Faber & Faber, 2014), p. 31.
4. See Alan Warner, 'Scottish Writers on the Referendum – Independence Day?', *The Guardian*, 19 July 2014, <http://www.theguardian.com/books/2014/jul/19/scottish-referendum-independence-uk-how-writers-vote> (last accessed 15 June 2016).
5. Alan Warner, *The Worms Can Carry Me to Heaven* (London: Vintage, 2007), p. 61. All quotations are from this edition; hereafter, page numbers will be given in the text, preceded by *TW*.
6. Alan Warner, *The Deadman's Pedal* (London: Jonathan Cape, 2012), p. 1. All quotations are from this edition; hereafter, page numbers will be given in the text, preceded by *DP*.
7. Fionn Mac Colla, *And the Cock Crew* (1945; Edinburgh: Canongate, 1995).
8. Cairns Craig, *The Modern Scottish Novel: Narrative and the National Imagination* (Edinburgh: Edinburgh University Press, 1999), pp. 239–40.
9. Ali Smith, *Artful* (London: Hamish Hamilton, 2012).

FURTHER READING

For an up-to-date list of Alan Warner's novels, see the British Council website: <https://literature.britishcouncil.org/writer/alan-warner> (last accessed 15 June 2016).

Brown, Ian, and Alan Riach (eds), *The Edinburgh Companion to Twentieth-Century Scottish Literature* (Edinburgh: Edinburgh University Press, 2009).
McGuire, Matt, *Contemporary Scottish Literature: A Reader's Guide to Essential Criticism* (Basingstoke: Palgrave Macmillan, 2008).

Schoene, Berthold (ed.), *The Edinburgh Companion to Contemporary Scottish Literature* (Edinburgh: Edinburgh University Press, 2007).

Warner, Alan, interview, in *The Scottish Review of Books*, 10 August 2011, <http://www.scottishreviewofbooks.org/index.php/back-issues/volume-seven-2011/volume-seven-issue-three/419-the-srb-interview-alan-warner-extended-version> (last accessed 15 June 2016).

—— 'Scottish Writers on the Referendum – Independence Day?', *The Guardian*, 19 July 2014, <http://www.theguardian.com/books/2014/jul/19/scottish-referendum-independence-uk-how-writers-vote> (last accessed 15 June 2016).

PART III

Postmodernism, Globalisation and Beyond

CHAPTER 9

Ali Smith: Strangers and Intrusions

Monica Germanà

Ali Smith's six novels – *Like* (1997), *Hotel World* (2001), *The Accidental* (2005), *Girl Meets Boy* (2007), *There but for the* (2011) and *How to be both* (2014) – are, with one exception, all products of the twenty-first century. We may take 2000 as the year of demarcation of a new cultural epoch, or we may agree with Brian McHale that the following year is a more significant threshold of a new cultural climate in the Western world.[1] More specifically, McHale views 2001 as the date marking the end of postmodernism and the beginning of 'post-post-modernism', a term he borrows from Jeffrey T. Nealon, to indicate 'the ways in which post-postmodernism *repeats*, albeit with a difference, the postmodernism that came before', and the 'new phase's continuity with postmodernism'.[2] Perhaps no British writer captures this transitional phase as well as Ali Smith, whose works may be seen to reflect a Janus-faced attitude towards postmodernism and its legacy.

Indeed, Smith's novels frequently challenge the real/imagined boundaries that postmodernism is preoccupied with.[3] In a typical reference to popular culture – another feature Smith's fiction shares with postmodernism – in *The Accidental*, Astrid describes the pop music video where 'the girl . . . is in a café having a cup of coffee and reading a comic then the comic comes alive and she becomes part of the story'.[4] The reference to a-ha's 1985 hit 'Take on Me' exposes the permeability of real/fictional worlds, which is also characteristic of postmodern narratives. If this exemplary passage from *The Accidental* can be held as representative of Smith's oeuvre, it would place it firmly within the ambit of postmodernism. Indeed, there is no doubt that her novels are often metaleptic – breaking down the boundaries between fiction and reality – as well as being intertextual (echoing other texts) and focused on the hyperreal, the simulated real that, according to Jean Baudrillard, has replaced the real in postmodern culture.[5] Her formal experimentation, while reminiscent of the modernist writings of Virginia Woolf and James Joyce, is also characteristic of a kind of writing that self-consciously reminds us of the skilled artifice at the heart of postmodern fiction.

Nevertheless, while we acknowledge the legacy of thematic, stylistic and ideological characteristics of postmodern narratives in Smith's fiction, her writing also departs from postmodernism in a way that not only displays innovative narrative techniques, but also combines formal experimentation with a strong ethical commitment to distinctly contemporary concerns. In particular, at the heart of Smith's fiction is a focus on the brokenness of the contemporary human condition, an experience intensified by an acute awareness of the temporariness of our existence. Significantly, while placing emphasis on the critical state of human relations in the twenty-first century, Smith's fiction also emerges as strongly life-assertive and redemptive, replacing the solipsistic alienation of contemporary living with a new kind of empathic *connectedness* that, arguably, constitutes a clear departure from the postmodern disaffection.

Responding to the contradictions of a globalised world whose shifting commercial frontiers coexist, paradoxically, with increasingly inflexible immigration policies, the attention to the other story throughout Smith's fiction is both a thematic and a formal feature that reveals political and ethical implications.[6] Thus her frequent emphasis on boundaries and the borderline condition is not just an engagement with postmodernist metalepsis, but a more complex commentary on the significance of borders and the liminal existence between them. This is something Smith reflects on, insightfully, in her critical work *Artful* (2012): 'Edges involve extremes. Edges are borders. Edges are very much about identity, about who you are.'[7] Smith's fiction is pervasively concerned with the unveiling of the other story, which exists beyond the border and the surface of things. The coexistence of multiple voices means that Smith's stories are always dialogical, based on a dialogue between different narrative voices and suggestive of the existence of multiple texts. Such dialogical structure of writing derives from Smith's specific interest in voice: 'everything is voice,' she explains. 'I don't think anything exists without voice. The first thing that anything written does is go to voice. . . . Even a monologue is never a monologue. It always implies.'[8] Smith's interest in voice gives rise to a polyphonic way of working with language, which is reminiscent of Mikhail Bakhtin's notion of heteroglossia: according to Bakhtin, the dialogical structure of language is also the foundation of the novel's polyphonic construction: 'The word is born in a dialogue as a living rejoinder within it; the word is shaped in dialogical interaction with an alien word that is already in the object.'[9] Bakhtin's organic notion of language revolves around the concept of heteroglossia, the language of the other, intended, very broadly, as any kind of linguistic deviation typically derived from the margins of society; consequently, heteroglossia acts as a centrifugal force within the centralised system of language, pulling it apart, subverting its norms, and disrupting its linearity. In Smith's fiction the voice of the other emerges particularly strongly through the character of the stranger – a recurrent feature in her work – who serves the purpose of disturbing the existing order and destabilising characters' identities, often with satirical and political intent. It is indeed the other that brings about the epiphany, that allows for the possibility, at least, of seeing things in a different way.

Set against the backdrop of the fictional Global Hotel, *Hotel World* is distinctly polyphonic. Narrating the stories are four voices and points of view, the first being that of the ghost of Sara Wilby, a nineteen-year-old hotel maid accidentally killed when she falls down a dumb-waiter shaft. While the novel's chapters – 'past', 'present historic', 'future conditional', 'perfect', 'future in the past' and 'present' – seemingly indicate the story's adherence to conventional time, chronological linearity is in fact replaced by the anachrony of spectrality.[10] In other words, the disruption to linear chronology, perpetuated by the haunting presence of Sara's ghost, poses a threat to the linear logic of the capitalist system embodied in the hotel: as Fiona McCulloch has observed, the novel's 'anti-linearity queers the straightforwardness of conventional time sequences, creating a spiralling network of intersecting narrative threads that shift between present, future, past and beyond the grave'.[11] Indeed, by telling the stories of marginal figures – a deceased chambermaid, a homeless woman (Else), a disaffected employee (Lise), a bereaved teenager (Clare) – the novel asserts its intention of pursuing the other story. The only exception is, of course, the hypocritical journalist (Penny), although her neurotic pro-establishment voice also serves the purpose of destabilising the voice of the centre.

Particularly relevant in this respect is the character of Else, whose language, reduced to the form of mutilated short-hand, is evocatively suggestive of her brokenness. Even her name implies the idea of otherness; her identity does not belong to the world of corporate hotels and their professional guests. She stands outside this world, distraught, watching its inhabitants: 'They hold mobile phones to their ears and it is as if they are holding the sides of their faces and heads in a new kind of agony. The ones with the new headset kind of mobile phone look like insane people, as if they're walking along talking to themselves in a world of their own.'[12] Such observations are a reminder of the post-millennial intensified virtuality McHale regards as a feature of the post-postmodern era.[13] Against this spectacle of globalised technological solipsism, Else's laughter – and cough – brings both disorder and subversion. The fact that she does not belong in this world is also symbolised by her inability to fully exploit the commodities of the Global Hotel, which Lise has offered her for free, in another act of corporate subversion.

More to the point, however, when Else meets Penny, who writes her a cheque she has no intention of honouring, she significantly asks her the meaning of the word 'rebegot', which Penny erroneously transcribes as 'rebiggot' (a pun, in turn, at the expense of her own bigotry). A reference to John Donne's poem 'A Nocturnal upon St Lucy's Day', the actual word 'rebegot' evokes the possibility of renewal, even at the darkest of times, as in Donne's mourning poem. Smith, significantly, returns to this word in her 'Manchester Sermon' presented in 2012: 'The begetting is a kind of revelation that time is chronological but life force is cyclic, a matter more of rhythm than of chronology. . . . When Donne invents the word rebegot, he is remaking everything – fathering, conceiving, the very deepest place of thought; almost, you could say, the place before thought, the original source of both birth and thought.'[14] In drawing attention to the notion of being 'rebegot', Else also embodies the concept of cyclical renewal that, in different ways, affects all the characters in *Hotel World*. Most importantly, as the last section in the novel suggests, such regenerative action – strongly linked to language, and its redemptive powers – is a way of reconnecting the centre with the margins, and of re-establishing new, invisible bonds with the others.

Like *Hotel World*, *The Accidental* is narrated from multiple points of view. The four members of the Smart family – Eve (mother), Michael (stepfather), Magnus (son) and Astrid (daughter) – are points of view represented in distinct chapters within the novel's three sections, 'The beginning', 'The middle' and 'The end'. As Ulrike Tancke rightly observes, the novel's apparent linear structure serves, in fact, the purpose of drawing attention to narrative deception and teleological disruption.[15] Framing each section is a first-person narrative by Amber, who, in this narrative frame that apparently tells the story of her origin, is named Alhambra. Amber is the stranger who causes major disruption to the Smart family, as they rent a holiday home in Norfolk. The name Alhambra, as well as bearing an association with the exotic Moorish palace in Granada, links Amber to the world of the cinema, which the novel frequently mentions. As Alhambra, Amber is born in a cinema 'just short of a century after the birth of the Frenchman whose name translates as Mr Light' – a playful reference to Auguste Lumière, who in 1894 created the first motion pictures.

As Amber, she simultaneously embodies notions of danger (an amber light draws attention to a potential hazard) and exoticism: 'Amber was an exotic fixative. Amber preserved things that weren't meant to last. Amber gave dead gone things a chance to live forever' (*TA*, 163). This is how Michael puts it, suggesting that Amber has come to the Smart holiday home to 'fix' their dysfunctional family. Smith does not lament the breakdown of the nuclear family as such, but rather the disconnectedness that characterises twenty-first-century human relationships. The consequence of this lack of authentic bonds leads to a sense of fragmentation, solipsism and isolation, which is what describes each single member of the Smart family. It is the rise of the other, Amber, that catalyses all sorts of processes which ultimately lead to a more aware – if still broken – family life. At a broader level, we can see how the disconnection of the Smart family can be read as a microcosmic projection of the contemporary condition, and the dangerous right-wing tendencies that speak of an increasing intolerance for the other (these are symbolically represented, locally, by the episodes of vandalism on the Indian restaurant in Norfolk, and, internationally, by the controversial war in Iraq, repeatedly referred to in the novel).

Nevertheless, there is a strong sense of redemption, with the novel pointing to Amber as, perhaps, an accidental saviour. Significantly, it is the Smart family's renewed language after Amber's intrusion that signals their potential salvation. Thus, while for Michael Amber is 'a word he hadn't known was in him' (*TA*, 61), the recovery of Magnus, whose brokenness is partially healed by his encounter with Amber, is evocatively expressed through his infatuation with the conjunction 'and'. 'And' is the ultimate connective word, or, as Magnus claims, to emphasise the breath of new life carried by the idea of reconnecting, 'The word *and* is a little bullet of oxygen' (*TA*, 155).[16]

Smith's next novel, *Girl Meets Boy*, has two levels: the first is in the present day, involving Midge (Imogen) and Anthea, who both work for Pure, a water company with dubious ethical foundations. The second level – taken from Ovid's *Metamorphoses* – is the story of Iphis, a girl raised as a boy by her mother in ancient Greece, because the family cannot afford to have a daughter. In Ovid's story, Iphis transforms into a boy on the eve of her wedding night. Such transformative power is reflected in the modern-day lesbian love story between Anthea and Robin, who uses the nickname of Iphis to sign her politically charged graffiti. As in the previous novels, the presence of the other – in this case, Robin/Iphis – has a kind of enlightening effect not just on Anthea, but also on her sister, Midge, who gradually begins to see Pure's problematic politics.

The question of sameness/difference pervades the novel from the start. The headings given to the novel's sections – 'I', 'you', 'us', 'them', 'all together now' – highlight, on one hand, the polyphonic structure of the novel, and, particularly in the last section, the notion of a connective simultaneity, whereby the different, previously clashing, voices merge into one choral narrative celebrating diversity in togetherness. Significantly, otherness is not merely opposed to sameness; on the contrary, the story deconstructs the same/other binary opposition in favour of a queer metamorphic discourse underpinned by the reference to Ovid's myth of Iphis and Ianthe.

The exploration of sameness/otherness is strongly associated with the global/local politics linked to the Pure water company, an international corporation which aims to exploit the right to drink water: 'water is the perfect commodity. Because water is running out,' Keith, 'the boss of bosses', claims in a team meeting.[17] This consumerist approach is also visible in the changes Anthea observes of Inverness, which now has 'all the same shops ... as in every big city' (GMB, 28), although 'the shopping centre was full of people who looked immensely sad, and the people working in the shops there looked even sadder' (GMB, 29). While the mythical frame of *Girl Meets Boy* does not directly engage with the motif of the zombie apocalypse shared in many post-millennial narratives, nevertheless, Anthea's reflection of the lifeless consumerist predicament of Inverness bears a comparison with many undead narratives of the twenty-first-century 'postmagical realism'.[18] Juxtaposed to the global politics of bottled water and the prefigured apocalypse of capitalist consumerism is Anthea's reflection on the local river Ness – 'The river laughed. I swear it did. It laughed and it changed as I watched. As it changed, it stayed the same' (GMB, 28) – which introduces the notion of dynamic identity, where sameness and difference can coexist, and celebrates the vitality of a natural world untouched by global capitalism.

Subverting the status quo is the queer character of Robin/Iphis, whose function in the novel appears similar, in this sense, to Amber's in *The Accidental*. Consumerist attitudes exist, in the twenty-first century, not only with respect to goods, but also with respect to human relationships, as demonstrated by dating websites promoting a rigorously heteronormative commerce of pre-packaged emotions. In the billboard advertising one such service, 'The difference between male and female was breasts and hair' (GMB, 31), Anthea notes. Within this context, Robin/Iphis shakes the foundations of both capitalist and patriarchal/heteronormative ways of thinking. Her voice, protesting against both, intrudes into the narrative, through a campaign of political slogans designed first to expose the Pure water company, then to draw attention to gender inequality in the world. Against the reductive gender and sexuality politics perpetuated by some members of the water company – '[lesbian] women. It's like, how can they? I just don't get it. It's a joke, Dominic says' (*GMB*, 71) – by being with Robin, Anthea learns what it means to be 'both genders, a whole new gender, no gender at all' (*GMB*, 104).

In *There but for the* Smith inverts the paradigm of the visiting stranger deployed in *The Accidental* by having a dinner party guest, Miles Garth, lock himself up in the house of his hosts, Gen and Eric Lee. As in *The Accidental*, the story is told from multiple points of view – Anna (an old friend of Miles); Mark, who brings Miles in as a guest to the party; May Young, an older woman Miles regularly visits; and Brooke, the daughter of Terence and Bernice Bayoude, who are also dinner party guests. As in *The Accidental*, it is the trespasser, the ultimately unwanted other, who throws satirical light on the hypocrisy of middle-class ways of living; the dinner party itself is an exercise in bourgeois political correctness: an 'alternative dinner party' (*TBFT*, 18), aiming to gather other people, people whom the 'generic' hosts would not normally interact with, in this case, two gay men (Mark and Miles) and a couple of black academics (Terence and Bernice).

This is highlighted through a preoccupation with boundaries, these being particularly relevant to the borough of Greenwich. As Mark says of the Observatory: '[it is] all about the visible-invisible borders, the thin lines between here and gone, there and now, random and meant, big and small' (*TBFT*, 112). Boundaries come up, too, as a pertinent topic of conversation at the dinner party, where a character named Richard remarks that the whole world is 'borderless'. He adds, however, that 'everywhere needs some defence against people just coming in and overrunning the place with their terrorisms or their deficiencies' (*TBFT*, 146). Significantly, the conversation moves on to Faye Palmer, Mark's late mother, and the political value of her art. 'Seeing a picture like one of Palmer's is very different from seeing something atrocious on a screen,' comments Terence. 'There *is* no screen. That's the point. There's nothing between you and it' (*TBFT*, 167). Such annihilation of borders between self and other, 'us' and 'them', clashes, ideologically, with what Gen and Eric – and their close friends – represent. As Terence puts it, the power of such art rests precisely on that notion of collective sharing which has been eroded from the contemporary 'communities' of the Western world: 'what it means [is] to have to bear the knowledge of inhumanity, having to bear it communally' (*TBFT*, 165).

Miles's refusal to leave the dinner party creates a paradoxical situation where, as Gen claims, '[a] stranger is living in our house against our will' (*TBFT*, 105). Miles, the unwanted other, occupies Gen and Eric's 'outstanding spare room', a room devoid of any purpose, other than that of showing off 'lovely, lovely furniture' (*TBFT*, 20). By agitating for his departure – while also, later on in the novel, trying to capitalise on his refusal to leave – the hypocrisy behind Gen's hospitality is laid bare. As in the previous novels, the intrusion of the unwanted other has a disruptive effect on the 'normal' people whose space he has, temporarily at least, altered: 'It is strange having a stranger in the house with you all the time. It makes you strangely self-aware, strange to yourself' (*TBFT*, 106). The result can be read in terms of the erosion of those fictitious boundaries that separate the self from the other, as Julia Kristeva, discussing Sigmund Freud's 'The Uncanny' (1919), argues: 'foreignness is within us: we are our own foreigners, we are divided.'[19]

Against the endemic discourse of inner/outer division, what Smith proposes, through the figure of the other, is the possibility for reconciliation. When Jennifer asks her mother, May, 'What are human beings for?', the answer is simple: 'It's for looking after each other' (*TBFT*, 258). Translated into the complex network of contemporary society, this implies a subversive re-assessment of the notion of twenty-first-century community: as Zygmunt Bauman has observed, 'The survival and well-being of *communitas* . . . depend on human imagination, inventiveness and courage in *breaking* the routine and trying the *untried* ways.'[20] Such imaginative powers, in *There but for the*, are the prerogative of the outsiders, namely Miles and Brooke, the child, who, as such, occupies a position outside the normative space which even her parents, though non-conformist, have to negotiate with. After all, it is Brooke who notes, at the end of the novel, that the beauty of the river Thames rests on its constant changeability. Thus the flow of the river becomes a broader metaphor for the flow of people who walk, underground, beneath the surface, and whose unknown stories constitute the invisible network that connects humanity in the twenty-first-century metropolis: 'It is a different possible river every second, and imagine all the *other* people under the water walking across to the other side and back to this side in the tunnel right now, because under the surface there is a whole other thing always happening' (*TBFT*, 356; italics mine).

The notion of simultaneity pervades both the form and the content of Smith's latest novel, *How to be both*. The novel consists of two apparently parallel narratives – that of fifteenth-century Italian painter Francesco del Cossa and modern-day British girl George – whose stories in fact intersect, as the ghost of Cossa, suspended in purgatory, haunts George's own story. As in *Boy Meets Girl*, here Smith plays with the gender/sex categories, having an androgynous teenage girl called George and imagining Cossa as a biological female who masqueraded as a male in order to train and work as a painter. As in the previous novels, there is a strong sense in which a story cannot be told in one way only, and, to enhance the non-linearity of the other story, the book was released in two alternative editions, one starting with Cossa's story, the other starting with George's.

At the threshold of each narrative are two drawings, a surveillance camera and a pair of eyes suggestive of the centrality of 'seeing' at the heart of the narrative. While the novel, thematically, approaches the notion of seeing in a variety of ways – Cossa is concerned with the reproduction of perspective in painting, and George is preoccupied by the ways in which we see things on a daily basis – it is the technique of frescoes that underpins Smith's dual narrative in *How to be both*. The coexistence of two 'narrative' layers in a fresco means that an earlier underdrawing, frequently depicting a different scene, lies beneath the final picture, which covers it completely. This, in Smith's words, reflects the paradoxical principle of narrative simultaneity: 'So you look at the wall, you see one thing, but something else is behind it, right in front of you, there but invisible. It's a perfect narrative structure.'[21] George's musing on the notion of narrative simultaneity addresses similar questions: 'Because if things really did happen simultaneously it'd be like reading a book but one in which all the lines of the text have been overprinted, like each page is actually two pages but with one superimposed on the other to make it unreadable.'[22]

Six hundred years earlier, Cossa is concerned with related issues, as an apprentice painter approaching the problem of perspective, or 'where to place things and tiles of a floor or across a landscape to show some things closer and some much further away. So things far away and close could be held together, in the same picture?' (*HTBB*, 219). Simultaneity, then, becomes a matter of perspective, which allows for things belonging to different planes to coexist. In other words, simultaneity is a different way of seeing, one that, like heteroglossia, facilitates the representation of otherness. The novel's title is indeed suggestive of the possibility of being something other than oneself, of expanding one's sense of identity and view of the world beyond the self/other binarism.

Such emphatic endorsement of multiple subjectivity is evident in George's reference to her friend Helena's mixed background: 'H's father is from Karachi and Copenhagen and ... according to her father, it is actually possible to be from the north and the south and the east and the west all at once' (*HTBB*, 88). Cossa reaches similar conclusions about painting, following Giambattista Alberti's teaching that 'beauty in its most completeness is never found in a single body but is something shared instead between more than one body' (*HTBB*, 276). Thus, in his/her paintings, he/she combines the features of the female prostitutes he/she has sketched at the brothel. Ultimately, what the novel – and Smith's work overall – appears to imply is well captured in George's words: 'nothing's not connected' (*HTBB*, 106).

Situated within the post-postmodernist cultural context, Smith's novels demonstrate the kind of continuity that exists between post-millennial fiction and the previous cultural epoch, or, to put it in McHale's words, 'the intensification and mutation of features and tendencies already present *within* postmodernism',[23] which characterises post-millennial fiction. In many ways, her fiction reflects some eminently postmodern preoccupations with the real and its boundaries with the fictional. Simultaneously, however, Smith's fiction also offers a manifest engagement with distinctly contemporary concerns. In particular, these are supported by her recurrent use of polyphony, a narrative strategy deployed to convey heteroglossia, the language of the other. Thus, Smith's experimental narratives appear to make strong statements about the acknowledgement of the other within ourselves, the erasure of neat borderlines separating us from the other, and the permeable coexistence of simultaneous identities within the post-millennial self.

NOTES

1. Brian McHale, *The Cambridge Introduction to Postmodernism* (Cambridge: Cambridge University Press, 2015), pp. 172–5.

2. Ibid., pp. 176–7. See also Jeffrey T. Nealon, *Post-Postmodernism, or the Cultural Logic of Just-in-Time Capitalism* (Stanford: Stanford University Press, 2012).
3. McHale, *The Cambridge Introduction to Postmodernism*, p. 15. See also Brian McHale, *Postmodernist Fiction* (London: Methuen, 1987), p. 10.
4. Ali Smith, *The Accidental* (London: Hamish Hamilton, 2005), p. 28. All quotations are from this edition; hereafter, page numbers will be given in the text, preceded by *TA*.
5. See Jean Baudrillard, *Simulacra and Simulation*, trans. Sheila Faria Glaser (1981; Ann Arbor: Michigan University Press, 2013).
6. Ali Smith has taken part in the Refugee Tales project, an initiative linked to the Gatwick Detainees Welfare Group. Smith's response to her involvement in the project, the story 'I Thought You Would Help Me', is available from <http://www.theguardian.com/books/2015/jun/27/ali-smith-so-far-the-detainees-tale-extract> (last accessed 16 June 2016).
7. Ali Smith, *Artful* (London: Hamish Hamilton, 2012), pp. 125–6.
8. 'Gillian Beer Interviews Ali Smith', in Monica Germanà and Emily Horton (eds), *Ali Smith: Contemporary Critical Perspectives* (London: Bloomsbury, 2013), pp. 137–53; p. 138.
9. M. M. Bakhtin, *The Dialogic Imagination: Four Essays*, ed. Michael Holquist, trans. Caryl Emerson and Michael Holquist (1981; Austin: University of Texas Press, 1982), p. 279.
10. See Jacques Derrida, *Spectres of Marx: The State of the Debt, the Work of Mourning, and the New International*, trans. Peggy Kamuf (New York: Routledge, 1994), pp. 6–7. Here Derrida reminds us that the apparition of a ghost 'de-synchronises. It recalls us to anachrony.'
11. Fiona McCulloch, *Cosmopolitanism in Contemporary British Fiction: Imagined Identities* (Basingstoke: Palgrave, 2012), p. 165.
12. Ali Smith, *Hotel World* (2001; London: Penguin, 2002), pp. 39–40. More recently, Smith has commented on the ambiguous function played by technologies of communication in the twenty-first century: 'In our own falling-faster-than-the-speed-of-sound world the screens of our phones and computers light up every dark, prove it by messaging us, we're not alone, keep us slavishly safe from ever thinking about one thing for too long and constantly bombarded with the newness of the new.' See Ali Smith, 'The Manchester Sermon 2012: Rebegot', p. 4; available at <http://www.manchesterliteraturefestival.co.uk/downloads/1213-4gde6ne45.pdf?f=manchester-sermon-2012---ali-smith> (last accessed 16 June 2016).
13. See McHale, *The Cambridge Introduction to Postmodernism*, p. 180.
14. Smith, 'The Manchester Sermon', p. 12.
15. See Ulrike Tancke, 'Narrating Intrusion: Deceptive Storytelling and Frustrated Desires in *The Accidental* and *There but for the*', in Germanà and Horton (eds), *Ali Smith*, pp. 75–88; p. 77.
16. The passage foreshadows a similar metalinguistic observation in *There but for the*, when Miles says of 'but' that it is 'a word that connects sentences, clauses and words one of the aspects of the planets, when two bodies have the same celestial longitude or the same right ascension'. See Ali Smith, *There but for the* (London: Hamish Hamilton, 2011), p. 195. All quotations are from this edition; hereafter, page numbers will be given in the text, preceded by *TBFT*.
17. Ali Smith, *Girl Meets Boy* (Edinburgh: Canongate, 2007), pp. 37, 34. All quotations are from this edition; hereafter, page numbers will be given in the text, preceded by *GMB*.
18. See McHale, *The Cambridge Introduction to Postmodernism*, p. 187. See also Alexandra Warwick and David Cunningham, 'The Ambassadors of Nil: Notes on the Zombie Apocalypse', in Monica Germanà and Aris Mousoutzanis (eds), *Apocalyptic Discourse in Contemporary Culture: Post-Millennial Perspectives on the End of the World* (New York: Routledge, 2014), pp. 175–89.
19. Julia Kristeva, *Strangers to Ourselves* (1988; London: Harvester Wheatsheaf, 1991), p. 181.
20. Zygmunt Bauman, *Liquid Love: On the Frailty of Human Love* (Cambridge: Polity, 2003), pp. 73–4.
21. Ali Smith et al., 'Man Booker Prize: The Six Shortlisted Authors Reveal the Story behind

the Book', *The Guardian*, 10 October 2014, <http://www.theguardian.com/books/2014/oct/10/man-booker-prize-shortlist-author-inspiration/print> (last accessed 16 June 2016).
22. Ali Smith, *How to be both* (London: Hamish Hamilton, 2014), p. 10. This edition begins with George's story. All quotations are from this edition; hereafter, page numbers will be given in the text, preceded by *HTBB*.
23. McHale, *The Cambridge Introduction to Postmodernism*, p. 178.

FURTHER READING

For an up-to-date list of Ali Smith's novels, see the British Council website: <https://literature.britishcouncil.org/writer/ali-smith> (last accessed 16 June 2016).

CHAPTER 10

Kazuo Ishiguro: Alternate Histories

Daniel Bedggood

Kazuo Ishiguro, a Japanese-born British writer, has built on his early success as one of the bright young writers of the late twentieth century, his recent mature work and cinematic adaptations adding to his reputation as a consummate artist and interrogator of social and individual crises. If his earlier work established a pattern of careful and creative historiography, personalised through the eyes of flawed narrators, his writing since the turn of the century has both extended and complicated such features, reflecting his taste for diversity, inconclusiveness and mistrust of nostalgia. This chapter looks especially at his recent work, focusing on Ishiguro's postmodern turn to the past and alternate histories and, in particular, to his narrative decolonisation, detection and misdirection in *When We Were Orphans* (2000); his speculation on alternatives in *Never Let Me Go* (2005); and his establishment of relationships between history and myth, trauma and forgetting in *The Buried Giant* (2015). In all of these works, I examine his development of unreliable first-person narrative traits, his manipulations of generic expectation and development, his manipulation of register, and his acts of narrative elision as techniques that serve his play on differences between individual and cultural memory.

His novels quite specifically interrogate contexts of history, part of what is perceived widely as 'changes in the fundamental attitude of some historical fiction . . . related to a parallel narrative turn in historical writing'.[1] Even though Ishiguro's first books appear to be purely historical novels, they arose from 'moments in history that would best serve my purposes. . . . I was conscious that I wasn't so interested in history *per se*, that I was using British history or Japanese history to illustrate something that was preoccupying me.'[2] His use of history continues into his later work, whether that of mid to late twentieth century or more experimentally located in the dimly recalled Dark Ages; this fascination is often a vehicle for exploring personal trauma and the mechanisms of remembering, his works evincing the psychological effects of wider history on the individual. Such a use of the past is consistent with the postmodern resurgence in the interest in and engagement with history, notably by critics such as Linda Hutcheon, who has identified the development of a special postmodernist genre, historiographic metafiction. As Hutcheon says, 'the postmodern ... effects two simultaneous moves. It reinstalls historical contexts as significant and even determining, but in so doing, it problematises the entire notion of historical knowledge.'[3] Part of Ishiguro's narrative trajectory seems to be about the turn away from lower-case 'history' or 'histories', in favour of alternative first-person accounts that embody one of the postmodern challenges to upper-case 'History' as a teleological, objective and monolithic embodiment of certainty.[4]

Alongside and emphasising his concerns with narrating the personal scale of experience and cultural history, Ishiguro's use of 'realism' is also complicated by the subjects of its discourse, and a tendency to introduce 'surrealist' or 'expressionist' elements into his narratives. These traits are also, in their own ways, attempts to render experiential reality, 'where everything is distorted to reflect the emotion of the artist who is looking at the world'.[5] Ishiguro's style of seemingly 'restrained' realism, expressed in 'prose [that] is precise, transparent, cautiously accessible',[6] is a matter of juxtaposing to well-observed attention to detail the accounts of often wildly unreliable narrators. As tellers of personal and unstable accounts that sample fantasy, nightmare and misremembering, Ishiguro's narrators are, as Brian Finney has observed, 'fixated with the past, especially with the trauma of leaving behind their protected childhood'.[7] Yet for these narrators, the telling of the past functions as an attempt at therapeutic displacement or elision, talking over and around the sites of trauma. Such a narrative methodology creates what Salman Rushdie has described as a turbulence 'just below the understatement of the [novels'] surface [that is] as immense as it is slow'.[8] Yet if Ishiguro's early work establishes alternative perspectives, his twenty-first-century novels more properly engage with 'alternative histories', and do so through a more thorough deconstruction of different genres that provide alternative modes of re-examining history.

It is important to recognise Ishiguro's praxis in his early work to consider how his later novels both build on this and yet also become distinct. His third and fourth novels in particular, the Booker-winning *The Remains of the Day* (1989) and the Whitbread Award-winning *The Unconsoled* (1995), play with suppressed pasts and masked role play that complicate the surface narrative. A book that at once 'perfects and subverts' a nostalgic literary tradition of portraying the relationship between the serving classes and their aristocratic 'masters',[9] *The Remains of the Day* centres on Stevens, the butler of the great house Darlington Hall, selectively remembering events from his service in the 1920s and 1930s narrated alongside a post-war journey to see a former co-worker. Stevens is a thoroughly 'buttoned-up' character, prioritising his performative 'role' based on conventions of recognised social class or 'place': 'The great butlers ... will not be shaken out by external events, however surprising, alarming or vexing. They wear their professionalism as a decent gentleman will wear his suit: he will not let ruffians or circumstance tear it off him in the public gaze.'[10] In contrast, and yet also by association undermining Stevens's dignified discretion, it is slowly revealed that his former master was not a 'decent gentleman' but rather an aristocratic fascist hosting 'house-party' sessions for Nazi sympathisers. Stevens's downplaying of such politics parallels his suppression of emotional responses, whether the possibility of affection towards a fellow servant, Miss Kenton, or sorrow at his father's death, remembered self-deludingly later as tests from which he has triumphed. Tellingly, slips in his 'front', such as the recent collection of 'small errors' in his work, trigger a professional response of misdirection: Stevens will manage these by drawing up a staff plan.

The Unconsoled, and its musician-protagonist, Ryder, again plays on the wilful suppression of the past by an unreliable narrator who is also obsessively professional in his outlook.[11] In this case, Ishiguro's international-pianist narrator inhabits a longer, more experimental text, where the oneiric domain is foregrounded more often; however, themes of self-delusion, cultural amnesia and the role of the artist in society repeat some of the concerns of his earlier novels and point to future 'self-fashioning' in later work. Ryder seems poised between nihilism and egomania in the stated importance of the concert performance and lecture in the unnamed European city, reflected also in other characters' reverence: 'I would remind you that we are not gathered here now to witness a cabaret. Gravely important issues lie behind tonight's occasion . . . relating to our future, to the very identity of our community.'[12] That the concert and lecture never take place renders this expectation not only bathetic but also consistent with an increasingly absurdist displacement and misdirection of action.[13] The Kafkaesque style of the text is 'simple, lucid, and "real" in the sense of never leaving any doubt concerning the reality of that which is narrated, described, or mediated . . . [despite] shockingly unbelievable' subject matter,[14] where the everyday realities of the city become littered with elastic perceptions of time and space, with minutes becoming hours, old friends and even bedrooms appearing out of context, and a random wall being built across a street, denying access to Ryder's concert hall.

Ishiguro develops his treatment of the past and relies more heavily on genre in his twenty-first-century work. In his fifth novel, When We Were Orphans, he expands upon the untrustworthiness of the narrator, demonstrating an even more extreme dream-like register in this character's observations; but in this narrative, the interrogation of 'golden age' detective-story framing is an effective device for revealing the narrator's self-deception and nostalgia for an 'imperial' past. Like Ryder in the case of his unfulfilled concert, 'renowned' detective Christopher Banks pursues an unrealisable goal of recovering his parents and recuperating his lost childhood in the international enclave of Shanghai decades after their disappearance. Having been 'orphaned' by the disappearance firstly of his father and then of his mother, Banks has been sent to England for his education, and then establishes himself as a successful detective, at least by his own account. In Brian Finney's analysis, Ishiguro develops the metaphor of the 'orphan' as a powerful figure throughout the novel, noting the repetition of characters 'orphaned', and further acts of abandonment.[15] As Peter Childs has observed, Banks 'abandons Sarah, as he abandons the orphan he adopts, Jennifer, and as indeed he once abandoned [his childhood friend] Akira, replaying his own abandonment by both parents and his "Uncle Philip"'.[16] Finney sees this figuration present in Banks's ambivalent separation from and haunting by his lost parents, much as 'happens to most ex-colonials after they have gained independence from their colonial occupiers'.[17]

Shaped by his early experiences of playing detective with his Japanese friend and also by this psyche-shaping unsolved case, Banks engages in an extended self-fashioning exercise, at once recreating himself as an archetypal 'private consultant' detective with all the trappings of a late Victorian dilettante, and yet blind to the obviousness of his act to others (who mockingly label him 'Sherlock').[18] It is a measure of his lack of self-awareness that Banks notes 'that not a single one of my fellows noticed anything odd or thought to make fun' (WO, 7). Even with a large magnifying glass in hand, Banks's childish fantasy view imposes simple *Boys' Own* solutions that obscure the real-world events surrounding him.

For Banks, then, detection is a kind of performative act of moral drama, which moulds reality into the archetypal narrative form. Hence his recognition of 'mission' as his reputation is beginning to be made: 'I was already beginning to appreciate for the first time the scale of responsibility that befalls a detective with any sort of renown. I had always understood, of course, that the task of rooting out evil in its most devious forms, often just when it is about to go unchecked, is a crucial and solemn undertaking' (WO, 30). Detective fiction in the inter-war period is a nostalgic domain, much about restoring order, and with much vested in looking backwards to an older, more simplified imperial moral domain. His fantasy of a return to Shanghai is formulated vaguely at first – 'it's always been my intention to return to Shanghai myself. I mean, to . . . to solve the problems there' – and then is more forcefully repeated: 'The last pieces of the jigsaw have come together. Surely the time has come to go out there myself . . . and – after all these years – "slay the serpent"' (WO, 144–5). Such broad terms of expression surely confirm Barry Lewis's view that 'Banks confuses his mission to rescue his parents with single-handedly averting the impending global catastrophe'.[19]

Once he is in China, the scale of self-delusion intensifies, with Banks's childhood fantasies mirrored in what he sees as others' belief in him, while the reader sees another narrative slip in his account. The first scene he relates here offers one official busy arranging a preposterous triumphant reception ceremony for his soon-to-be-found parents, while another offers sound advice and suggestion of local support: his 'recognition' of their true roles, one a functionary and the other a spy, is later revealed as the opposite of the reality. Banks's claim, 'I left England only once I'd formed a clear view of the case. In other words, my arrival here isn't a starting point, but the culmination of many years' work', is similarly misguided (WO, 155). Paralleling the failed diplomatic mission of a character who has succumbed to alcohol and gambling, such certainty from afar is maintained in Banks's increasingly wishful interpretation of events, rather than in the events themselves. In recounting his understanding that the current Chinese owners of his childhood house would be happy to move out to accommodate him once he has found his parents (WO, 188–9), or his pleasure at finding his childhood friend, 'Akira', in the form of a wounded Japanese soldier on the battlefield, Banks demonstrates a myopic vision that is compellingly regressive. In perhaps the most deranged scene of all, Banks insists on being taken through the nightmare battleground landscape of the contested and ruined Chapei district of Shanghai to search for the house of his parents' imagined gangster abductors.

Once rescued by the Japanese, Banks begins to register that 'many things aren't as I supposed', and his host replies that 'our childhood becomes like a foreign land once we have grown' (WO, 277). At the end of the novel this sense of alienation from his past and his expectations is confirmed more fully: his 'Uncle Philip' reveals that his mother had agreed to be the concubine of a Chinese warlord in exchange for him supporting Banks through his education and early career. Compared to his father's adulterous abandonment, the warlord's honouring of a bargain offers a far more complex vision of morality than Banks has expressed earlier, and at the very end he is granted a partial consolation: locating his mother after the war, he finds that she is too mentally incapacitated to recognise him.[20] The 'closed world' of the detective tale is demonstrated as a defective escapist fantasy, which Ishiguro effectively parodies by contrast with the narrative of a confused period of history.

Ishiguro's next novel, *Never Let Me Go*, also manages to challenge genre expectations by presenting a story of human clones who are raised to provide bodily organs for transplants. This novel most specifically deals with concepts of 'alternate history', based as it is on the science fiction trope of 'alternate' or 'parallel' worlds; paradoxically, these concepts emphasise the 'normality' of the world presented.[21] If his previous novel interrogates detective fiction as a flawed mode artificially closed in its scope of reference, this book also projects a strange insularity and introversion in its narration of events in this parallel setting. Partly this is to do with the sheltered upbringing of the characters, but, considering the narrator's fascination with the past, the very telling produces an obscure, forgetful, de-historicised account. Kathy H., the first-person narrator, is one of several clones brought up in the relatively humane Hailsham, a traditional-seeming boarding school. Looking back, Kathy notes this apparent privilege: 'Kathy H. they say, she gets to pick and choose, and she always chooses her own kind: people from Hailsham, or one of the other privileged estates.'[22] Yet this is only *relative* privilege; at this point, Kathy is a 'carer' charged with looking after 'donors' – the euphemistic term for the clones' central purpose, organ harvesting that will lead to 'completion' at a very early age. Such euphemisms are common in the novel, where Kathy and her kind are repeatedly infantilised and objectified, and mundane elements (like the 'token' system for buying junk objects) are elevated as a distraction. Even when one of the teachers, Lucy Wainwright, reveals the central truth of their role as a product for human use, the trauma is buried in the narrative, which is consistently redirected to the past and the reclamation of 'innocence' rather than to the future.[23]

Hailsham itself, it is explained later, was an important experiment in the displacement and subjugation of their future:

> we were able to give you something, something which even now no one will ever take from you, and we were able to do that principally by *sheltering* you. ... Sometimes that meant we kept things from you, lied to you. Yes, in many ways we *fooled* you. ... But we sheltered you during those years, and we gave

you your childhoods. . . . You wouldn't be who you are today if we'd not protected you. (NLG, 262–3)

In part, this 'programmed' childhood shapes Kathy's adult fixations on past relationships, and also sets up a curious vacant 'present' in the text: 'who [they] are today' is less concrete than Miss Emily suggests. As Mark Currie notes, Kathy's obsessive remembering of the past manifests itself in multiple retellings and misrememberings; often her recollection is of an earlier event, and there is a sense of 'aporia' present in the difficulties of recalling the appropriate sequence of events as opposed to how her friends Tommy and Ruth remember them.[24] Kathy's fixation is a move towards historiography, trying to place events into a sequence and thus narrate a sense of causal connection, but through the constant play on revisiting the memories, and remembered forgetting, the sequence and its apparent meaning will never be fully articulated, especially as the story is strangely hopeful at the same time as fatalistic.

Characteristically for Ishiguro, the expected recognition and resistance of the clones is never fully realised, beyond seeking small extensions in the process towards 'completion': as one critic notes, 'the book is not really about cloning, but about mortality'.[25] To this end, the novel provides displaced awareness of the fate of the clones through outsiders' observations, and even more attention paid by the clones to their surrounding human culture. Some of the teachers at Hailsham are sympathetic to the clones' fate, with the art competition's potential to signal the 'humanity' of the students; however, the final collector of the art, 'Madame', reveals such projects as failed disputations of the clones' human-like 'education and culture', ignored by a 'more scientific . . . harsh, cruel world' (NLG, 267). Ultimately, the main trauma of unrequited past love with Tommy haunts Kathy more in her consideration of approaching death; and as a crucial displacement of the clones' object status, their observation of a version of recent British society reveals patterns of dehumanisation and consumption that challenge where the readers' sympathies should be directed.[26] Hence, as Margaret Atwood suggests, the book is all the more 'disquieting' in the way it manipulates expectations: 'the reader reaches the end of the book wondering exactly where the walls of his or her own invisible box begin and end.'[27]

Ishiguro's most recent novel, The Buried Giant, is a further interrogation of attitudes to the past and of problems with cultural memory. Here he returns to such weighty topics as the atrocities of war and the processes of hiding or displacing personal culpability through cultivating forgetting in the process of retelling. In this novel, though, Ishiguro chooses to play with what Tolkien terms the 'arresting strangeness' of 'fantasy',[28] dealing with Arthurian traditions and mythical features in the tale which are yet treated as concrete. In this telling, ogres, pixies and giants appear as 'real' beings to be dealt with, and the 'mist' attributed to a wholesale cultural forgetting is the product of the dragon Querig's magic breath, summoned by Merlin to obscure the memory of genocide on the part of Britons and Saxons. Instead of one unreliable narrator, this book has various first-person narrative voices, including the sinister 'I' of a lurking boatman at the end of the tale, perhaps recalling the role of Charon, the mythological Greek ferryman who conveys the dead to the underworld. If there are main characters, these are a pair of elderly Britons, Axl and Beatrice, intent on a confused quest to locate their son and reclaim their memories by seeking the source of the all-pervading mist. Yet in this quest, they are joined by an addled boy rescued from a Grendel-like abduction, and also by the Saxon warrior Wistan, himself intent on the death of the dragon and the restorative justice that will follow. The dispersal of the quest into the differing perspectives and aims of these characters complicates the resolution and symbolism of the quest's 'fulfilment'.

Nathaniel Rich has noted the departure from some of Ishiguro's common concerns: 'it is hard to shake the sense that Ishiguro is up to his old tricks: one expects the ogres to be revealed as members of a rival village, the dragon to be some kind of communal delusion, and Merlin to be a crackpot.'[29] Yet if Ishiguro's inclusion of various features of the Arthurian legend aligns the text with fantasy genre expectations, these are altered in ways that ironise and challenge the nostalgia and conservative mythopoeia often associated with this domain.[30] King Arthur's youngest knight, Gawain, is transformed into a figure marked by age and dishevelled nobility: 'the knight was no threatening figure. . . . His armour was frayed and rusted . . . his tunic, once white, showed repeated mending . . . He might have been a sorry sight . . . except the sun falling through the branches above . . . made him look almost like one enthroned.'[31] Complementing such shifts, Ishiguro continues to make play of the delusional narration and displacement familiar to readers of his earlier work, further altering expectation and perception. The 'mist' is the central conceit of the novel, affecting not just Axl and Beatrice but the majority of the other characters besides. As they approach the source of this forgetfulness, though, the two ageing Britons begin to recollect personal anxieties and doubts over their past relationship. Such doubts and emerging recognitions draw attention to the wider site of historical elision and the question of whether the general amnesia faced by the communities of Britain is partly self-imposed forgetfulness. The killing of Querig retrieves the 'real history' of the peoples and their genocidal behaviours, and also reveals the book as a reflection on modern conditions: the 'cognitive estrangement' technique of displacing a concern from today into an unfamiliar setting forces the reader to focus on the issues at hand.[32]

In an interview with Alex Clark, Ishiguro poses a number of questions relating to ways people remember their countries' history:

> What are the main mechanisms by which a country like Britain or France or Japan remembers? Is it by means of the literature, is it by means of museums, is it official history books? What is it? It's some mixture of all those things, but in the end it comes down to what ordinary people actually have in their heads about what happened in their country.[33]

Personal and cultural traumas have had a history of suppression; Ishiguro notes the historical revisionism at work in post-war Japan, Vichy France and, more recently, the former Yugoslavia.[34] Yet even in redressing and remembering such sites of horror and attempted amnesia, regret is evident. Wistan's slaying of the dragon is presented as necessary, yet there is also ambivalence towards the 'justice and vengeance' (BG, 322) he sees as initiated by this act:

> The giant, once well buried, now stirs. When soon he rises, as surely he will, the friendly bonds between us will prove as knots young girls make with the stems of small flowers. Men will burn their neighbours' houses by night. Hang children from trees at dawn. The rivers will stink with corpses bloated from their days of voyaging. (BG, 324)

In such commentary as this, Ishiguro reminds us that remembering can also be a dangerous activity, spurring the possibility of further trauma to come. For his protagonist couple, such remembering of the larger cultural rifts between peoples is also matched by pain in recalling personal betrayals and the loss of their son, and the tentative hope voiced at the end in seeking sanctuary together on an enchanted isle is undercut by the intimations that this will be a final separation.

Ishiguro's treatment of indirectly revealed personal and cultural trauma, and his fascination with the interplay between wider historical events and their negotiation in writerly accounts, seems a consistent feature throughout his novels. However, his increasing experimentation with form and forays into the oneiric, speculative and fantastic registers signals a new interest in narrating alternate history. While still manifestly 'realist' in his surface writing, this experimentation traces a new direction for 'historiographic metafiction' in the new century, yet one rooted in exposing the fallacy of 'return[ing] to some point in your childhood, or your distant past, when you suppose things went wrong, when your world went askew, . . . and undo what happened'.[35]

NOTES

1. Suzanne Keen, 'The Historical Turn in British Fiction', in James F. English (ed.), *A Concise Companion to Contemporary British Fiction* (Oxford: Blackwell, 2006), pp. 167–87; p. 171. Keen is amongst a number of critics who note the late twentieth-century rise in both the prominence of historical material in fiction and the focus on narrative elements in historiography.
2. Kenzaburo Oe and Kazuo Ishiguro, 'The Novelist in Today's World: A Conversation', *Boundary*, 2.18 (1991), 115.
3. Linda Hutcheon, *A Poetics of Postmodernism: History, Theory, Fiction* (London: Routledge, 1988), p. 89.
4. See, for example, Hayden White, 'Historical Emplotment and the Problem of Truth', in Keith Jenkins (ed.), *The Postmodern History Reader* (London: Routledge, 1997), pp. 392–6. White gives an excellent account of the possibilities and effects of different modes of narrative on the interpretation of historical 'fact' as received wisdom.
5. Frederick M. Holmes, 'Realism, Dreams and the Unconscious in the Novels of Kazuo Ishiguro', in James Acheson and Sarah C. E. Ross (eds), *The Contemporary British Novel* (Edinburgh: Edinburgh University Press, 2005), pp. 11–22; p. 12; see also Ishiguro's own description, quoted in Linda Richards, 'January Interview: Kazuo Ishiguro', *January Magazine*, January 2000, <http:///www.januarymagazine.com/profiles/ishiguro.html> (last accessed 16 June 2016).

6. Richard Bradford, *The Novel Now: Contemporary British Fiction* (Malden, MA: Blackwell Publishing, 2007), p. 214.
7. Brian Finney, *English Fiction Since 1984: Narrating a Nation* (Basingstoke and New York: Palgrave Macmillan, 2006), p. 139.
8. Salman Rushdie, 'What the Butler Didn't See', *The Observer*, 21 May 1989, p. 53.
9. Ihab Hassan, 'An Extravagant Reticence', *The World and I*, 5.2 (February 1990), 374; see also Kazuo Ishiguro, 'Ishiguro in Toronto', Interview with Suanne Kelman, in Linda Spalding and Michael Ondaatje (eds), *The Brick Reader* (Toronto: Coach House, 1991), pp. 71–7; p. 73. This novel clearly sets up the kind of genre iconoclasm to come in Ishiguro's more recent work.
10. Kazuo Ishiguro, *The Remains of the Day* (1989; London: Faber & Faber, 1999), pp. 43–4.
11. See Richard Rorty, 'Consolation Prize', *Village Voice Literary Supplement*, October 1995, p. 13; Bradford, *The Novel Now*, p. 215.
12. Kazuo Ishiguro, *The Unconsoled* (1995; London: Faber & Faber, 2005), p. 482.
13. Variations on the significance of music are prominent in Ishiguro's later collection of stories, *Nocturnes: Five Stories of Music and Nightfall* (London: Faber & Faber, 2009).
14. Brian W. Shaffer, *Understanding Kazuo Ishiguro* (Columbia: University of South Carolina Press, 1998), p. 97, quoting Erich Heller on Kafka's style.
15. Finney, *English Fiction Since 1984*, p. 144.
16. Peter Childs, *Contemporary Novelists: British Fiction Since 1970* (Basingstoke: Palgrave Macmillan, 2005), p. 126.
17. Finney, *English Fiction Since 1984*, p. 144.
18. Kazuo Ishiguro, *When We Were Orphans* (2000; London: Faber & Faber, 2001), pp. 10, 15, 3, 8–10. All quotations are from this edition; hereafter, page numbers will be given in the text, preceded by *WO*.
19. Barry Lewis, *Kazuo Ishiguro* (Manchester: Manchester University Press, 2000), pp. 148–9.
20. See Finney, *English Fiction Since 1984*, p. 154; Holmes, 'Realism, Dreams and the Unconscious', p. 19.
21. See Brian Stableford, 'Alternate Worlds', in John Clute and Peter Nicholls (eds), *The Encyclopaedia of Science Fiction* (London: Orbit, 1999), pp. 23–5, for discussion of the history of this genre.
22. Kazuo Ishiguro, *Never Let Me Go* (2005; London: Faber & Faber, 2006), pp. 3–4. All quotations are from this edition; hereafter, page numbers will be given in the text, preceded by *NLG*.
23. See Finney, *English Fiction Since 1984*, p. 139.
24. Mark Currie, 'Controlling Time: Kazuo Ishiguro's *Never Let Me Go*', in Sean Matthews and Sebastian Groes (eds), *Kazuo Ishiguro* (London: Continuum, 2010), pp. 92–103; pp. 94–5.
25. Alex Clark, 'Kazuo Ishiguro's Turn to Fantasy', *The Guardian*, 19 February 2015, <http://www.theguardian.com/books/2015/feb/19/kazuo-ishiguro-the-buried-giant-novel-interview> (last accessed 16 June 2016).
26. Bradford, *The Novel Now*, p. 217.
27. Margaret Atwood, *In Other Worlds: SF and the Human Imagination* (London: Virago, 2011), p. 168.
28. J. R. R. Tolkien, 'On Fairy-Stories', in *The Monsters and the Critics, and Other Essays*, ed. Christopher Tolkien (London: George Allen & Unwin, 1983), pp. 109–61; p. 139.
29. Nathaniel Rich, 'The Book of Sorrow and Forgetting', *The Atlantic*, March 2015, <http://www.theatlantic.com/magazine/archive/2015/03/the-book-of-sorrow-and-forgetting/384968> (last accessed 16 June 2016).
30. Even so, Ishiguro has had to defend his use of 'fantasy genre' elements against the criticism of exemplary critic and fantasy writer Ursula K. Le Guin; Ishiguro counters suggestions that he is being elitist: 'I am on the side of the pixies and giants.' See Sian Cain, 'Writer's

Indignation: Kazuo Ishiguro Rejects Claims of Genre Snobbery', *The Guardian*, 8 March 2015, <http://www.theguardian.com/books/2015/mar/08/kazuo-ishiguro-rebuffs-genre-snobbery> (last accessed 16 June 2016).
31. Kazuo Ishiguro, *The Buried Giant* (London: Faber & Faber, 2015), pp. 113–14. All quotations are from this edition; hereafter, page numbers will be given in the text, preceded by *BG*.
32. See Darko Suvin, *Positions and Suppositions in Science Fiction* (London: Macmillan, 1988). Suvin argues that speculative fictions function through transplanting a familiar idea into a strange context, an alternative to the writer's own setting, to enable special attention to and recognition of the idea.
33. Ishiguro, quoted in Clark, 'Kazuo Ishiguro's Turn to Fantasy'.
34. Ibid.
35. Ishiguro, quoted in Finney, *English Fiction Since 1984*, p. 148.

FURTHER READING

Booker, M. Keith, 'The Other Side of History: Fantasy, Romance, Horror, and Science Fiction', in Robert L. Caserio (ed.), *The Cambridge Companion to the Twentieth-Century English Novel* (Cambridge and New York: Cambridge University Press, 2009).

Huggan, Graham, *The Postcolonial Exotic: Marketing the Margins* (London and New York: Routledge, 2001).

Hutcheon, Linda, *A Poetics of Postmodernism: History, Theory, Fiction* (London: Routledge, 1988).

Matthews, Sean, and Sebastian Groes (eds), *Kazuo Ishiguro* (London: Continuum, 2010).

Shaffer, Brian W., *Understanding Kazuo Ishiguro* (Columbia: University of South Carolina Press, 1998).

CHAPTER 11

Kate Atkinson: Plotting to Be Read

Glenda Norquay

In a review of Kate Atkinson's 2015 novel *A God in Ruins*, Lesley McDowell asks whether her 'warm and approachable characters [and] her smart ... funny ... compassionate prose count against her when it comes to intellectual literary awards like the Booker? Even the new literary prize, the Folio, ignored the more experimental *Life After Life*.'[1] While literary innovation need not be assessed by prize-winning recognition, accessibility is a key aspect of Kate Atkinson's fiction. Working in genres that might be defined as popular (or at least familiar to a wide readership) – detective fiction, family saga, English country house fiction, historical fiction – she writes novels that deeply engage the reader in emotions, plots and characters, so as to make for a pleasurable, joyful, moving, affirmative and affective reading experience. From her early fiction onwards Atkinson has demonstrated a 'postmodern' interest in the ontological, in 'world-making and modes of being'.[2] In her first novels that was expressed in explicitly experimental strategies. In her later writing she inhabits narrative convention more comfortably while simultaneously interrogating it in more fundamental ways. In its underlying challenges to normative understanding of being in the world, her fiction has grown in daring and profundity.

Through charting shifts in her deployment of different fictional forms, this chapter suggests that Atkinson's emphasis on plotting, which emerges in the combination of familiar and defamiliarising constructions of 'events' and 'characters', is part of a strategic attempt to produce novels that can be pleasurable and meaningful yet disruptive in their challenges to our thinking about time, history, justice and love. Atkinson's trajectory of experimentation and her unique pattern of generic shifts, from the 'Case Histories' series to the recent *Life After Life* (2013) and *A God in Ruins*,[3] reveal that although her novels have been described as combining an interest in 'history, family and identity within a postmodern aesthetic', the increasing sophistication of that dynamic has made them both more complex and more commercially successful.[4]

Kate Atkinson's first novel, *Behind the Scenes at the Museum* (1995), was an immediate success, an acclaimed first novel easily situated within a 1990s interest in both metafiction and the historical.[5] It also offered an analysis of the determinants – family, location, culture and imagination – of the individual life that is touching, comic and more traditionally associated with the concerns of realist fiction. Since then she has maintained an interest in the shaping forces of historical moments and individual lives, as in *Human Croquet* (1997) and *Emotionally Weird* (2000), but has developed increasingly innovative but compelling fictional forms through which to explore these concerns.[6] Written at the turn of the twenty-first century, *Emotionally Weird* articulates a tension central to Atkinson's fiction and indicates the emergence of changing interests with the new millennium and its re-evaluation of historical formations. Through the device of a university literature tutorial, she rehearses a familiar opposition between post-structuralist thinking (Archie McCue's pontifications on 'the autonomous work of fiction') and traditional humanist perspectives (Professor Cousin's suggestion that 'all literature is about the search for *identity*, [and] the *meaning* of life') before producing a novel that conforms to neither literary agenda.[7] Her later novels – postmodern and realist, interrogating and mocking grand narratives while clinging to notions of truth and value associated with a more conventional humanism – work to accommodate but move beyond these apparently conflicting notions of fiction.

Atkinson's highly successful and innovative explorations of these tensions can be traced though 'Case Histories', a group of novels which, by playing with 'mystery' and telling their stories in interweaving, overlapping narratives, ironise understanding of a shared human condition but nevertheless endorse the value of an individual life. Deploying comedy and tragedy with equal effect, Atkinson finds in crime fiction a genre that allows her to engage with agency and chance, justice and retribution, and to explore tensions between social institutions and the individual imagination. The serial nature of these novels featuring Jackson Brodie – *Case Histories* (2004), *One Good Turn* (2006), *When Will There Be Good News?* (2008) and *Started Early, Took My Dog* (2010) – reinforces the ironic engagement with genre fiction suggested by the 2006 novel's subtitle, 'A Jolly Murder Mystery', and provides extended opportunity to examine the plotting of the self in wider narratives.[8]

Atkinson's more recent twenty-first-century novels, *Life After Life* and *A God in Ruins*, abandon the playful dynamic with popular forms and return to her earlier concerns with the life in history. With her focus on both the First and Second World Wars, and in that respect on the 'historical', Atkinson produces impressive research into under-narrated aspects of that period, while openly acknowledging her inheritance from E. M. Forster and Virginia Woolf. In that sense, as with 'Case Histories' and its interaction with detective fiction, the novels work to defamiliarise a recognised literary mode, producing a deeply unsettling experience for their readers through experiments with chronology. With their combination of innovation and familiarity the novels address complex questions about the nature of history, the value of human relationships and the response of the self to the darkest of moments. In each tour de force of experimental writing Atkinson retains that compelling and characteristic engagement with each individual life but uses the plotting of the self to explore the subject within larger historical narratives.

Atkinson's first crime novel *Case Histories*, whose title then became the overarching name for a television series bringing together all the 'Jackson Brodie' novels, is fundamentally interested in and structured by the relationship between apparently random forces and the making of narrative patterns through the tragedies and triumphs of individual lives.[9] Although she dislikes the label 'crime fiction', its central character, Jackson Brodie, acts in pursuit of a number of mysteries, or 'case histories'.[10] In *One Good Turn*, *When Will There Be Good News?* and *Started Early, Took My Dog*, Brodie acts as a catalyst for each novel's adventures, becomes unwittingly implicated in them and attempts to 'solve' their mysteries. A dominant question that emerges from the novels is: can there be such a thing as an 'innocent bystander'? Levels of public engagement with crime are mocked in *One Good Turn* when all witnesses questioned after a road rage incident can describe the dog involved but not the car registration number. In *Started Early, Took My Dog*, Jackson, frequently positioned as observer, is enmeshed in a plot hinging upon the complicity of inaction as much as action. 'Is anyone really a bystander?' he asks, suggesting 'you could say that we are all bystanders' (*SE*, 238). As Atkinson explores the complexities of retribution and justice, the relationship between victimhood and communal human responsibility, 'Case Histories' introduces characters who are victims, perpetrators, detectives, figures of retribution and apparently innocent bystanders, increasingly blurring the lines between these demarcations. While navigating the relationship between narratives of personal tragedy and the public spheres of criminal investigation and legal justice, Atkinson also poses larger questions about agency and determinism.

In the context of contemporary Scottish writing, crime fiction has a well-established reputation for addressing social and political issues.[11] Atkinson herself notes the pleasure of 'taking stock elements and then playing around with them'. More interestingly, she adds: 'Mainstream crime is very end-driven: there's a plot that goes directly from A to B, and all the detective is doing is going about picking up clues. That's important, but it's not what these books are about. The interesting thing to me is character.'[12] One way in which Atkinson works to subvert the dominant modes of crime fiction is indeed by the detailing of character: this is achieved less through narrative exposition but with the iteration of details which add specificity so that each individual life, each victim, is delineated. The first and most striking example of this is in *Case Histories*, where Theo Wyre returns again and again to what made his murdered daughter, Laura, herself: 'Laura, who slept curled up in a ball, who liked hot buttered toast and all the Indiana Jones movies but not *Star Wars*, whose first word was 'dog', who liked the wind but not the rain, who planned to have three children, Laura who would forever be standing by the photocopier in the office in Parkside waiting for the stranger and his knife' (*CH*, 54). Atkinson thus exploits realism, the appeal of knowable character, to make the reader feel loss. This recovery of a self is articulated as an impulse of literary realism but also that of an ethics of 'detection'.

Detection is thus given a moral imperative. 'Inside Jackson', we are told, 'there remained a belief – a small, battered and buried belief – that his job was to help people to be good rather than punish them for being bad' (CH, 81). This drive, counter to the punishment thrust of conventional crime fiction, illuminates the structuring principle of Atkinson's texts: an emphasis on the individual and the fragile possibility of creating a positive narrative. Atkinson's 'case histories' work in contradictory directions. On the one hand they suggest that violence is random, that chance makes people victims, damaged or lost; and on the other, that the patterns that emerge from violence suggest the possibility of 'balance' rather than justice. Jackson mentally tallies his lost and found accounts – dead daughter, missing sister, murdered sister, lost daughter – but by the end of the first novel a daughter has been replaced and a sister in some ways 'compensated' for the loss of another. This is not the justice of the symbolic order: when Jackson finds out the name of Laura's killer he puts it on a card to Theo rather than tell the police; he does not tell both sisters what happened to Olivia and Sylvia's role; he never finds out whether Nicola Spencer is having an affair. But although the narratives appear to depend upon chance, there is tangential acknowledgement of underlying explanations: Laura's deployment of her father's name actually leads to the stalker looking for her father, then murdering her; Victor's abuse of Sylvia means she descends into madness, hears voices and murders her sister, his daughter, so that he has to conceal the body, a punishment both for him and for Sylvia in terms of loss and complicity. Cause and effect may be unexpected and continually ironised but also impossible to ignore. Jackson's own position, meanwhile, also rests upon contradiction: he 'liked to think truth was an absolute but maybe that just made him into a tight-arsed moral fascist' (CH, 318).

Atkinson's subsequent novels in this series more confidently parody the crime genre. In *One Good Turn*, Martin, the mild-mannered surprise hero of the opening scenes, is himself a crime writer, producing novels that he thought were pastiches of the 'old-fashioned soft-boiled' genre of the 1940s but in fact have been successfully marketed as 'jolly murder mysteries' and turned into a television series: 'Perfect fodder for the Sunday evening slot, the BBC producer said, making it sound like an insult, which of course it was' (OGT, 26). Equally heroic housewife Gloria in the same novel 'had no enthusiasm for crime writing. It had sucked the life out of her father, and anyway wasn't there enough crime in the world without adding to it, even if it was fictional?' (OGT, 37). In *Started Early, Took My Dog*, a minor character, Marilyn Nettles, is a writer of 'true noir' fiction: '"Women in Jeopardy," she commented, handing Jackson a mug of coffee. "Very popular. You have to wonder"' (SE, 250).

As this comment suggests, the intersections of women's lives and criminality become an increasing focus of attention in the series. Without asserting an explicitly feminist agenda, each novel's plot revolves around missing or lost women and the challenges faced by women who are not lost. *One Good Turn* and *When Will There Be Good News?* continue the unfulfilled relationship, dogged by bad timing, between police detective Louise Murdoch, locked into the system, and the outsider, Jackson Brodie. While differing in their missions, both are shown to operate in the same arena defined by the victimhood or not of women. Jackson, we are told, 'cared about missing girls, he wanted them all found. Louise didn't want them to get lost in the first place' (*WWT*, 170). *When Will There Be Good News?* examines the possibilities but also the dangers of women enacting justice for themselves. By contextualising its plot through the 1970s and Ripper murders, *Started Early, Took My Dog* situates Jackson's search 'for all the lost girls' within a more specifically historicised understanding of women in jeopardy: 'The past was a dark place, a man's world' (*SE*, 329). As the power to enact justice increasingly comes from outside the law, Jackson becomes feminised by both his apparent powerlessness and his need to redress justice through private means: '"The older you get, the more like a woman you become," Julia said' (*SE*, 50).

Atkinson's self-conscious relationship to crime writing, part of her broader gesture towards postmodernism, means that her attention to individual character is balanced by a knowingness about self-fashioning. In *One Good Turn* the sinister 'Ray', who has invented his name because he likes its ambiguous possibilities and because he likes slipping between identities, is positioned against Martin, who has little control in formulating his own identity, leaving that to his father, and to his publisher whose insistence that he was a monk then becomes the fulcrum of interviews even as he denies it (*OGT*, 22). But rather than an easy questioning of the 'fictions' of identity, Atkinson's novels use the plotting of selves and the careful chronologies of crime writing to raise much larger questions around agency, historical determinism, the nature of victimhood and survival. The 'Case Histories' series, as its first title suggests, attempts to make sense of different moments in time and the connections between them, an interest extended by Atkinson's subsequent novels.

In *Case Histories* this interest in temporality is evident through highly specific dates, increasingly given meaning in relation to each other. *One Good Turn* is organised around days, while in *When Will There Be Good News?* the different sections of the novel are 'In the Past', 'Today', 'Tomorrow' and 'And Tomorrow'. *Started Early, Took My Dog* is structured in more abstract terms – 'Treasure', 'Sacrifice', 'Jeopardy' – but again moves backwards and forwards in time, returning to the Yorkshire Ripper murders of the 1970s. In *Case Histories* a character reflects: 'That was how history worked, wasn't it? If it wasn't written down it never existed. You might leave behind jewellery and pottery, ornamental tombs, you might leave behind your own bones to be dug up in a later age, but none of those artefacts could explain how you *felt*' (*CH*, 96). All these novels explore how 'feeling' might be understood within time, what makes for a 'valuable' life, and what are the forces that might determine the feelings of an individual. This interest in chronology and temporality becomes increasingly complicated in Atkinson's later fiction. *A God in Ruins* has Teddy asking Bertie to 'promise to make the most of your life' but Bertie 'already at twenty-four knowing it was unlikely she would be able to do so' (*AGR*, 112). In *Life After Life* Ursula states: 'I believe we have just one life and I believe that Teddy lived his perfectly' (*LAL*, 376).

The 'Case Histories' series also shares with the later novels a fascination with the ways in which narratives of 'perfection' shape desires and feelings and are expressed in fantasies of both time and place. These novels anticipate Atkinson's later interest in versions of Englishness, possessing a dominant power in the literary imagination, set in stark contrast to the Scottish or northern English landscapes which construct their settings. When Martin in *One Good Turn* worries why everyone doesn't live in the world of the imagination because it is so much better than the real one, he defines the constituents of that world as: 'Scones, home-made blackcurrant jam, clotted cream. Overhead, swallows sliced through the blue, blue sky, swooping and diving like Battle of Britain pilots. The distant *thock* of leather on willows. The scent of hot, strong tea and new mown grass' (*OGT*, 21). In her most recent novels Atkinson lovingly recreates this world, symbolic of a desired social order, then brings it, if not to ruins, at least into question by positioning it within darker and more historically inflected contexts.

While this shift towards Englishness appears to make her novels more mainstream, that lost world is presented as increasingly impossible. And their greatest challenge is to conventional temporality: by engaging with a past prior to the war 'when people still believed in the dependable nature of time' (*AGR*, 73), Atkinson develops both structural and thematic challenges to our notions of time and history. In *Life After Life* she offers us plenty of signposting as to the nature of her experiment: the novel opens with an epigraph voiced by one of its characters – 'What if we had a chance to do it again and again until we finally got it right?' – which becomes the central question in the book. Beginning in 1910 and ending, arguably, in 1967, the novel works and reworks the life possibilities of Ursula Beresford Fox, recreating a range of life stories that are shaped by chance, by larger historical forces, and increasingly, as she experiences a kind of déjà vu, by Ursula herself. Characters constantly pronounce on the nature of time: Sylvie, Ursula's mother, says 'we all end up in the same place', while her daughter insists that 'it's how you got there that matters' (*LAL*, 240). 'Hindsight is a wonderful thing,' adds her friend Klara. 'If we all had it there would be no history to write about' (*LAL*, 327). Ursula tells her therapist that time 'isn't circular . . . it's a palimpsest' (*LAL*, 456); when a co-worker misquotes John Donne's Holy Sonnet 13, 'What if this were the world's last night?', Ursula corrects him: 'What if this present were the world's last night?', reflecting, '"The word 'present' makes all the difference, don't you think? It makes it seem as if one's somehow in the thick of it, which we are, rather than simply contemplating a theoretical concept"' (*LAL*, 375). Key to the whole text, the question of what it means to be 'in the thick of it' has two aspects. Can one change history? And can one change the understanding of history?

Characterising its response to both questions – how is agency to be achieved and what might historical agency actually mean in the context of a new millennium – is the novel's attentiveness to gender and the 'historicised' acquisition by women of the power to change events, embodied by developments in the period the novel covers. In the section entitled 'A Lovely Day Tomorrow', the sixteen-year-old Ursula has to live through various iterations of sexual assault by a visiting American, each time responding with a more vigorous rejection and each time shaping her subsequent life as one of lesser misery, oppression and passivity. A personal history can therefore be 'remastered'. In an early version of Ursula's life the clumsy rape attempt leads to an unwanted pregnancy, disastrous marriage and drink. Only in later versions can she slap down the aggressor, escape and shape her life differently.

Political history is less easy to determine than a personal narrative but Ursula nevertheless has a go. The novel's most obvious 'what if' – and one Atkinson herself admits inspired the novel – is what if someone shot Hitler? When one of Ursula's incarnations leads her to this point, it is a particularly gendered moment, a collision of the public and domestic. Ursula insinuates herself into Hitler's inner circle through friendship with Eva Braun, meets these powerful men in the feminised atmosphere of a German café, where they are indulging in hot chocolate and luscious cakes, produces a gun out of her handbag, having just dabbed at her lips with a lacy handkerchief, and points it at the Führer.

This is the most striking example of the way in which a 'womanly sphere' can be brought to change history, but in addition to this dramatic plot device the novel frequently articulates a Woolfian awareness of the gendering of perspective and the 'difference of value'.[13] When Ursula's father signs up at the outbreak of the First World War because 'it may be the only adventure I ever have', her mother shouts at him, 'Adventure? . . . what about your children? What about your *wife*?' (*LAL*, 60). The novel continues to interrogate such rhetoric, with the notion of life as an 'adventure' being set against Sylvie's idea of life as an endurance race or an obstacle course (*LAL*, 180). Through its narrative structure, the nature of its events and in its explicit observations on time, *Life After Life* echoes Woolf's oft-quoted statement in 'Modern Fiction' that life is more than just 'a series of gig lamps symmetrically arranged'.[14] The past may be 'a straight line' for Pamela but it is 'a jumble in her mind' for Ursula (*LAL*, 79): 'Her memories seemed like a cascade of echoes. Could echoes cascade?' (*LAL*, 156). The novel not only presents a challenge to gendered versions of history but begins to interrogate progressional versions of temporality.

Life After Life and *A God in Ruins* could be read as melding the various responses of women to history identified by Julia Kristeva in her essay 'Women's Time': the early attempts of the women's movement to gain a place in linear time, a second phase in which 'linear temporality has been almost totally refused, and as a consequence there has arisen an exacerbated distrust of the entire political dimension', and then the third phase mixing the two attitudes: 'insertion into history and the radical refusal of the subjective limitations imposed by this history's time on an experiment carried out in the name of irreducible difference' so that 'the very dichotomy man/woman as an opposition between two rival entities may be understood as belonging to metaphysics'.[15] Yet ironically, given the family-focused nature of her fiction, Atkinson goes further, challenging what Judith Halberstam describes as 'the force of middle-class logic of reproductive temporality'. Halberstam argues, 'in Western cultures, we chart the emergence of the adult from the dangerous and unruly period of adolescence as a desired period of maturation; and we create longevity as the most desirable future . . . and pathologize modes of living that show little or no concern for longevity.'[16] In their refusal to adhere to that model of temporality, in their playing with 'then and now' and with the dissolving of those separations, Atkinson's most recent novels partake in what Carolyn Dinshaw has described as the 'difficult work of thinking outside narrative history, reworking linear temporality'.[17]

The novels achieve this in various ways. They do it first, and most obviously, in the very structure of their fictions. In its emphasis on a reiterated now-ness, *Life After Life* could be read as a manifestation of Walter Benjamin's advocacy of 'history' as 'time filled by the presence of the now'.[18] Atkinson's most recent novel, *A God in Ruins*, appears to move back and forwards in time but comes to rest in a moment of present that dissolves and, to an extent, denies everything that has gone before. Secondly, her fiction provides an explicit critique of 'history as linear narrative', in the many comments about time as chaos and jumble. *Life After Life* further challenges assumptions about history in terms of a political imagination. When Ursula realises that 'most people muddled through events and only in retrospect realised their significance. The Führer was different, he was consciously *making* history for the future. Only a true narcissist could do that' (*LAL*, 324), she is offering a critique, in psychological terms, of the notion that 'politics is a name for the temporalisation of desire, for its translation into a narrative, for its teleological determination'. Hitler might be read as embodying an extreme version of what Lee Edelman has described as 'the coercive belief in the paramount value of futurity'.[19]

If these novels critique normative temporality, they also begin to offer alternatives. Atkinson does this by focusing on death, structuring her narratives in terms of the formal repetition distinctive of the death drive. This is achieved in *Life After Life* by presenting many different narratives for Ursula Beresford's life, a constant movement towards her survival, towards self-realisation, but with most of them ending in annihilation – with the words 'Darkness fell' – before beginning again. *A God in Ruins* is death-centred in a more public way, focusing as it does on the lives of Halifax bomber crews during the Second World War. As the novel progresses, the repeated accounts of bombing raids over Germany, indicating the similar yet different dangers of each raid, become representative of a 'life after life', which each time is nearer to a death. The death at the centre of these accounts both creates and annihilates the whole narrative the novel contains: Teddy's life. It also creates that stasis in the present – Teddy's death in the air – which then becomes the model of a life 'lived perfectly' (*AGR*, 376).

Because of their apparent realism, the focus on relationships and individuals, and their interest in the tiniest details of the everyday, Atkinson's novels could be read as constructing what Lauren Berlant describes as an 'intimate public sphere' and has condemned because of the ways in which 'questions of intimacy, sexuality, reproduction and the family', while properly interrelated with questions of identity and inequality, become 'over-organising' in terms of public discussions about power, ethics and the nation.[20] Yet, arguably, what the novels and their predecessors in the 'Case Histories' series achieve is to take our engagement with these intimate spheres, our willingness to feel through character and plot, and force us as readers to develop new modes of organising our understanding. As a result Atkinson offers her readers pleasure but never complacency.

In some respects Atkinson's fiction might appear to have become less obviously 'postmodern', satisfying her readers with the kind of textual engagement familiar from a realist novel, yet they retain that impulse to 'trouble and volatise' identified with postmodernism.[21] If 'plotting' remains a consistent concern, the dimensions in which it is understood have shifted to encompass larger questions about how the self might be understood in terms of past, present and future. While the 'Case Histories' series addresses hard questions about the plotting of individual and social justice and the tensions between them, *Life After Life* and *A God in Ruins* struggle with the more general possibilities of plotting in a world without 'the tenses that Western civilisation was constructed on' (AGR, 73).

NOTES

1. Lesley McDowell, 'Book of the Week: *A God in Ruins* by Kate Atkinson', <http://www.thenational.scot/culture/book-of-the-week-a-god-in-ruins-by-kate-atkinson-doubleday-20.3077> (last accessed 17 June 2016).
2. See Brian McHale, *The Cambridge Introduction to Postmodernism* (Cambridge: Cambridge University Press, 2015), p. 15.
3. All quotations are from Kate Atkinson, *Life After Life* (London: Doubleday, 2013) and *A God in Ruins* (London: Doubleday, 2015). Hereafter, page numbers will be given in the text, preceded by LAL and AGR respectively.
4. Fiona Tolan, '"Everyone Has Left Something Here": The Storyteller-Historian in Kate Atkinson's *Behind the Scenes at the Museum*', *Critique: Studies in Contemporary Fiction*, 50 (2009), 275–92; 276.
5. Kate Atkinson, *Behind the Scenes at the Museum* (London: Doubleday, 1995).
6. Kate Atkinson, *Human Croquet* (London: Doubleday, 1997); *Emotionally Weird: A Comic Novel* (London: Doubleday, 2000).
7. Atkinson, *Emotionally Weird*, pp. 38–9.
8. Kate Atkinson, *Case Histories* (London: Doubleday, 2004), *One Good Turn: A Jolly Murder Mystery* (London: Doubleday, 2006), *When Will There Be Good News?* (London: Doubleday, 2008), *Started Early, Took My Dog* (London: Doubleday, 2010). All quotations are from these editions; hereafter, page numbers will be given in the text, preceded by CH, OGT, WWT and SE respectively.
9. The first three novels were adapted for series one of the BBC television drama *Case Histories*. *Started Early, Took My Dog* formed the basis of episode one of a second series; two new stories were written for two further episodes. See 'On Screen', <http://www.kateatkinson.co.uk/on_screen.php> (last accessed 17 June 2016).
10. See 'Interview: Kate Atkinson, Author', *The Scotsman*, 13 August 2010, <http://www.scotsman.com/news/interview-kate-atkinson-author-1-821075> (last accessed 17 June 2016).
11. William McIlvanney and Ian Rankin were trailblazers; Louise Welsh and Denise Mina continue to explore the form's potential.
12. 'Interview: Kate Atkinson, Author'.
13. Virginia Woolf, *A Room of One's Own*: 'But it is obvious that the values of women differ very often from the values which have been made by the other sex' (1929; London: Grafton, 1977), p. 70.
14. Virginia Woolf, 'Modern Fiction', in *The Common Reader* (1925; London: Hogarth Press, 1951), pp. 184–95.
15. Julie Kristeva, 'Women's Time', trans. Alice Jardine and Harry Blake, *Signs: Journal of Women in Culture and Society*, 7 (1981), 13–35; 19, 20, 34.
16. Judith Halberstam, *In a Queer Time and Place: Transgender Bodies, Subcultural Lives (Sexual Cultures)* (New York: New York University Press, 2004), p. 4.
17. Carolyn Dinshaw et al., 'Theorising Queer Temporalities: A Roundtable Discussion', *GLQ: A Journal of Lesbian and Gay Studies*, 13 (2007), 177–95; 185.
18. Walter Benjamin, 'Theses on the Philosophy of History', in *Illuminations*, ed. Hannah Arendt, trans. Harry Zorn (London: Pimlico, 1999), p. 252.

19. Lee Edelman, *No Future: Queer Theory and the Death Drive* (Durham, NC: Duke University Press, 2004), p. 6.
20. Lauren Berlant, *The Queen of America Goes to Washington* (Durham, NC, and London: Duke University Press, 1997), p. 8.
21. McHale, *The Cambridge Introduction to Postmodernism*, p. 15.

FURTHER READING

For an up-to-date list of Kate Atkinson's novels, see the British Council website: <https://literature.britishcouncil.org/writer/kate-atkinson> (last accessed 17 June 2016).

Berlant, Lauren, *The Queen of America Goes to Washington* (Durham, NC, and London: Duke University Press, 1997).

Halberstam, Judith, *In a Queer Time and Place: Transgender Bodies, Subcultural Lives (Sexual Cultures)* (New York: New York University Press, 2004).

Norquay, Glenda, 'Genre Fiction', in Norquay (ed.), *The Edinburgh Companion to Scottish Women's Writing* (Edinburgh: Edinburgh University Press, 2012), pp. 130–9.

Tew, Philip, and Fiona Tolan (eds), *Writers Talk: Conversations with Contemporary British Novelists* (London: Continuum, 2008).

CHAPTER 12

Salman Rushdie: Archival Modernism

Vijay Mishra

Although Rushdie makes reference to Sanskrit and Old Hindi texts in his fiction, his archival modernism draws primarily on medieval Islamic and European archives. I use the term 'archival modernism' to mean the manner in which earlier modernities, earlier and including pre-European Enlightenment modernities, inform the works of a late modernist writer. Instead of looking at modernity as a purely post-Kantian and, more generally, a European legacy with literary modernism as its direct outcome, in this chapter I make creative use of what Susan Stanford Friedman has called 'planetary modernisms'.[1] Setting aside Friedman's category error in conflating modernism and modernity, what is of value is her claim that modernist writers have self-consciously turned to the past, indeed to the entire cross-cultural global enterprise of modernism, to energise their works. In novels earlier than the ones discussed in this chapter, Salman Rushdie had used Farid Ud-din Attar's Persian-Sufi poem *The Conference of the Birds* (c. 1187) in *Grimus* (1975); subversive medieval commentaries on the Qur'an in *The Satanic Verses* (1988); *The Arabian Nights* and early Indian tales (notably the *Kathāsaritasāgara*, composed in the second half of the eleventh century) in *Haroun and the Sea of Stories* (1990); and the history of Moorish Spain in *The Moor's Last Sigh* (1995). Embedded in more recent novels, *The Ground Beneath Her Feet* (1999) and *Fury* (2001), are classical myths, those of Orpheus and the Furies respectively. In *Shalimar the Clown* (2005) medieval pastoral serenity is destroyed by jihadist as well as state terror, while in *The Enchantress of Florence* (2008) Rushdie turns to Mughal India as a Renaissance site equal to Florence, and in *Luka and the Fire of Life* (2010) to the traditions of Oriental storytelling. His latest work, *Two Years Eight Months and Twenty-Eight Nights* (2015), projects a crisis in modernity (Western secularism versus Islamic fundamentalism) on to the battle between two medieval Islamic thinkers, known in the West as Avicenna and Averroës.

In this admittedly schematic account of archival modernism in Rushdie's later novels, I begin with *The Ground Beneath Her Feet*, where Rushdie's turn to archival modernism is informed by a reading of the Orpheus myth as one composite text in a number of versions. The versions may be read as five phases of the myth: the classical (Virgil, Ovid), the medieval (the Middle English *Sir Orfeo*, Henryson's *Orpheus and Eurydice*, and Chaucer's translation of Boethius's *The Consolation of Philosophy*),[2] the revisionist (Gluck's *Orfeo ed Euridice*), the pre-modernist (Rilke's poem 'Orpheus. Eurydike. Hermes'), and the late modern (Cocteau's *Le Testament d'Orphée*, 1950, and the carnivalesque *Orfeu Negro*, 1960). The opening chapter of *The Ground Beneath Her Feet*, entitled 'The Keeper of Bees', with its anthemic song 'All my life, I worshipped her' reprised towards the end of the novel, gives the secret of the Orpheus intertext away at the outset.[3] The archive is classical, in fact clearly Virgil's *The Georgics*, but no Virgil is ever unmediated, which is Salman Rushdie's point throughout this new imposed allegory of reading, this new medieval *moralitas* as modernist novel. A disoriented Vina Apsara, the once great but now waning popular singer, is saved by the photographer Umeed Merchant (Rai), her occasional lover and the novel's narrator. His is an unrequited love, although in an echo of Princess Diana's death, he 'would have crashed into a concrete wall for her if it had been her desire to die' (GB, 4). He flies with Vina to Tequila, where Don Ángel Cruz, a plantation owner, and himself a good countertenor, has invited Vina to a banquet. En route we are told that earthquakes are becoming common in that part of the world due to French nuclear explosions in the Pacific, one of the many anachronistic references (the explosions took place in the 1960s) that are littered throughout the novel. At the banquet Don Ángel Cruz sings in a voice which with its 'sidereal sweetness' is (after John Donne) 'like the music of the spheres' a chorus, 'Trionfi Amore' (Temple of Love), from Gluck's *Orfeo ed Euridice* (1762), with the libretto by Ranieri de' Calzabigi. Vina Apsara herself joins in and sings the soprano parts, celebrating as she does so the power of beauty and the tormented heart as the emblem of happiness. As she finishes, there is an earthquake, the symbolical crevice to the underworld, the ground beneath our feet, the 'unsolidity of solid ground . . . the gaps in the earth through which our history seeps' (GB, 54), which in the time of Voltaire (a favourite source for Rushdie) was seen as spaces filled with sulphur with 'its stench of Hell' (GB, 465). The returning helicopter manages to take Vina away but Umeed never sees her again. Rai (Umeed) is left behind; as Aristaeus, the Keeper of the Bees, he will narrate the retrospective tale, a modernist fable of a pop singer through whom an allegory of the greatest decades of popular music will be given figurative form. Like Rushdie, Rai the narrator was born in 1947, and again like Rushdie, he will create a historical pastiche in the manner of the medieval minstrels, in the manner of Scheherazade, in the manner of Vyasa, the putative narrator of the great Indian epic and many Puranas, and more precisely of Aristaeus in Virgil's *Georgics* (IV, 453–527). In this historical pastiche synchronicity will distort chronology as European modernism with its discrete post-Enlightenment historicity pays homage to the planetary, 'with the echoes of the high old yarn of, oh, Helen, Eurydice, Sita, Rati and Persephone' (GB, 58).

With Umeed as the narrator, the personalities in this mythic re-enactment are three, not two. Two names had been mentioned and the typological connections with the myth already foregrounded: Eurydice-Vina Apsara ('Vina, the Indian lyre' (GB, 55), 'Apsara, from *apsaras*, a swanlike water nymph' (GB, 55)), and Aristaeus-Umeed Merchant (Rai), the photographer. The triad needs completing and we turn, as already foreshadowed, to Orpheus-Ormus Cama, son of Sir Darius Xerxes Cama, named after Kama, the Hindu god of love (GB, 148). Sir Darius is an amateur classicist living in the appropriately named Bombay suburb Apollo Bunder (he is called 'the Apollonian of Apollo Bunder' (GB, 26)). Born on 27 May 1937, Ormus meets the very young Vina-Eurydice at the 'Rhythm Center store in Fort, Bombay' (GB, 90), where he hears his compositions being pilfered by the great popular singers of the age. It is Vina Apsara who salutes this genius and recognises Ormus's regressive telepathic ingenuity. From here on their lives become intertwined: the composer-musician and the singer, Orpheus's great talents now manifest through both Shiva and Shakti, as also through Orpheus and Eurydice.

The great earthquake swallows Vina like a latter-day Sita but without the latter's splendour or place in the unsullied pantheon of womanhood. Can she be sung back to life? When Ormus himself arrives (in 1989 he is fifty-two) at the El Huracán, Guadalajara, Mexico, in a 'black linen suit and matching velvet eye patch', one hears the sound on an acoustic guitar, and the reprise of the old song. The song has new words, modelled, in melodic terms, and perhaps even in substance, it seems, on John Lennon's 'A Hard Day's Night': *All my life, I worshipped her* . . . (GB, 475). She cannot be brought back to life, this much is true, but these are not ancient times. The tale cannot end, as dead Vina is reincarnated, supplanting 'dread Persephone' (GB, 479). Her afterlife spirals uncontrollably, the outpouring of grief reminiscent of that which followed the death of Princess Diana (GB, 480). Singers, pop stars, gurus declare that Vina 'has become the patron divinity of the age of uncertainty' (GB, 483), people impersonate her, and there is no end to the impersonation craze. Ormus too, a recluse, is dragged into the craze and, equipped with Vina recordings, he visits the impersonators and finds in one Mira, an uncanny impersonator, someone who could replace Vina and in an ironic echo of Gluck's *Orfeo ed Euridice* lead to their reunion through love (Amor). It is left to 'Doorman Shetty', Vina's biological father, to provide us with the accusation made against Orpheus (Ormus) by Plato in *The Symposium*: if Orpheus had truly loved Eurydice (Vina) he would have killed himself to be forever with her (GB, 498).[4]

For Rushdie the myth that informs the novel raises a number of questions about love and art: does love always die? Is art incapable of raising the dead? Is love always cowardly? Are the gods dead against lovers? (GB, 499). Was Eurydice, as Rilke intimated, from the underworld herself, a satanic force, a Queen of Darkness, who steals Orpheus's heart and destroys the idea of love?[5] In the novel the afterlife of Vina haunts not only Ormus but also Rai, who wants to declare that he and not Ormus was Vina's great love. The new Orpheus-Ormus, despondent but incapable of making the ultimate sacrifice, gives a final performance with 'The Ground Beneath Her Feet' as the farewell song. The stage is a version of Hades with Mira, the ideal Vina impersonator, featured in the centre. In this final performance Ormus recognises that only Death could set him free – only Death could unite them in the 'forest of the forever dead' (GB, 563). And Death is finally embraced by Ormus too, shot as he is (by the many Vina wannabes in a reprise of Orpheus's own death at the hands of the Dionysiac Maenads whom Orpheus had condemned because of their promiscuity, or perhaps by the spectre of Vina herself) at the entrance of the Rhodopé Building, near Central Park, New York, on a cold wintry day. The reference to John Lennon's assassination by Mark David Chapman at the entrance of The Dakota on 8 December 1980 is consciously foregrounded.

'The Furies' hearts', Ovid tells us, 'were assuaged by the song, and the story goes / that they wept real tears for the very first time'.[6] The song was of course Orpheus's, and Rushdie, in researching the myth of Orpheus for *The Ground Beneath Her Feet*, would have been struck by the grief of these otherwise heartless harpies, whose tears moved Pluto to release Eurydice. In Virgil and Dante the Furies' names are specified (Alecto, Megaera and Tisiphone), and their origin as daughters of Chaos predating the arrival of the gods is given greater prominence.[7] What form does this instance of archival modernism take in the next novel? In *Fury* the story of the Furies is not invoked in any systemic fashion as the Orpheus myth is in *The Ground Beneath Her Feet*. In fact the word 'Furies' (in the plural) is used less often than the common word 'fury', with its meaning of anger, vehemence, unrestrained frenzy or passion. *Fury* is a novel about getting to know a city, New York, the writer's third metropolis after Bombay and London, and of all his novels, it is the most clearly simulacral. In *Fury* the city exists not so much as an objective fact that can be fixed in any descriptive sense but one that is formed and re-formed through technological lenses that keep changing. It is therefore both real and simulacral, both near and far, both being and non-being, both existential and spectral. In this quasi-illusory cityscape the kind of allegory that Dante wrote by informing his grand poem with myth lacks depth because the city itself is all surfaces; it is a city where the 'exceptional was as commonplace as diet soda'[8] and the phony Assyrian Palace is the city's 'best simulacrum of a *Viennese Kaffeehaus*' (F, 44).

In this city we find fifty-five-year-old Professor Malik Solanka, 'retired historian of ideas, irascible dollmaker' and celibate (F, 3). In retirement Solanka lives very comfortably in an apartment complex in New York on the proceeds of his very successful talking doll named Little Brain which, as the character in the TV cult classic *The Adventures of Little Brain* (itself disingenuously modelled on Monty Python's *Life of Brian* (1979)), impersonates and interviews 'Great Minds'. He has had his fifteen minutes of Andy Warhol glory because Woody Allen's *Husbands and Wives* is partly filmed in his rented apartment (F, 40). This momentary glory notwithstanding, Solanka is traumatised by the loss of his family. He has left his son Asmaan and wife Eleanor Masters back in England. Like Rushdie's own son Milan, who was too young to understand why his father left Elizabeth West, his mother, for Padma Lakshmi, Asmaan cannot understand why his father walked out on them. 'The Furies pursue us,' Malik consoles himself, adding that 'Shiva dances his furious dance to create and also to destroy' (F, 31). Although it seems that now he does not need gods to understand both fury and the Furies, there is one incident which haunts him. The night before he left his son and wife to fly to New York he had 'brought a carving knife upstairs and stood for a terrible, dumb minute over the body of his sleeping wife' (F, 39), an image that recurs later (F, 79) when he links it to Macbeth's '*Is this a dagger which I see before me, the handle towards my hand?*'. The incident is repeated in the flashback section where he once again remembers 'he was standing above them in the dark and here in his hand was the carving knife' (F, 107). He had panicked and blamed the satanic doll he had created. And so he flies to America to '*unwrite*' this story or event: America, the land of self-creation, the 'country whose paradigmatic modern fiction was the story of a man who remade himself' (F, 79).

Furies shadow all his relationships with women. There is Mila Milo, originally Milosevic (F, 90), admirer of Solanka's *Little Brain* TV episodes, and a lover whose presence provokes a clearer statement of the Furies. The imagery of Mila Milo as Fury extends to premonitions of 'dark goddesses' (F, 130) hovering over him and nightmares about crows as Furies, all of which also bring back memories of a father holding a knife before his son and wife. And then early one morning, with Neela, the misguided revolutionary fighting for her diasporic homeland Lilliput-Blefuscu in the Pacific, in bed with him, he is confronted with the other women in his life, Mila and Eleanor. We read: 'Here they were, the three Furies, the "good-tempered ones" themselves, in full possession of the physical bodies of the women to whom his life was most profoundly joined. . . . The fury that had once possessed him was now theirs' (F, 233). Himself a victim of child abuse – his stepfather Dr Solanka dressed him up as a girl for a long time (F, 220) – an inner fury, the fury that damages one forever, had always possessed him.

In his last days Oedipus, through the voice of the Chorus, had turned to the Furies for peace of mind in the pastoral surroundings of Athens: 'Dark Furies! Goddesses of the Earth . . . of eternal sleep, I call to you, let Oedipus rest forever' (Sophocles, *Oedipus at Colonus*, 377). *Fury*, the novel, also ends with Solanka looking at his son Asmaan on a glorious April day on Hampstead Heath. This is the closest we come to a structural homology because in *Fury*, unlike in *The Ground Beneath Her Feet*, earlier archives function as 'shadows' that haunt the lives of people. In the next novel, *Shalimar the Clown*, the Furies are transformed into Oriental cosmology and local memories.

In *Shalimar the Clown* Rushdie turns to medieval Hindu cosmology, whereby astrology (and cosmology more generally) is invoked as a prescient principle governing human desire. The influence of the seven known planets including the Sun and the Moon (Surya, Soma) and the shadow planets Rahu and Ketu is present everywhere. The shadow planets especially have a greater influence because they were 'heavenly bodies without bodies', without physical form, but this very fact makes them spectacularly influential since they have power over human emotions: 'Kaam the Passion, Krodh the Anger, Madh the Intoxicant . . . Moh the Attachment, Lobh the Greed and Matsaya the Jealousy.'[9] Over these emotions Rahu and Ketu are in an eternal moral combat. As Rahu intensifies, Ketu blocks and suppresses. There will be lovers, one an acrobat, Noman Sher Noman (known as Shalimar the Clown), the other an alluring Bhoomi (or Boonyi), the great dancer whose signature performance was the dance of the Mughal courtesan Anarkali. In the idyllic pastoral landscapes of Kashmir they would meet, one a Muslim, the other a Hindu, at a time when to be a Kashmiri was to be something apart. But is passion something to be blocked, repressed, thinks Boonyi? She recalls how patriarchy blamed Sita for Rama's troubles in the other great epic. But passion (with the conflicting tendencies of the shadow planets) had its own laws, its own course. In the epic Sita succumbs to the wily language of Ravana (dressed as a mendicant) and lets him cross the magic line (the Lakshman Rekhā), an act that brings about the catastrophic narrative of violation, war and reprisal. But when Boonyi thinks about it she feels that 'what had to happen should be allowed to happen or it could never be overcome' (SC, 50). In Rushdie's hands, archival medievalism (since the modern Indian has access to the text through its medieval variants) is again reworked, and Sita's abduction (unconsciously desired) will replicate itself in Boonyi's own life as she leaves her husband Noman for the American ambassador, Maximilian Ophuls, named by Rushdie after the great German-American filmmaker. The shadow planets Rahu and Ketu are always there: 'Was he [Noman] her [Boonyi's] epic hero or her demon king, or both?' (SC, 50). Was he in fact both Rama and Ravana?

The jilted lover Shalimar takes to honour killing and will murder both Boonyi and her ex-lover Maximilian and almost kill their illegitimate daughter India (Kashmira). This was not, as the narrator tells, how things were 'supposed to go according to the old story':

> In the old story Sita the pure is kidnapped and Ram fought a war to win her back. In the modern world everything had been turned upside down and inside out. Sita, or rather Boonyi in the Sita role, had freely chosen to run off with her American Ravan and willingly became his mistress and bore him a child . . . (SC, 263)

Boonyi lights no fire for ritual purification; nor does the earth open so that she can depart with all her innocence intact as, in an ironic reversal, Vina Apsara did in *The Ground Beneath Her Feet*. All Shalimar knows is slaughter, slaughter of Boonyi's daughter India. As the latter takes her own revenge, she recalls the earlier Furies: 'Blood called out for blood and she wanted the ancient Furies to descend shrieking from the sky and give her father's unquiet spirit peace' (SC, 331).

The turn to the local for archival modernism continues with *The Enchantress of Florence*.[10] Susan Stanford Friedman speaks of an 'early modernity' in the fourteenth and fifteenth centuries in India centred on Mughal rulers. She uses the syncretic devotional (*bhakti*) poet Kabir (c. 1448–1518), Hindu by birth, Muslim weaver by profession, as an instance of an oral poet who uses the vernacular to create local, discrepant and challenging beliefs against the transcendental claims of high Hinduism and orthodox Islam. Kabir was easily incorporated into the tradition of the medieval saint singers of India who espoused the religion of love in both its *nirguṇa* (God as One) and *saguṇa* (God as Many) forms.[11] In *Shalimar the Clown* Boonyi's father Pyarelal Kaul speaks of Kabir, who espoused the value of bringing together the personal soul (*jivātma*) and the divine over-soul (*paramātma*) into a state of union (SC, 234). A century after his birth Kabir's vernacular syncretism receives regnal endorsement from Akbar (1542–1605), the greatest of all Mughal emperors, whose reign (1556–1605) closely coincides with that of Elizabeth I. Friedman concedes that in Akbar's reign there was 'a particular cosmopolitanism in which a multicultural blend of religion, knowledge, and the arts flourished'.[12] Salman Rushdie's *The Enchantress of Florence* is a celebration of this vital modernity and the global linkages that Akbar sought to establish. Against the internecine religious wars of Europe around the same time, Akbar's India offered a model of tolerance and peace. Although battles continued to be fought and Akbar was merciless when it came to beheading rebels and upstart princes, there was nevertheless a kind of 'Pax Indica' that prevailed and dialogue was encouraged. What then does a writer – who is himself an exemplary latter-day cosmopolitan – do with this Oriental medieval modernity? We need to let the novel speak for itself.

A traveller from Renaissance Florence calling himself Mogor dell'Amore ('The Mughal of Love', '*Mughal born out of wedlock*' (*EF*, 93)) heads for the court of another Renaissance man, a philosopher king who was to become the greatest ruler the nation had ever known. In *The Ground Beneath Her Feet* an archival modernism is used to connect the lives of contemporary pop stars with the foundational myth of love and desire, and in *Two Years Eight Months and Twenty-Eight Nights* again an Islamic medieval modernism is used to explore current debates about God and truth. In *The Enchantress of Florence* the two modernities are historically parallel and Rushdie uses the traveller's story and his Florentine background to create a dialogue between cultures. In doing so, though, Rushdie utilises his considerable craft as a writer of fiction thoroughly acquainted with its global intertexts. The cultures connect and disperse as the traveller's alluring tale – a tale given in parts like Scheherazade's to defer death itself – is unravelled.

The stranger, variously named Uccello di Firenzi, Mogor dell'Amore and Niccolò Vespucci (after the political theorist and the explorer), tells the Emperor that his mother Angelica, named by Rushdie it seems after a character in Ariosto's *Orlando Furioso*,[13] but better known as Qara Köz, was a princess of the true Chaghatai blood, a direct descendant of Genghis Khan, a member of the house of Timur, the sister of the First Mughal Emperor of India, whom she called 'the Beaver' (Babur, grandfather of Akbar (*EF*, 107)), and therefore the Emperor's grand aunt. As his grand aunt's son he is the Emperor's uncle, albeit many years younger. To make his case the stranger has to tell a love story, which, as Rushdie himself explained at the 2008 Miami Book Fair International, is also a kind of 'road novel'. In this tale the lives of three Florentine youths (one of whom is none other than Machiavelli) will intertwine with that of Princess Qara Köz ('Black Eyes'). It is an intriguing tale which draws extensively on earlier archives of modernity and the point of the tale lies in its telling. Fantasist or beguiling human, the stranger fascinates but fails to convince the Emperor that the claim he makes about his birth is correct.

It is a fascinating tale about two parallel modernities, the ideological strength of which lies precisely in a later modernity's homage to an earlier planetary modernism and one which dispenses with an exclusive definition of a (Western) humanism. The traveller's tale, the tale of the road, the picaresque story – a traveller comes, he tells his fantastic tale and then he departs – affirms the power of story, a point made with great effect in Rushdie's next novel, *Luka and the Fire of Life*, where Nobodaddy berates Luka, who had said 'But that's just a story': 'You of all the boys should know that Man is the Storytelling Animal, and that in stories are his identity, his meaning and his lifeblood. Do rats tell tales? Do porpoises have narrative purposes? Do elephants ele-phantasise? You know as well as I do that they do not. Man alone burns with books.'[14] In *The Enchantress of Florence* the stranger is a teller of tales and it so happens that language is the subject of debates in Akbar's enlightened court. These debates replay or re-enact the struggle between reason, 'a mortal divinity' (*EF*, 80), supported by Abul Fazl, and dogma, fanatically defended by Badauni, that found its grand moment in Islamic culture in the debates between Ibn Rushd and Al-Ghazali that Rushdie returns to in *Two Years Eight Months and Twenty-Eight Nights*.

In her discussion of Abbasid modernity Susan Stanford Friedman notes that the Abbasid Caliphate controlled the vast Arab-Islamic Empire from Baghdad from 750 to 1258 CE.[15] Baghdad, with Basra as the major port city, became a thriving centre with a flourishing artistic culture under the benign patronage of its Caliphs, notably Harun al-Rashid, a key figure in *The Thousand and One Nights*. Scholars drew on Greek classics and science, and advances in navigation took their sailors and merchants across the Indian Ocean, past the Straits of Malacca to China. The Friedman thesis is based on principles that collapse discrepant modernities in favour of interconnected influences which, at times, are forced analogies. Inasmuch as the thesis has great heuristic value in the context of Rushdie's own work, it is a useful starting point, even when critically invoked. For even as the Abbasid Caliphate reigned supreme, elsewhere in the Islamic-Arab world something more decisive was taking shape. What was at stake was the place of knowledge itself within a religion that declared itself as the final and absolute will of God, to whom a believer submitted without question. The challenge is not taken up by Friedman in her discussion of modernity. To Rushdie the philosophical challenge is pivotal. At the height of the Abbasid Caliphate the seeds of a religious reformation were being scattered. In Rushdie's *Two Years Eight Months and Twenty-Eight Nights*[16] the debate about religious reformation and its consequences affected the history of the world to the extent that a thousand years later the consequence led to the near end of the world as we know it. A battle raged between the forces of Good and Evil and luckily Good was triumphant. Another thousand years later – that is, 2,000 years after the debate – one can look back at that battle of two years, eight months and twenty-eight nights (or 1,001 nights) that almost brought civilisation to an end. The novel is based on this great conceit and it seems Rushdie felt that the conceit was necessary to establish a much larger principle about the power of the imagination, a point underlined in the Goya etching that serves as an epigraph to the novel.

In *Two Years Eight Months and Twenty-Eight Nights* Rushdie turns to medieval Islamic thinkers – Avicenna (Al-Ghazali), the Islamic literalist, and Averroës (Ibn Rushd), the grand Aristotelian rationalist – to examine the nature of a 'right war', noted in his *Joseph Anton*.[17] This is the war of aesthetics versus blind ideology, the war of art over righteousness, the war that would find place for both sense (reason) and sensibility (art), temporarily fought with disastrous consequences for the author (the fatwa of death, the isolation of the artist, the deaths of people associated with the novel's publication). It was a war that insinuated that freedom of expression was at an end. That 'right war', it was felt, required an extended commentary, in short a lengthy allegory of meaning in the tradition of Bunyan, Swift and all those writers who always felt that fiction was after all allegorical: it said one thing but meant another. Rushdie returns to the battle of the books, of ideas, and enlarges that brief war into a catastrophic encounter in which the future (a thousand years hence) looks back at the crisis of the end of the second millennium. How to give it form? Allegory, the genre of understatement and critique, the genre of evasion and at the same time of forthright critique, the genre at once objective and self-reflective, offers its services to the writer. And Rushdie grasps it; the world indeed reached a crisis point because of the competing forces of irrational belief and critical philosophy, and that crisis could be understood only with historical hindsight by looking forward a thousand years and then looking back. And for the allegory to work, archival modernism provided the necessary conceit. 'To tell a story about the past', the narrator tells us, 'is to tell a story about the present' (*TY*, 207).

Rushdie turns to archival modernism to write an allegory of Islamic fundamentalism, and what better way of doing it than to return to Islamic modernity itself, a time when debates were not uncommon, even if in that flowering of modernity absolutism and unreason triumphed? It is therefore the dialectic that works, but only as an allegory, not the allegory itself as a form in its own right. This is the enigma of the work: where the form fails but the lesson has a tenacity and force, even if it remains too early to tell if indeed Ibn Rushd triumphs over Al-Ghazali.

To reprise the argument of the chapter itself and get back to the texts that precede *Two Years Eight Months and Twenty-Eight Nights*, the case presented here is that Rushdie's understanding of archival modernism is something apart. To him archival modernism excavates from earlier archives ideas that a later, modern writer uses to disrupt rigid periodisation and suggest that the modern is precisely the creative and ever-changing use of epistemologies that, with the availability of different discourses, radical linguistic usages, both informs the modern and blasts open its claims of exclusiveness.[18] For Rushdie modernity is a contested space, a contested narrative and a contested idea with earlier 'planetary' manifestations. Modernity in a sense pays homage to a history or more precisely a historical formation that has not been self-evidently incorporated into a hitherto largely unproblematic grand narrative of modernity. Archival modernism in its turn to medieval archives does something different. By turning to both European and non-European medievalisms Rushdie adds to the great tradition of the European high modernists who were conscious of non-European medievalisms (one is reminded yet again of Pound with classical Chinese, Eliot with Sanskrit, and Joyce with almost everything else). Indeed, one may locate Rushdie in a commentarial tradition that should inform all Western discussions of modernity.

NOTES

1. See Susan Stanford Friedman, *Planetary Modernisms* (New York: Columbia University Press, 2015).
2. This was such an influential text that C. S. Lewis could enthusiastically state: 'Until about two hundred years ago it would, I think, have been hard to find an educated man in any

European country who did not love it. To acquire a taste for it is almost to become naturalised in the Middle Ages'; C. S. Lewis, *The Discarded Image: An Introduction to Medieval and Renaissance Literature* (Cambridge: Cambridge University Press, 1967), p. 75.
3. Salman Rushdie, *The Ground Beneath Her Feet* (London: Jonathan Cape, 1999), p. 475. All quotations are from this edition; hereafter, page numbers will be given in the text, preceded by GB. The song has been made famous by Bono and U2.
4. Rushdie returns to Plato's *The Symposium* in *The Enchantress of Florence*, pp. 290–1 (see note 10).
5. In Rilke's poem 'Orpheus. Eurydike. Hermes' Eurydike (Eurydice) has difficulty remembering Orpheus when he turns around to see her in the underworld of Hermes, a point noted by Rushdie in *The Ground Beneath Her Feet* (p. 499). 'And when suddenly the god stopped her and, with anguish in his cry, uttered the words: "He has turned around" – she comprehended nothing and said softly: "Who?" [begriff sie nichts unde sagte leise: Wer?]'
6. Ovid, *Metamorphoses*, X, 384.
7. See Virgil, *The Aeneid*, VII, 323–31; Dante, *Hell*, IX, 38–48.
8. Salman Rushdie, *Fury* (London: Jonathan Cape, 2001), p. 39. All quotations are from this edition; hereafter, page numbers will be given in the text, preceded by F.
9. Salman Rushdie, *Shalimar the Clown* (London: Jonathan Cape, 2005), p. 48. All quotations are from this edition; hereafter, page numbers will be given in the text, preceded by SC.
10. Salman Rushdie, *The Enchantress of Florence* (London: Jonathan Cape, 2008), p. 82. All quotations are from this edition; hereafter, page numbers will be given in the text, preceded by EF.
11. Friedman, *Planetary Modernisms*, pp. 204–13.
12. Ibid., p. 205.
13. Angelica is described by the text's translator, Barbara Reynolds, as 'daughter of the Great Khan of Cathay; loved and pursued by numerous knights, both Christian and pagan; marries Medoro', an African soldier. See Reynolds's 'Introduction', in Ludovico Ariosto, *Orlando Furioso* (Harmondsworth: Penguin Books, 1975), p. 107.
14. Salman Rushdie, *Luka and the Fire of Life* (London: Jonathan Cape, 2010), p. 34.
15. Friedman, *Planetary Modernisms*, pp. 199–204.
16. Salman Rushdie, *Two Years Eight Months and Twenty-Eight Nights* (New York: Random House, 2015), p. 207. All quotations are from this edition; hereafter, page numbers will be given in the text, preceded by TY.
17. Salman Rushdie, *Joseph Anton: A Memoir* (London: Jonathan Cape, 2012), p. 23.
18. Rushdie, it seems, does not follow the synchronously present notion of modernity as suggested by Friedman, to whom the later, modern deployment of a Sanskrit word such as *ādhuniktā* (to mean 'modernity') is meant to signify modernity as a planetary and not simply Eurocentric understanding of reason and enlightenment (Friedman, *Planetary Modernisms*, pp. 47–9). However, a closer look reveals a linguistic fallacy because in Sanskrit the word never had the meaning 'modernity' in its historical usage. It may be used in any vernacular translation of 'modernity' if the current vernacular does not have such a word. This does not mean that the redeploying of an earlier word and infusing it with connotative value present in the here and now gives retrospective meaning and value to the word. Friedman does not quite see this distinction.

FURTHER READING

For an up-to-date list of Rushdie's novels, see the British Council website: <https://literature.britishcouncil.org/writer/salman-rushdie> (last accessed 21 June 2016).

Ariosto, Ludovico, *Orlando Furioso*, trans. and intro. Barbara Reynolds (Harmondsworth: Penguin Books, 1975).

Attar, Farid Ud-din, *The Conference of the Birds*, trans. and intro. Afkham Darbandi and Dick Davis (London: Penguin, 2011).
Boethius, *The Consolation of Philosophy*, trans. Victor Watts (London: Penguin Books, 1999).
Chaucer, Geoffrey, *Chaucer: Complete Works*, ed. Walter W Skeat (London: Oxford University Press, 1967).
Dante Alighieri, *The Divine Comedy I: Hell (L'Inferno)*, trans. Dorothy L. Sayers (Harmondsworth: Penguin Books, 1969).
Friedman, Susan Stanford, *Planetary Modernisms* (New York: Columbia University Press, 2015).
Henryson, Robert, 'Orpheus and Eurydice', ed. David J. Parkinson, Robbins Library Digital Projects (Middle English Texts Series, University of Rochester), <http://d.lib.rochester.edu/teams/text/parkinson-henryson-complete-works-orpheus-and-eurydice> (last accessed 21 June 2016).
Lewis, C. S., *The Discarded Image: An Introduction to Medieval and Renaissance Literature* (Cambridge: Cambridge University Press, 1967).
Ovid, *Metamorphoses*, trans. David Raeburn, intro. Denis Feeney (London: Penguin Books, 2004).
Plato, *The Symposium*, trans. Walter Hamilton (Harmondsworth: Penguin Books, 1973).
Rilke, Rainer Maria, *Selected Poems*, <http://www.poetryintranslation.com/PITBR/German/MoreRilke.htm#anchor_Toc527606964> (last accessed 21 June 2016).
Sands, Donald B. (ed.), *Middle English Verse Romances* (New York: Holt, Rinehart and Winston, Inc., 1966).
Somadeva, *The Ocean of the Rivers of Story (Kathāsaritasāgara)*, vol. 1, trans. Sir James Mallinson (New York: New York University Press, 2006).
Sophocles, *The Three Theban Plays*, trans. Robert Fagles (New York: Penguin Books, 1984).
Virgil, *The Aeneid*, trans. Frank O. Copley (New York: Bobbs-Merrill, 1965).
Virgil, *The Georgics: A Poem of the Land*, trans. and ed. Kimberly Johnson (London: Penguin Books, 2010).

PART IV

Realism, Postmodernism and Beyond: Historical Fiction

CHAPTER 13

Adam Foulds: Fictions of Past and Present

Dominic Head

Adam Foulds has a growing reputation as one of the more significant twenty-first-century British novelists. An intimation as to why this might be is the seriousness with which he views the craft of writing. In a short essay for *The Guardian* on the importance of description in fiction, Foulds writes that '[t]hrough description, reality is broken down and reassembled according to what you, the author, desire'. Foulds continues this thought by prioritising aesthetic composition in the pursuit of verisimilitude: 'The resulting words must be formally satisfying, finding an artistic pattern that has only tangentially to do with lived experience per se and yet somehow renders it with the greatest possible intensity.'[1] This is a writer's way of engaging with the debate about realism, a suggestion that a convincing mimetic presentation is always an intense kind of re-presentation. Thea Lenarduzzi puts this another way, suggesting that one 'broader theme' in Foulds's novels is his concern 'with different ways of seeing, and the gaps between things as they are perceived and things as they are'.[2] This elevation of the conventional account of literary insight to the status of a *theme* signals the literariness of Foulds, an emphasis that issues especially in an examination of his literary influences and inheritance.

His first novel, *The Truth about These Strange Times* (2007), is chiefly an examination of contemporary British social concerns. The plot is centred on an improbable relationship between ten-year-old Saul, a prodigy on the brink of winning the World Memory Championships, and the social failure Howard McNamee, who is without a career at twenty-eight, overweight, friendless, and haunted not only by his traumatic childhood in Glasgow but also by the recent death of his mother. Howard is representative of those dispossessed in a Britain obsessed with economic success and physical beauty. Yet it is he who supplies the understanding that Saul's over-ambitious parents cannot muster, and in turn Saul gives Howard the modicum of respect lacking in his life, as well as being the focus for Howard's undeveloped skills in care and responsibility. The use of the naïve protagonist abroad has been a staple feature of the British novel, of course. Walter Scott's *Waverley* (1814) is a prominent example, but the origins lie in the sentimental novel of the eighteenth century: Henry Fielding's *Joseph Andrews* (1742) is one of the earliest examples in English fiction. This convention allows Foulds to resuscitate the idea that 'feelings' can provide the moral compass for characters in an alienated world.

The motif of the attraction of opposites can make the novel seem rather clumsily written, with 'outlandish, almost cartoon characters', as James Procter has it.[3] Yet Foulds's binarism allows him to identify a social moment with acuity. This is especially the case when Howard and Saul flee from the World Memory Championships, in the process escaping the breakdown for which Saul seems to be heading. Predictably, Howard is perceived to have abducted Saul for a sexual motive, and their flight is dogged by news headlines and moments of recognition. There is a chilling scene in a hotel when another guest deems Howard to be a fellow paedophile, and requests 'a little time' with Saul in exchange for not turning Howard in to the authorities. The pent-up violence of Howard's repressed existence fuses with resentment at the man's imputation, and he grabs at his throat:

> 'I ... will call ... police,' the man said, thick-tongued, lightly holding Howard's wrist.
>
> 'You will not, you fuck,' Howard said quietly. 'Because I have done nothing to that boy, who's my friend by the way, and if the police start on investigating *you* they're gonnee find some filth, eh?'
>
> The man's eyes grew fat; his lips writhed to form words he could give no sound.[4]

This is a rare moment of assertion against the prevailing view. Yet it is also another instance of an extreme mental state, like the bullying Howard endured as a child, the hothousing mentality of Saul's parents, and the idea of excelling in a memory competition. Psychological extremity creates a claustrophobic atmosphere, and there is seemingly no way for Howard to escape the social nets that enclose him. The paedophile in the hotel shares the general assumption – also enunciated by a 'tramp' (*TT*, 291) – that Howard's flight with Saul is explicable only as the act of a child molester. The penultimate section of the novel ends with the police about to arrest Howard, with retribution being apparently inevitable.

There is another plotline, however, which produces a more hopeful outcome. This concerns a group of Russians working in London, who use Howard as a potential husband-of-convenience for the character Irina, who arrives in England in the novel's final section. This sub-plot exacerbates the sense of Howard's victimhood, whilst providing an oblique commentary on the era of migrancy: in a dog-eat-dog world, small collectives survive, but only by, in turn, finding weaker people to exploit. Howard, who has fallen in love with his internet 'girlfriend' Irina, is unable to avoid his fate, although the imprisonment we feel to be inescapable might thwart the marriage to her. Yet, in the closing section, Howard is in the party that meets her at the airport, and here we learn that he appears to be a 'lunatic' (*TT*, 324). In an unforeseen move, however, Foulds succeeds in turning his readers' expectations around with the novel's final sentence, which presents Irina's first estimation of Howard: 'She couldn't help noticing, as they stepped out through sliding doors into a bitter, damp wind, that Howard, wearing only a shirt and no jumper or coat, didn't seem to feel the cold, like a true Russian' (*TT*, 324). Howard's mere presence at the scene of Irina's arrival surprises our expectations about the social retribution that he must face over the 'abduction' of Saul; and this hint that Irina has instantly found grounds for affinity with him begins to reverse his position as victim. In an improbable and wilful gesture, Foulds suggests that Howard's essential goodness has the power to transform the social dynamic of exploitation.

Foulds's second book, *The Broken Word* (2008), continues an important tradition since World War II of British re-evaluations of colonialism in which the colonial psyche under pressure is meticulously dissected. Paul Scott's *Staying On* (1977) and J. G. Farrell's 'Empire Trilogy', *Troubles* (1970), *The Siege of Krishnapur* (1973) and *The Singapore Grip* (1978), are some of the finest works in this tradition. *The Broken Word* is not a novel, however, but a long narrative poem about the violent Mau Mau uprising in Kenya in the 1950s (which expedited Kenyan independence in 1963), and the ruthless British response. Although it is not a novel, there are elements of this book that are key to understanding Foulds's developing uses of narrative. The main character, Tom, a young man about to go up to Oxford, finds himself caught up in the violence while visiting his father's farm in Kenya. Swift to meet violence with violence, the British settlers show how the brutality of conflict is infectious and dehumanising. On his return to England, the privileged university life Tom finds at Oxford emerges as an idyll apparently quite distinct from the violence of colonial Africa, but expressly linked to it by Foulds. The fact that Tom feels no overt guilt or remorse – although violent scenes haunt his dreams – underscores the suggestion that individuals are powerless to resist the pull of larger historical forces, and it is from this point that the most troubling aspect of *The Broken Word* emerges: what the narrative illustrates is how swiftly 'tribal' behaviour takes hold as a group acts to defend its interests, and how that imperative trumps any latent moral sense. Soon Tom is inured to the violence, a transformation encapsulated in this account of beatings meted out to rebel prisoners:

> Tom watched for a bit. He'd grown a connoisseur
> Of beatings: the first blows stunning and accurate,
> With feints or not, and large, like sculpture.
> But quickly the prisoner couldn't focus,
> Looked ridiculous, bewildered, lonely
> Before they blacked out completely and lay there.[5]

This is an illustration of how specifically poetic effects are made to render the impercipience of the colonial mindset. Where J. G. Farrell uses extended comic effects, Foulds here uses a single arresting image. The transition from perceiving the torturer's blows as 'large, like sculpture' to the brutalised acceptance of the routine conveys the process of desensitised moral collapse in six lines.

Overall, however, the book's accomplishment is defined by its narrative thread.

Tom's time in Kenya ends abruptly after he shoots a prisoner in the head, apparently troubled by the prisoner's account of how the rebel leader (Dedan Kimathi) will evade capture, by becoming a bird, or a snake, or the wind, or a drop of water (*BW*, 43–4). In this key moment in the poem, the evocation of an ineffable and undefeatable 'other' – the Mau Mau culture – provokes murderous refusal. Back in England, Tom is interrogated by his parents, who think he has left Kenya under a cloud and feel he should go back. His response is to hurl a teacup against the wall, the first of several indications of how he has been brutalised. Of course, it is not that he has become uncivilised, but that he now sees the viciousness beneath the veneer of civilised English society (*BW*, 48).

The concerns of Foulds's first two books evolve in satisfying ways in the next two, which are works of greater maturity. *The Quickening Maze* (2009) concentrates on an episode in the life of the poet John Clare while he was a patient at High Beech Asylum, the private institution in Essex founded by Matthew Allen. Allen is presented in Foulds's novel as an exuberant but overreaching Victorian, pursuing enlightened ideas, but flawed by his entrepreneurial ambitions. Expectations of an involved form of fictional biography are raised by the arrival of the young Alfred Tennyson at High Beech, accompanying his brother Septimus. But Tennyson's function is not causal in relation to Clare's creativity: the two never meet. Foulds simply presents us with the juxtaposition of different worlds and different forms of poetic inspiration, where Tennyson's muse is made to seem more formulaic than Clare's, partly through arch narratorial intervention: 'Tennyson sat by his fire, sinking into the grief that will make him famous.'[6]

Matthew Allen's plan to design a wood-carving machine for the manufacture of ecclesiastical furniture symbolises the flawed progression of modernity, and this serves to particularise our sense of a world that disregards the sources of inspiration of a John Clare. Clare's creativity is contrasted with a machine intended to supplant the craft of traditional artisans. Foulds finds Clare a compelling subject for other reasons as well, and in an essay on Clare he emphasises that the poet's famous long walk from the asylum to Cambridgeshire was pivotal to the composition of *The Quickening Maze*.[7] Clare's poems, Foulds argues, are 'compelling to so many' because we all share the experience of a vanishing 'childhood world'; but for Clare the loss was intensified: 'For him, home had been doubly abolished, in part by the alienation brought by literary achievement, and in part because it simply no longer existed. The rural world Clare grew up in had been dismantled around him. His fate was to be everywhere an exile.'[8]

In this account, Clare's experience is compelling because it chimes with the psychological exile that is a consequence for everyone of the transition from childhood to adulthood. What is specific to Clare is the historical circumstance of enclosure – or, rather, that final stage in a centuries-long process of enclosure that was modernity's final *coup de grâce* for the traditional rural community. Clare's representativeness in a psychological sense is diluted by the specificity of historical circumstance. Yet, in an intriguing move in his discussion, Foulds then finds occasion to make the longer march of history reinstall Clare's emblematic status, because 'the enclosure acts' began 'a denuding of the environment, a stripping out of habitat and human diversity that ... now represents a potential ecological and cultural catastrophe'. Clare's significance is, then, not just that he is 'a key figure of ecological literature' – indeed, 'our greatest ecological poet' – but that his plight anticipates our plight, in a continuum of ecological disaster through modernity.[9]

This extrapolation of the general from the particular is implicit throughout Foulds's portrayal of Clare. For example, when he is at work gardening, as part of his therapy at High Beech, Clare has a moment of communion with nature, after feeding a worm to a robin, and observing it at its meal:

> Watching this, being there, given time, the world revealed itself again in silence, coming to him. Gently it breathed around him its atmosphere: vulnerable, benign, full of secrets, his. A lost thing returning. How it waited for him in eternity and almost knew him. He'd known and sung it all his life. Perception of it now, amid all his truancy and suffering, made his eyes thicken with warm tears. (QM, 17)

This is a fine illustration of Foulds's method in this novel. The sense of Clare's mental fragility is sharply evoked, the communion with nature tipping the poet over into emotional instability. While this helps create a convincing psychological portrait of Clare, it also reinforces the idea of his emblematic role in the treatment of a slowly evolving ecological crisis – the brittleness is produced by his exile from his rural home, but the exile is a general one in this novel suggestive of historical ecological malaise through modernity, his nostalgia for communion with nature indicative of humanity's banishment in general.

This dynamic, in which Foulds makes the biographical portrait emblematic, is quietly suggested in Foulds's rewriting of perhaps the best-known episode of Clare's life, his eighty-mile walk home from the asylum, over four days, to Werrington (and then to Northborough in Cambridgeshire by cart). It is, in fact, a subtle appropriation of Clare's famous 'Journey Out of Essex', which Foulds condenses and rewrites in the third person. This rewriting is largely faithful to the encounters, conversations and moods of Clare's own account, but there are some notable differences. Most obvious is the interjection of an omniscient paragraph that foretells the aftermath of the journey home, his incarceration in the asylum at Northampton, and his obscure death (QM, 253). When he calls upon neighbouring gypsies for help, Clare finds that they have moved on, and recounts finding 'an old wide awake hat' (as well as an old straw bonnet) left behind in their camp.[10] He takes the hat – apparently thinking it might come in useful as a disguise when he makes his escape. In Foulds's version, Clare has already set off, and the hat is disregarded: 'it provoked a melancholy emotion, looking at that hat, but he had no time for it. . . . Friendless and lawless and unreliable, they'd upped and gone' (QM, 253). Such changes place emphasis on Clare's mental instability. There is another similar change to the entry for 21 July, as Clare approaches the Tollgate south of St Neots, where 'doubt and hopelessness made me turn so feeble that I was scarcely able to walk yet I could not sit down or give up' becomes 'He heard himself whimpering with the misery, almost too feeble to keep walking, shuffling forward in the dark' (QM, 256).[11] Again, the change emphasises Clare's mental fragility, as does the incorporation of a footnote in which Clare claims Queen Victoria as his daughter (QM, 257).[12]

Foulds's most recent book, *In the Wolf's Mouth* (2014), is a very different novel; yet it has a strong connection with *The Quickening Maze* in its reliance on a well-known rural English literary author and text (in this case, Kenneth Grahame's *The Wind in the Willows* (1908)) as a counterpoint to its central concerns. *In the Wolf's Mouth* is set largely in Sicily at the end of the Second World War, although it also embraces the North African campaign of 1942, and there is an important 'Prologue' set in 1926. It concerns four men, who are 'types' bordering on caricature. Their lives intersect in the clumsy end of conflict – in the muddled efforts to establish a new political order. These four are: Will Walker, an idealistic Englishman working in field security; Ray Marfione, a Sicilian-American; Cirò Albanese, a Mafioso returning to Sicily having gone into exile in the 1920s; and Angilù, the shepherd whose life epitomises one of Foulds's central themes: that individuals are at the mercy of systemic human failings. Rebecca Abrams reminds us that 'in the wolf's mouth' is 'a translation of the Italian expression for good luck, "in bocca al lupo", to which the correct response is "crepi il lupo", or "may the wolf die"'. Abrams's gloss on this shows how Foulds may have appropriated the metaphor: 'As this superb novel makes clear, to evade the wolf takes more than good luck, for the wolf is out there in the woods, and sipping coffee at the kitchen table, and within us.'[13] This propensity to be dehumanised is most clearly presented in the career of Will Walker, who is a extension of Tom in *The Broken Word*.

Walker is disabused of his youthful enthusiasm for the Allied involvement in the 'defascistification' of Sicily through his role as an AMGOT Civil Affairs Officer.[14] His psychological identity is (understandably) determined by the fear of death, and this is made tangible by the sense of what he would lose, all of which is concentrated in nostalgia for his Warwickshire riverside home. The key book he decides to take with him is Grahame's *The Wind in the Willows*, and evidently the edition illustrated by E. H. Shepard, originally issued in 1931.[15] The book fills him 'with a large nostalgia' for the house he grew up in, 'and the landscape and his childhood' (*IWM*, 40). It is a recurring theme in accounts of the English military (in both World Wars) that their purpose was sharpened by false ideas of an enduring verdant rural England – false (so this line of argument goes) in failing to register the march of modernity, and false in obscuring the power relations that upheld the traditional rural order. Foulds is responding to the view that the ruralism of the inter-war period (Walker's formative years) was fashioned by earlier rural fantasy.[16]

He seems, however, to be doing something a little richer with this idea, to be examining the continuing resonance of the rural. Indeed, snatches of *The Wind in the Willows* resonate in Walker's mind, supplying a commentary that is not ironic in a simple or obvious way. The most telling of these moments occurs in Sicily, where Walker comes across a hellish scene of Allied soldiers queuing for sex with local young women, sent out by their starving families to sell themselves for cans of food. One especially beautiful girl has the longest queue, and a pile of cans. The scene condenses in his mind the horror of war on the ground: 'And this was the whole thing. You killed people with guns and machines, smashed homes to bits, and in the ruins you fucked hungry survivors in exchange for tins of meat. . . . Everything was floating, everything was sliding apart' (IWM, 187–8). In an attempt to anchor himself, he falls asleep reading *The Wind in the Willows*, including a passage from chapter two, 'The Open Road', where Toad, Rat and Mole finish their first day caravanning, 'tired and happy and miles from home'.[17] Toad joshes Rat for hankering after the riverbank, which he thinks about 'all the time' (IWM, 40). It is a scene of camaraderie (before Toad's first encounter with a motor-car) that forms an obvious contrast with Walker's own adventures away from the riverbank.

We are left to ponder the contrast. Is this innocent moment in a children's book simply an inadequate parallel? Or does it form a moral corrective of some sort? It certainly embodies the identity (rooted in his home) – and the moral rectitude – that Walker is losing. Rather than acting to stop the corruption, he returns to the scene in pursuit of the beautiful girl (whom he has idealised); but, finding her absent, 'in exchange for a tin of mackerel, he lost his virginity to someone else' (IWM, 200). *The Wind in the Willows* here stands for a rural English upbringing in which – whatever else one may think of it – overt inhumanity and exploitation are unthinkable. It is an 'unworldly' model that leaves Walker unprepared for the tests of war. Yet it also retains its capacity to comment on his career, and help fashion his psychological development.

One of his other horrifying experiences, earlier in North Africa – and a still worse atrocity – is the discovery of a sewer, within a gaol, dubbed 'the fish pond', and filled with prisoners left to rot (IWM, 113). These formative experiences come together in a dream of a woodland war scene, which includes Will's dead father, unable to speak, and in which '*The Wind in the Willows* was somehow involved' (IWM, 307). The woodland animals in the dream 'weren't like they were in the book'. Instead, they are 'disgusting, low to the ground', and Will 'needed to chase them'. Looking for 'information' and 'pattern' in the trees, he wakes up, feeling that the appearance of the book in his dream 'was particularly ridiculous and shaming'. Yet this shame mutates, and intensifies, 'as he remembered another part: he was back at the fish pond. The cover was off. With a kind of tingling pleasure he was dropping tins of food down to the shivering prisoners below, naked in their filth' (IWM, 307–8). Here *The Wind in the Willows* sparks a subconscious process of moral assertion. In the absence of paternal guidance, Walker identifies 'animal' behaviour to condemn; and he makes mental reparation for the two scenes of social and institutional horror, taking the tins of food out of the scene of prostitution and putting them to a better purpose in 'the fish pond', a gesture which is itself not unconnected with the simple beneficence of food in Grahame's tales of the riverbank. (A subterranean supper is planned around a tin of sardines when Rat and Mole return to 'Mole End', for example.[18])

The aspect of *In the Wolf's Mouth* that best locates Foulds's recurring preoccupations is the career of the shepherd Angilù Cassini, who becomes the right-hand man of Prince Adriano, helping to run his estate from 1926, when the Prince first encounters him, seeing him as the idealised embodiment of a shepherd, protecting his flock:

All shepherds were great, the true and ancient Sicily, classical Sicily. Someone had described Sicilian shepherds in a poem a long time ago. Angilù had shown great courage defending his flock against the bandits and it was the Prince's turn to do the same, to return from Palermo to protect his flock. Now that the Fascists were in power things would be different. (*IWM*, 20)

The vague classical allusion may be to the *Idylls* of Theocritus, or to Virgil's *Eclogues*, and it indicates a conservative cultural assumption of the value of pastoral literature per se, here appropriated for the Prince's own political ideology: the Fascists will supply the stability for a traditional social hierarchy to endure. When Cirò Albanese effects his disappearance, to escape the Fascists, Angilù is installed in the house he had occupied. In the closing chapters of the book, Albanese terrorises Angilù, in the hope of driving him out of the property. Angilù, realising that he is unlikely to be protected by the Allied forces on their mission of 'defascistification', resolves to shoot Albanese, which he does before being killed himself in reprisal (*IWM*, 320–1).

This conclusion re-emphasises the point that human actions are determined by larger historical forces. Particularly at fault is the crude Allied understanding of the political situation, which paves the way for the reassertion of Mafia power in Sicily. Foulds's larger idea, however, retrieves the idealism of classical pastoral, and that powerful enduring current in European literature, and in this respect *In the Wolf's Mouth* reveals further affinities with *The Quickening Maze*. Angilù, his vocation already compromised by Sicilian politics in the 1920s, and especially by the idealisation of Prince Adriano, which appropriates his life for an ideological schema, becomes the novel's major victim. This is especially so because Foulds hints at the value latent in the pastoral ideal, and in the elemental existence of Angilù outdoors in the novel's most poetic passages. Yet the nature he communes with is also the landscape in which he shoots a bandit in the opening scene, a scene of some kind of portentous Fall (*IWM*, 15).

Foulds's conscious attention to literary tradition begins with his appropriation of a central device of the sentimental novel in his first novel, and continues in *The Broken Word* with his thoughtful contribution to the twentieth-century tradition of colonial critique. In *The Quickening Maze* and *In the Wolf's Mouth*, Foulds taps into sources in both English and European literature, beginning a process of working through his literary inheritance in the elaboration of post-millennial themes of exile and deracination. This is an exemplary instance of a writer's development of T. S. Eliot's conviction about literary tradition: 'the conscious present is an awareness of the past'.[19] In the essay cited at the beginning of this chapter, Foulds explains his craft with reference to a roll call of European artists and writers – Picasso, Joyce, Flaubert, Waugh, Eliot himself – to show how the premise that description 'remakes the world' is always a matter of literary inheritance.[20]

NOTES

1. Adam Foulds, 'How to Write Fiction: Adam Foulds on Description with Meaning', *The Guardian*, 20 October 2011, <http://www.theguardian.com/books/2011/oct/20/how-to-write-fiction-adam-foulds> (last accessed 21 June 2016).
2. Thea Lenarduzzi, 'Left in Suspension' (review of *In the Wolf's Mouth*), *The Times Literary Supplement*, 7 February 2014, p. 19.
3. James Procter, entry on Foulds for the British Council: <http://literature.britishcouncil.org/adam-foulds> (last accessed 21 June 2016).
4. Adam Foulds, *The Truth about These Strange Times* (London: Weidenfeld & Nicolson, 2007), p. 281. All quotations are from this edition; hereafter, page numbers will be given in the text, preceded by TT.
5. Adam Foulds, *The Broken Word* (London: Jonathan Cape, 2008), p. 34. All quotations are from this edition; hereafter, page numbers will be given in the text, preceded by BW.
6. Adam Foulds, *The Quickening Maze* (London: Jonathan Cape, 2009), p. 216. All quotations are from this edition; hereafter, page numbers will be given in the text, preceded by QM.
7. Adam Foulds, 'Everywhere an Exile', *The Guardian*, 23 May 2009, <http://www.theguardian.com/books/2009/may/23/john-clare-poetry> (last accessed 21 June 2016). In his acknowledgements to *The Quickening Maze*, Foulds points out that he takes 'a number of liberties' with the historical record, 'compressing events that occurred over several years'. This seems to have concentrated his theme of home and exile.
8. Foulds, 'Everywhere an Exile'.
9. Ibid.
10. John Clare, 'Journey Out of Essex', in *Major Works*, ed. Eric Robinson and David Powell (Oxford: Oxford University Press, 2008), pp. 432–7 and p. 498; p. 432.
11. Ibid., p. 434.
12. Ibid., p. 498.
13. Rebecca Abrams, 'In the Wolf's Mouth, by Adam Foulds', *Financial Times*, 7 February 2014, <http://www.ft.com/cms/s/2/055e735e-8cc7-11e3-ad57-00144feab7de.html> (last accessed 21 June 2016).
14. Adam Foulds, *In the Wolf's Mouth* (London: Jonathan Cape, 2014), p. 179. All quotations are from this edition; hereafter, page numbers will be given in the text, preceded by IWM. The AMGOT (Allied Military Government of Occupied Territories) mission was to 'recreate all the complex services of a civilian administration'. Foulds's aim is to present a revisionist view to the contemporaneous understanding of how this operation functioned, where 'the general avoidance of disorder' was felt to have justified 'the selection and training of the Civil Affairs Officers now at work in Sicily'. See Peter Matthews, 'AMGOT Men', *The Spectator*, 26 August 1943, p. 6. Available at <http://archive.spectator.co.uk/article/27th-august-1943/6/amgot-men> (last accessed 21 June 2016).
15. See Foulds, *In the Wolf's Mouth*, pp. 40–1.
16. Valentine Cunningham shows the significance of Grahame's book to the cult of the rural in the 1930s. See *British Writers of the Thirties* (Oxford: Oxford University Press, 1988), p. 229.
17. Kenneth Grahame, *The Wind in the Willows*, illustrated by Ernest H. Shepard (London: Methuen & Co., 1954), p. 40.
18. Ibid., p. 117.
19. T. S Eliot, 'Tradition and the Individual Talent', in *Selected Essays* (London: Faber & Faber, 1932), pp. 13–22; p. 16.
20. Foulds, 'How to Write Fiction'.

FURTHER READING

For an up-to-date list of Adam Foulds's novels, see the British Council website: <https://literature.britishcouncil.org/writer/adam-foulds> (last accessed 21 June 2016).

Laing, Olivia, 'Adam Foulds: Writing Has Warped Me', *The Observer*, 10 May 2009, <http://www.theguardian.com/books/2009/may/10/adam-foulds-the-quickening-maze> (last accessed 21 June 2016).

Motion, Andrew, 'The Asylum in the Forest', *The Guardian*, 2 May 2009, <http://www.theguardian.com/books/2009/may/02/the-quickening-maze> (last accessed 21 June 2016).

Wood, James, 'Asylum: A Novel about the Poet John Clare', *The New Yorker*, 28 June 2010, <http://www.newyorker.com/magazine/2010/06/28/asylum-2> (last accessed 21 June 2016).

CHAPTER 14

Sarah Waters: Representing Marginal Groups and Individuals

Susana Onega

Sarah Waters is the author of six bestselling and prize-winning novels: *Tipping the Velvet* (1998), *Affinity* (1999), *Fingersmith* (2002), *The Night Watch* (2006), *The Little Stranger* (2009) and *The Paying Guests* (2014). Described by reviewers as lesbian fictions with metafictional, metahistorical and neo-Gothic traits, these novels display a striking generic hybridity, with elements of the sensation novel, the historical romance, the war novel, the London novel and the trauma novel, among others. Waters herself has acknowledged the influence of Dickens and of nineteenth-century 'gothic writers' like Wilkie Collins, Mary Shelley and the Brontës, alongside twentieth-century writers like John Fowles and A. S. Byatt, 'who were at the heart of a sort of postmodern return to Victorian life and fiction'. Angela Carter also had a big impact on her, and in addition her work evinces the influence of Virginia Woolf and other early feminist writers like Elizabeth Bowen and Elizabeth Taylor. These influences situate Waters as a feminist writer with a thematic focus on lesbianism and as a postmodernist writer of historiographic metafictions.[1]

A salient effect of feminist activism since the 1960s has been the appearance of feminist imprints of mainstream publishers, like Pandora Press, Virago Press and The Women's Press, and of radical/lesbian/women-of-colour-identified imprints such as Sheba Feminist Publishers, Onlywomen and Silver Moon Books.[2] This phenomenon facilitated the general public's access to fictions traditionally catering for marginal cultural groups that triggered the popularity of British writers like Alan Hollinghurst and Jeanette Winterson. Sarah Waters belongs in the generation after Winterson, together with 'contemporary writers like Stella Duffy, Ali Smith, Charlotte Mendelson and Joanna Briscoe'.[3] Unlike Winterson, who is placed in the 'posh' and 'exotic' lesbian trend associated with Radclyffe Hall, Djuna Barnes and Daphne du Maurier, Waters insists on the unexceptionality of herself and her work. Her fictions are highly readable historical romances aimed at decentring totalising perspectives on sexuality and gender by bringing to the fore not just the existence but the *normality* of homosexuality in a largely heterosexual world. Before becoming a writer, Waters taught literature at a university and wrote a PhD thesis on lesbian and gay historical fiction.[4] This would explain why her first three novels are neo-Victorian romances with a wealth of intertextual echoes to both canonical and popular texts. Indeed, her first three novels display a characteristically postmodernist combination of the high and the low, and the historical with the fictional, and blend the lesbian topos of coming-out with a coming-of-age quest structure saturated with picaresque and romance overtones, narrated retrospectively by the protagonists.

Given the focus of this volume, we will begin the analysis with *Fingersmith*, a bawdy lesbian picaresque intrigue that combines elements of the 'seduced and abandoned maiden' romance, the 'rags-to-riches tale', and the classical topos of the exchange or confusion of identical children. The narration alternates the retrospective soliloquies of the protagonists, Sue Trinket and Maud Lilly, addressed to each other. This fact allows them to compare the contradictory versions of their closely related pasts and, eventually, to discover that Sue, the thief apprentice raised by Mrs Sucksby at her 'baby farm', was in fact the daughter of Marianne Lilly, a seduced and abandoned gentlewoman; and that Maud was Mrs Sucksby's biological daughter. As Tom Gilling has noted, 'Sucksby is a shamelessly Dickensian name, and baby-farming an authentically Dickensian trade.'[5] This and Sue's mention of a theatrical performance of *Oliver Twist* point to the figure of Oliver as a literary model for Sue: both children are raised in a dreadful baby farm and become apprentice thieves.[6] But while Oliver's marginality is a question of temporary ill fortune that a benevolent Providence would eventually redress, Sue's fate was determined by her dying mother's ardent desire to protect her baby from her vindictive and pervert brother; and that of Maud by Grace Sucksby's prospect of making a gentlewoman of her daughter. However, by putting her in Mr Lilly's hands, she condemned Maud to a worse fate than that of Sue.

In the 'Notes' at the end of the novel, Waters acknowledges that Mr Lilly's library is based on that of Henry Spencer Ashbee, a wealthy Victorian gentleman, who 'became the first bibliographer of pornographic literature'.[7] But Mr Lilly's name and self-designed emblem also associate him with Angela Carter's Marquis in 'The Bloody Chamber', and so with the 'sex wars' between anti-censorship and anti-pornography feminists of the 1970s and 1980s.[8] In brief, anti-porn feminists argued that pornography represents or describes sexual behaviour that is degrading for at least one partner, and can lead to violence.[9] Anti-censorship feminists responded that pornography is a symptom, not the cause, of dysfunctional sexual relations in patriarchal societies, and that it can be rethought and liberated from the constraints imposed by the dominant ideology. This is the reforming task allotted by Carter to the 'moral pornographer': 'an artist who uses pornographic material as part of the acceptance of the logic of a world of absolute licence for all the genders, and projects a model of the way such a world might work'.[10] A similar moral aim lies behind Waters's depiction of Victorian London as a world of total corruption and greed organised to meet the sexual fantasies of dominant males. The physical and psychological punishments Mr Lilly systematically inflicts on Maud soon teach her to hide her feelings under a façade of meekness and imperturbability and to suppress her capacity for love and empathy, thus becoming a Sadeian woman: that utterly free, and therefore monstrous, type of woman Angela Carter imagined as the counterpart to the Marquis de Sade's sexually voracious and murderous statesmen and popes.[11] However, after meeting Sue, Maud discovers that there are alternatives to sadomasochism, and this discovery transforms her from Sadeian woman to moral pornographer, someone charged with the task of rethinking and liberating sexuality from all sorts of ideological constraints. This is why, after Mr Lilly's death, Maud destroys his library and begins writing a new type of pornography based on mutual *jouissance* and the abolition of inequality between subject and object of desire, which is a basic demand of feminism.

After her third neo-Victorian fiction, Waters decided to 'move in a slightly different direction'.[12] Her next two novels, *The Night Watch* and *The Little Stranger*, are situated in the 1940s, while *The Paying Guests* is set in 1922. That is, they are set in periods of crisis that brought about radical changes in class structures and gender roles. In *The Night Watch*, Waters sets 'lesbian culture at the hub of a broader cultural picture of the role played, during wartime, by the "illicit", either with regard to personal relationships or social activities'.[13] Accordingly, together with lesbians like Kay Langrey, Iris Carmichael ('Mickey'), Helen Giniver and Julia Cavendish, we find gays like Duncan Pearce and his 'uncle' Horace Mundy, and heterosexuals like Robert Fraser, or Viv Pearce and Reggie Negri. Some belong to the upper-middle class, like Kay, Julia and Robert, while others are working class, like Mickey, Viv and Duncan. Two served time in Wormwood Scrubs during the war: Robert, because he was a conscientious objector; and Duncan because he was a pacifist involved in the suicide of his gay lover. All these characters lead parallel lives in various areas of London until their paths cross, sometimes in decisive ways. For all their differences in social status, ideology, gender and sexual orientation, they share a traumatic memory of loss, and/or shame involving some form of deviance from patriarchal norms. This traumatic element and the general impression of collective stagnation and grief point to an evolution in Waters's writing towards trauma fiction, a generically hybrid and multifaceted type of novel combining realist, modernist and postmodernist traits with the excessiveness of the romance that has been steadily developing since the 1990s,[14] in response to the traumas of the Holocaust, the Vietnam War and other armed conflicts of our recent past.[15]

The Night Watch is divided into three sections, each containing various one-day chapters presented in reverse chronological order: the first section is situated in 1947, the second in 1944, and the third in 1941. The narration is carried out by an external author-narrator with access to the characters' actions and innermost thoughts, but with limited omniscience, as the events are focalised from the characters' perspectives and reported with minimal narratorial intervention. The text alternates italics with standard type to distinguish the characters' stream of consciousness from the narrator's comments in a free indirect style that is strongly reminiscent of Woolf's technique in *Mrs Dalloway*. The novel begins with Kay observing from her garret window the cripples who come for faith healing with her host, on the morning of a Tuesday in September 1947:

> *So this*, said Kay to herself, *is the sort of person you have become: a person whose clocks and wrist-watches have stopped, and who tells the time, instead, by the particular type of cripple arriving at her landlord's door.*
>
> For she was standing at her open window, in a collarless shirt and a pair of greyish underpants, smoking a cigarette and watching the comings and goings of Mr Leonard's patients.[16]

Like Clarissa Dalloway, Kay Langrey is upper-middle class, but while for the former the opening of the French window with which she begins the day is an experience of exhilaration and happiness that triggers fond memories of her youth at Bourton, for Kay – a traumatised middle-aged butch who lost her job and her lover at the end of the war – it only serves to provide her with incontestable evidence of the ailing condition of post-war Londoners.

In *Mrs Dalloway*, the narrator records the actions and thoughts of Clarissa along one day, using time montage to achieve chronological freedom and the possibility of intermingling Clarissa's memories with her thoughts about the present and the future, while she remains in the same space. Waters employs the same technique throughout the novel, as the events narrated in each chapter cover roughly one day from morning to night and are focalised from the perspective of a single character. However, unlike Woolf, Waters must portray the actions and thoughts of several characters existing simultaneously in various areas of London; that is, she has to spatialise time. And again, *Mrs Dalloway* provides the solution, this time in the form of space montage, a technique that allows for the space to change while the time remains static, thus giving an impression of simultaneity in the actions and thoughts of various characters. This effect was achieved by Woolf for the first time in the famous scene of the sky-writing plane, when five characters, including Mrs Dalloway, look up at the sky from different places and respond to the vision of the aeroplane in their own ways.[17] Waters creates an equivalent of this, for example, whenever various characters experience the bombing of London from different places, but she also uses space montage structurally by dividing each chapter into sections separated by a blank space to indicate a change of place and focaliser while the time remains the same. Thus, after Kay decides to close the window and start her daily walk, a blank space indicates the change of focalisation from her to Duncan and Mr Mundy, who are approaching the house. This change of perspective provides a new, sympathetic outlook on Kay, nicknamed 'Colonel Barker' by Mr Mundy, and introduces readers to the closeted gay couple formed by Duncan Pearce, an ex-convict, and his former prison guard at Wormwood Scrubs. A similar blank line and change of focalisation serve to introduce Viv and Helen, two middle-aged women who are working at a thriving dating agency in another part of London at the same time. Viv is Duncan's older sister and, ironically for a dating advisor, the long-time mistress of a married man, Reggie Negri. This is the secret she tries to preserve at all costs. The illegal relation has led Viv to a life-endangering, traumatic abortion that has revealed Reggie's callousness. The ambulance driver who makes a false report of miscarriage and puts her own wedding ring on Viv's finger to prevent her imprisonment is Kay, but neither Viv nor the readers know at this stage that the ring is the precious symbol of Kay's love for Helen.

Although Viv and Helen have been working together for more than a year, they know very little of each other's past. Any attempts at intimacy are invariably stopped by what Helen describes as Viv's sudden drawing of a '*curtain*' whenever 'she thought she had given away too much' (*NW*, 19). This reluctance to speak about the past is shared by every character, including Helen, for, if Viv cannot talk about her illicit affair and abortion, or the shame she feels for the imprisonment of her brother, neither can Helen tell Viv that her present partner, Julia Cavendish, a writer of detective novels and Kay's former lover, has initiated her into masochism and is driving her mad with jealousy, so that she has secretly started injuring herself (*NW*, 153–5).

Given the reverse chronological order of the novel, the reasons for the characters' secrets and traumas can only be gathered fragmentarily, through the accumulation of passing remarks or thoughts whose true significance does not become apparent until the end of the novel. Kaye Mitchell considers this backward chronology a 'temporal oddness' reflecting both the ghostliness and invisibility of the lesbian characters and 'the subversion (or *inversion*)' of 'queer temporality'.[18] She contends that, by putting both the homosexual and heterosexual characters 'into some kind of perpetual present' and denying them the possibility of making 'plans for some nominal future', Waters is asserting that 'queer temporalities prevail in wartime' and that lesbianism is 'paradigmatic', rather than 'a second-order sexuality'.[19] This interpretation is problematic in that it takes for granted the traditional association of queerness with trauma and ignores the fact that Kay does make plans for the future which conform to the heteronormative linearity of romance, marriage and childbearing: 'It was one of the tragedies of [Kay's] life, that she couldn't be like a man to Helen – make her a wife, give her children . . .' (*NW*, 326). Further, Mitchell's reading does not take into consideration Waters's remark that the key to the understanding of *The Night Watch* is that 'everybody in the book was engaged in illicit or clandestine activities' and that: 'Actually, I don't think of them as marginal people at all; I just think of them as perfectly ordinary people from the 1940s, but they happen to have these things going on in their lives.'[20]

Rather than the odd expression of queer temporality, the backward chronology of the novel may be said to reflect the belatedness of trauma, just as the immediacy, fragmentariness, repetitiveness and incompleteness of the narration mimic the structure of traumatic memory during the 'acting out' phase.[21] Only by realising that the form of the novel echoes the traumatised condition of a representative number of 'perfectly ordinary' Londoners living through the war can we gauge the true significance of the title. As Mr Leonard's fierce prayer sent out to London during his 'night watch' makes clear, the only way out of this never-ending acting out of trauma is that we 'learn to look away from perishable things' (*NW*, 169), deny the existence of evil and pain, and fill and surround ourselves with love. Whether this imaginative alternative to the suffering imposed on all sorts of trespassers by the ideological state apparatus is life-affirming and liberating or self-deluding and escapist is an issue for readers to decide.

Waters's fifth novel, *The Little Stranger*, is, like the first section of *The Night Watch*, situated in 1947, and also displays 'a wonderfully evoked atmosphere of postwar anxiety'.[22] But it takes place in rural Warwickshire, rather than London, and instead of following modernist models, it parodies the generic conventions of the Gothic historical romance, with overt intertextual allusions, for example, to *The Castle of Otranto*, *Jane Eyre*, *Great Expectations*, 'The Turn of the Screw', 'La Belle au bois dormant' and 'The Yellow Wall-Paper'. The novel tells the story of Hundreds Hall, a beautiful Georgian mansion, and the passing of its last owners: Roderick Ayres, his mother Mrs Ayres, and his sister Caroline. A key element of this Gothic subgenre is the uncanny feeling of its inhabitants that the haunted mansion is alive and is actively seeking their destruction. Echoing this, the supernatural phenomena seem to start spontaneously and take different forms depending on the intended victim, as if the house were responding to the fears, weaknesses and shameful secrets of each family member. The puzzle the novel sets is, therefore, what the reason might be for the house's determination to annihilate the remaining members of the Ayres dynasty at the cost of its own destruction.

The answer to this question is complicated by the unreliability of the narrator, Dr Faraday, a middle-aged GP who starts paying regular visits to the Hall after being called to attend to Betty, a teenaged parlour maid who has feigned an indisposition after undergoing an uncanny experience. Although Betty conforms to a centuries-long literary tradition of unhappy adolescent servants acting as catalysts for supernatural phenomena, the fact that she was forced into service by her father, in spite of her ardent wish to be a factory worker, establishes a significant parallelism between the rural aristocracy and their servants, two interdependent classes that were bound to disappear after the war due to the Welfare State reforms launched by Clement Attlee's Labour government. Roderick, the young master of Hundreds Hall, is the perfect embodiment of the extremely conservative ideology of the rural gentry: he served in the RAF during the war and returned to the Hall with a smashed knee, a badly scarred face and 'a touch of nervous trouble' provoked by survivor guilt, as he lost his navigator in the crash of the aircraft he piloted.[23] He becomes the victim of the first of a series of poltergeist attacks when he is dressing up for a party organised by his mother in honour of new neighbours, the Baker-Hydes. This family represents the upstart business class that had made a fortune during the war and was attempting to 'gentrify' itself by buying land (*LS*, 70). Mrs Ayres and Caroline's dismay at the boorishness of Mr Morley, a bachelor who had been seriously discussed as a possible match for Caroline, points to class bias as a precipitating agent for the supernatural phenomena. The Baker-Hydes' plan to acquire another Georgian mansion in the area is put to an abrupt end when Gyp, Caroline's dog, unexpectedly bites Gillian, the Baker-Hydes' little daughter, in the face.

After this, Roderick's nervous condition deteriorates and the poltergeist phenomena increase exponentially, to the distress of Mrs Ayres. Educated in the upper-class tradition of emotional dissimulation and secrecy, Mrs Ayres has been unable to mourn the death of her first daughter, Susan. She has blocked her feelings to the point of never pronouncing her name, so that Roderick and Caroline do not know they had an elder sister. However, Mrs Ayres has in fact transmitted her secret trauma to her children empathically, through her lovelessness and pregnant silences.[24] These contribute decisively to their feelings of inadequacy and shame, expressed in Roderick's case in the form of masochistic behaviour, and in Caroline's in aloofness and self-denial.

The novel ends with the distracted Dr Faraday roaming the derelict Hall three years after the extinction of the dynasty. Before that, his colleague Dr Seely had offered him a rational and a supernatural interpretation for the supernatural phenomena. The first was that 'Hundreds was, in effect, defeated by history, destroyed by its own failure to keep pace with a rapidly changing world' (LS, 498), and the second that it was 'consumed by some dark germ, some ravenous shadow creature, some "little stranger" spawned from the troubled unconscious of someone connected with the house itself' (LS, 498). Drawing on the rational explanation, Georges Letissier argues that the spectrality of the novel should be read in Derridean terms as the effect of history.[25] But the supernatural interpretation places Dr Faraday at centre stage, as he has a troubled conscience and is closely connected with the house. The son of a grocer's boy and a nursemaid who had worked at the Hall, Dr Faraday has made the difficult climb from the menial to the professional class and stands in an in-between social position that provokes in him mixed feelings of shame and guilt, expressed in an obsessive love-hate relationship with the mansion and its owners. Further, according to popular lore, the little stranger that haunted the Hall was female, 'the spirit of a servant-girl who was badly treated by a cruel master' (LS, 495). This suggests that the suppressed rage provoked by the pain of a maid (like Dr Faraday's mother) had been transmitted along successive generations of servants until it reached the declassed and obsessed narrator and transformed him into the unwitting catalyst of this collective rage. Thus, while the rational version signals history as the necessary agent of social change, the supernatural explanation explicitly connects the extinction of the rural gentry with the unrest of the servants. In Dr Faraday's proleptic words: 'After two hundred years, [the servants] had begun to withdraw their labour, their belief in the house; and the house was collapsing, like a pyramid of cards' (LS, 27).

Waters's sixth novel, The Paying Guests, takes readers from the aftermath of the Second World War to that of the First. Divided into three sections and narrated by an external narrator with fixed focalisation through the protagonist, it reads as a pastiche of 'the domestic novel', a deceptively transparent type of novel created by early feminist writers like Elizabeth Taylor, the author of shrewd but affectionate portrayals of middle-class and upper-middle-class English life, and Elizabeth Bowen, whose first novel, The Last Testament (1929), shows the characters attempting to live their lives in the aftermath of the First World War, while her later The Heat of Day (1948) provides an accurate expression of life in London during the Second.[26] Echoing this trend, The Paying Guests begins with a slow-moving and detailed description of the uneventful life of Frances Wray, a twenty-six-year-old middle-class spinster living with her mother in the family mansion in South London, in 1922. After the loss of her brothers, Noel and John Arthur, in the First World War, and the untimely death of her father, Frances renounced a fulfilling lesbian relation and the unprecedented autonomy gained by women during the war, in order to take care of her mother. This decision, prompted by her sense of duty, echoes that of Caroline Ayres when she complies with her mother's demand that she give up her career as a Wren and return to Hundreds Hall to nurse her ailing brother.

Mr Wray's disastrous attempt to imitate the thriving business class by 'putting the family money into one bad speculation after another' has left the family in a desperate financial position that Frances tries to solve by drastically reducing expenses, doing herself the exacting work of the absent servants and, finally, renting most of the upper floor to paying guests.[27] While in *The Little Stranger* the incompatibility of the Ayres and the Baker-Hydes is obvious from the start, in *The Paying Guests* the arrival of Lilian and Leonard Barber, a modern young couple of the 'clerk class', is perceived by Frances simply as a partial renunciation of her privacy and an alteration of her routine, as well as a source of amusement, for, as she tells her ex-lover Christina, the news of having the Barbers as paying guests would 'cause a stir in Champion Hill', where being reduced to taking in lodgers is all but unheard of (PG, 46). However, the exotic lifestyle and shocking behaviour of the Barbers soon start having ever more acute transformative effects on Frances. What at first seem minor disturbances of her orderly life soon become transgressive and shocking occurrences that take the repressed lesbian spinster to situations beyond her control: Mrs Barber's charm and sex-appeal are difficult to resist and the friendship she offers Frances soon turns into unrestrained passion. But by falling in love with a married woman she knows nothing about, Frances initiates a journey that will end with her collaboration in two ghastly criminal acts: Lilian's (second) abortion and Leonard's murder. Thus, Frances will discover in herself a degree of energy and resourcefulness and a capacity for secrecy and deceit she had never thought she had. Her metamorphosis is accomplished during the murder trial, when she discards the values that had cost the lives of her two brothers and the apoplexy of her father, 'brought on by reading something he disagreed with in *The Times*' (PG, 84), in the realisation that 'They [the jury] had no idea how decency, loyalty, courage, how it all shrivelled away when one was frightened' (PG, 561).

At this stage, Frances is placed in the dilemma of either keeping silent, to save Lilian and herself, or confessing the truth, to save the life of Spencer Ward, a boorish boy accused of Leonard's murder. At the last minute, however, Spencer's innocence is proved by a reluctant witness, a war veteran who teaches Frances an ethical lesson by choosing to testify at the cost of his badly needed job (PG, 559). This and the fact that the novel ends with Frances giving up the idea of committing suicide and contemplating a happy future with Lilian (PG, 564) deprives her Darwinian metamorphosis of a dramatic climax, suggesting that her adaptation to the new times and mores means exchanging the middle-class values of duty and honour for the relentless self-interest and pursuit of pleasure of the new moneyed class. Though Frances's expectations of happiness might be illusory, given Lilian's waywardness and egotism, the very fact that Frances is able to change provides an optimistic alternative to the tragic end of Miss Margaret Prior in *Affinity*, thus rounding off Waters's portrayal of lesbianism in the nineteenth and twentieth centuries.[28]

NOTES

1. See Linda Hutcheon, *A Poetics of Postmodernism: History, Theory, Fiction* (London: Routledge, 1988), p. 5.
2. See Simone Murray, *Mixed Media: Feminist Presses and Publishing Politics* (London: Pluto Press, 2004), pp. 4–5.
3. Robert McCrum, 'What Lies Beneath', *The Observer*, 10 May 2009, <http://www.guardian.co.uk/books/2009/may/10/books-sarah-waters> (last accessed 22 June 2016).
4. Sarah Ann Waters, 'Wolfskins and Togas: Lesbian and Gay Historical Fictions, 1870 to the Present', PhD thesis, Queen Mary and Westfield College, University of London, 1995, <https://masterofants.files.wordpress.com/2013/09/393332.pdf> (last accessed 22 June 2016).
5. Tom Gilling, '*Fingersmith*: An Alternative Dickensian Fiction', *New York Times*, 24 February 2002, <http://www.nytimes.com/2002/02/24/books/review/24GILLINT.html> (last accessed 22 June 2016).
6. Sarah Waters, *Fingersmith* (2002; London: Virago, 2003), p. 3.
7. Kathleen Frederickson, 'Victorian Pornography and the Laws of Genre', *Literature Compass*, 8.5 (2000), 304–12; 304.
8. For Mr Lilly's name and emblem, see Waters, *Fingersmith*, p. 218. For a fuller discussion of *Fingersmith*, see Susana Onega, 'Pornography and the Crossing of Class, Gender and Moral Boundaries in Sarah Waters' *Fingersmith*', *Études britanniques contemporaines*, 48 (2015), 1–11; 4. Published online on 23 March 2015, <http://ebc.revues.org/2053> (last accessed 22 June 2016).
9. See Robin Morgan, *Going Too Far: The Personal Chronicle of a Feminist* (London: Vintage, 1978).
10. Angela Carter, *The Sadeian Woman* (1979; London: Virago, 1992), p. 19.
11. Ibid., p. 27.
12. Abigail Dennis, '"Ladies in Peril": Sarah Waters on Neo-Victorian Narrative Celebrations and Why She Stopped Writing about the Victorian Era', *Neo-Victorian Studies*, 1.1 (Autumn 2008), 41–52; 51.
13. Lucie Armitt, 'Interview with Sarah Waters (CWWN Conference, University of Wales, Bangor, 22 April 2006)', *Feminist Review*, 85 (2007), 'Political Hystories', 116–27; 122.
14. On the generic hybridity and thematic complexity of contemporary trauma fiction, see Michael Rothberg, *Traumatic Realism: The Demands of Holocaust Representation* (Minneapolis and London: University of Minnesota Press, 2000), and Jean-Michel Ganteau and Susana Onega, *Contemporary Trauma Narratives: Liminality and the Ethics of Form* (London and New York: Routledge, 2014).
15. See Jean-Michel Ganteau and Susana Onega, *Ethics and Trauma in Contemporary British Fiction* (Amsterdam and New York: Rodopi, 2011).
16. Sarah Waters, *The Night Watch* (2006; London: Virago, 2009), p. 3. All quotations are from this edition; hereafter, page numbers will be given in the text, preceded by NW.
17. See Cornelia Klecker's analysis of time and space montage in *Mrs Dalloway* and in Stephen Daldry's film version of Michael Cunningham's *The Hours*, another possible intertext of *The Night Watch*: Cornelia Klecker, 'Time- and Space-Montage in *Mrs Dalloway* and *The Hours*', *Swiss Papers in English Language and Literature*, 26 (2011), 209–23. Available at <http://dx.doi.org/10.5169/seals-283973> (last accessed 22 June 2016).
18. Kaye Mitchell, '"What does it feel like to be an anachronism?": Time in *The Night Watch*', in Mitchell (ed.), *Sarah Waters* (London and New York: Bloomsbury, 2013), pp. 84–98; pp. 86–7.
19. Ibid., p. 86.
20. Armitt, 'Interview with Sarah Waters', p. 122.

21. See Cathy Caruth, *Trauma: Explorations in Memory* (Baltimore and London: Johns Hopkins University Press, 1995), pp. 4–5.
22. Scarlett Thomas, 'House Calls', *New York Times*, 29 May 2009, <http://www.nytimes.com/2009/05/31/books/review/Thomas-t.html?pagewanted=all> (last accessed 22 June 2016).
23. Sarah Waters, *The Little Stranger* (2009; London: Virago, 2010), pp. 34, 22. All quotations are from this edition; hereafter, page numbers will be given in the text, preceded by *LS*.
24. See Onega, Susana, 'Class Trauma, Shame and Spectrality in Sarah Waters's *The Little Stranger*', unpublished paper read at the Conference: 'Acts of Remembrance in Contemporary Narratives in English: Opening the Past for the Future', Dept. of English and German Philology, University of Zaragoza (Spain) 24-26 April 2013. In *Traumatic Memory and the Ethical, Political and Transhistorical Function of Literature*, Palgrave Studies in Cultural Heritage and Conflict Series, ed. Susana Onega, Constanza del Río and Maite Escudero (Basingstoke: Palgrave Macmillan, forthcoming).
25. See Georges Letissier, 'Hauntology as Compromise between Traumatic Realism and Spooky Romance in Sarah Waters's *The Little Stranger*', in Jean-Michel Ganteau and Susana Onega (eds), *Trauma and Romance in Contemporary British Literature* (London and New York: Routledge, 2013), pp. 34–50; p. 38.
26. See Rachel Cusk, '*The Paying Guests* by Sarah Waters (review)', *The Guardian*, 15 August 2014, <http://www.theguardian.com/books/2014/aug/14/paying-guests-sarah-waters-review-satire-costume-drama> (last accessed 22 June 2016).
27. Sarah Waters, *The Paying Guests* (London: Virago, 2014), p. 84. All quotations are from this edition; hereafter, page numbers will be given in the text, preceded by *PG*.
28. The research carried out for the writing of this chapter is part of a project financed by the Spanish Ministry of Economy and Competitiveness (MINECO) (code FFI2015-65775-P). The author is also grateful for the support of the Government of Aragón and the European Social Fund (ESF) (code H05).

FURTHER READING

For an up-to-date list of Sarah Waters's novels, see the British Council website: <https://literature.britishcouncil.org/writer/sarah-waters> (last accessed 22 June 2016).

Arias, Rosario, 'Female Confinement in Sarah Waters's Neo-Victorian Fiction', in Jan Alber and Frank Lauterbach (eds), *Stones of Law, Bricks of Shame: Narrating Imprisonment in the Victorian Age* (Toronto: University of Toronto Press, 2009), pp. 256–77.

Doan, Laura, and Sarah Waters, 'Making Up Lost Time: Contemporary Lesbian Writing and the Invention of History', in David Alderson and Linda Alderson (eds), *Territories of Desire in Queer Culture: Refiguring Contemporary Boundaries* (Manchester: Manchester University Press, 2000), pp. 12–28.

Mitchell, Kaye (ed.), *Sarah Waters* (London and New York: Bloomsbury, 2013).

Waters, Sarah, '"A Girton Girl on a Throne": Queen Christina and Versions of Lesbianism, 1906–1933', *Feminist Review*, 46 (Spring 1994), 41–60.

Wormald, Mark, 'Prior Knowledge: Sarah Waters and the Victorians', in Rod Mengham and Philip Tew (eds), *British Fiction Today* (New York and London: Bloomsbury, 2006), pp. 186–97.

CHAPTER 15

James Robertson: In the Margins of History

Cairns Craig

The action of James Robertson's *The Fanatic* (2000) is split between 1997, in the weeks before the Labour Party's election victory that led to the establishment of a Scottish parliament, and the seventeenth century when, in the 1670s, James Mitchel is tried and executed for the attempted assassination of Archbishop Sharp, betrayer of the principles of the Scottish Covenant.[1] The two periods are linked by Andrew Carlin, a former history student so ghostlike in appearance that he is asked to perform in a 'ghost tour' of Edinburgh's Old Town, playing Major Weir, an associate of Mitchel's who was executed for incest and diabolism in 1670. Carlin becomes obsessed with understanding Mitchel, one who had the opportunity to make history – 'Now is Mitchel's time, now he is *in* history' (*TF*, 138) – but failed. 'History betrays him' (*TF*, 138). Carlin's obsession is mirrored in the seventeenth-century scenes by John Lauder, who is desperate to understand the 'fanaticism' that drives someone like Mitchel to the gallows for his faith. Doing research on the period, Carlin uncovers 'a secret book' supposedly written by Lauder, which brings him so close to the events of the past he feels 'It's like the past isna past. It's right there happenin in front o me' (*TF*, 52). Before Carlin can finish Lauder's book, however, both the book and the librarian who provided it disappear, leaving no record of their existence. The history which Robertson's novel recounts may seem very real, but it is based either on absent textual evidence (even though the novel shows Lauder beginning to write his 'secret book' (*TF*, 287)) or, as in the case of Weir, on a surfeit of textual evidence known to have been invented for propaganda purposes: the narrative veers between characters like Mitchel, who fail to make their mark on history, and other characters like Weir, who go down in history so wreathed in interminglings of the speculative and the supernatural – many of them gathered in Robertson's own collection of *Scottish Ghost Stories* (1996) – that 'historical truth' is impossible to establish.

The Fanatic sets in conjunction a seventeenth-century Scotland in which religious commitment made possible the survival of the national church and, therefore, the survival of the nation after its 'incorporating union' with England in 1707, and a twentieth-century Scotland that is waking from a long period of being apparently without history but, by the re-establishment of its parliament, may be about to reassert an independent national narrative. Carlin, like modern Scotland, 'looks like he's been wandering around there for centuries trying to find a way out' (*TF*, 149), while Mitchel regards his life in history as only of symbolic significance, for after

> his trial and death, for *not* having killed the Archbishop, did this not show God's people the true spirit of their enemies in an even harsher light? God was ... about to do James Mitchel the greatest honour, and raise him up as upon a cross. It was the most a true Christian could hope for. (*TF*, 290)

Mitchel's execution proves that he has been God's instrument in 'an age when Scotland had been smiled on by God' (*TF*, 290), while Carlin is haunted by his childhood experience of Pieter Brueghel's 'Triumph of Death', with its 'total absence of hope; the total lack of either God or reason' (*TF*, 195). Mitchel's sense of 'election', retrospectively justifying his every action, contrasts with Carlin's failure to vote in the election of 1997: Carlin is the ghostly absence of narrative in a country that sells fragments of its past to tourists and waits to have its fate decided elsewhere – 'He inhabited his days like a man in a dream, or like a man in other people's dreams' (*TF*, 22).

The double structure of *The Fanatic* is built around a crisis that Robertson had analysed in his doctoral thesis on 'The Construction and Expression of Scottish Patriotism in the Works of Walter Scott' (1988), which argued that Scott created a version of *Scottish* patriotism that was contained safely in the past so that it would not conflict with the *British* patriotism of a Scotland now committed to Union and Empire. Scott had made Scottish history famous by, effectively, bringing it to an end, confining it to the era when 'passion', rather than 'prudential reason', ruled men's actions. This Scott-inspired version of Scotland had, by the 1980s, come into conflict with the unanticipated rise of Scottish nationalism, a nationalism which its critics declared to be a regression to the world of passion but which nonetheless opened up the possibility of alternative versions of Scotland's future. *The Fanatic* is located in the interstices between possible Scotlands – Carlin is 'a man that might slip between worlds, if such a thing were possible' (*TF*, 22) – but also in the interstices between literature and modes of historical writing that had been revealed by postmodernist theories such as Hayden White's *Metahistory* (1973) to be governed, however unconsciously, by literary genres. As the librarian who provides Carlin with Lauder's narrative (before disappearing and taking the text with him) warns him: 'What's real, Mr Carlin? We say history's real. It really happened. But we can't prove it. We can't touch it. All we have is hearsay and handed down stories and a lot of paper that somebody else tells us is the genuine article' (*TF*, 197).

But if the text of history turns into literature, do the texts of literature point to truths to which history is blind? It is a possibility that Robertson envisaged when, in the introduction to *Scottish Ghost Stories*, he noted that although 'I am . . . highly sceptical of that kind of absolute certainty which categorically denies there can be any such thing as a ghost', it nonetheless may be 'that reason and science are not the keys to every locked door; it may be that our ancestors had access to doors now locked and bolted to all but a few of us'.[2] The 'ghost' opens a door which empirical, realist narrative does not know exists and points to possibilities that are excluded by the mode in which modern history is written. Robertson's novels develop out of this haunted nexus of intersecting concerns about the reality of Scotland's history – 'an unreal picture of an unreal country' (*TF*, 25); about how literature and history intertwine and undermine one another – 'lurid tales of witchcraft and Satanism, it seemed, had been spread like a coverlet over the truth' (*TF*, 39); and about the possibility of truthful supernatural tale – 'because you lost sight of ghosts did not mean they had gone' (*TF*, 75).

The ghost which inspires Robertson's second novel, *Joseph Knight* (2003),[3] is Scottish historiography's lack of acknowledgement that the profits of slavery fuelled the country's industrial development.[4] Robertson explores this issue in a narrative set in motion by the 1745 Jacobite Rebellion and insistently contrasted with Walter Scott's version of those events in *Waverley* (1814). Waverley was 'out' with the Jacobites but, through the conventions of romance, is allowed to evade the loss of liberty and property such rebellion normally incurred. In *Joseph Knight*, John Bellenden was also 'out' with his Jacobite father at Culloden but loses everything and has to flee to Jamaica, where, after his father's execution, he and his brother James restore the family fortunes as owners of a slave plantation. The black magic of money achieves for them what the white magic of romance does for Waverley. In Waverley's home is a painting of himself as a Jacobite – 'the scene a wild, rocky, and mountainous pass, down which the clan were descending in the background'[5] – which symbolises how his Jacobite past is now aesthetically contained and separated from his British present, leaving it like 'a dream, strange, horrible, and unnatural'.[6] Bellenden's escape is equally a 'dream-like flight' (*JK*, 50), and while Waverley, as his name implies, is a man 'blown about by every wind of doctrine',[7] Bellenden hesitates over the execution of a rebellious slave – ironically named Charlie – and is told by his brother James, 'Do not waver. I can read you like a book. If you waver you will lose everything' (*JK*, 125). In Bellenden's restored home in Scotland there is also a prominent painting, one of himself and his brothers in Jamaica, painted by the one brother not represented, Sandy, whose diary of life in Jamaica Bellenden keeps as a memento of the brother who did not make it back, despite the fact its contents disgust him. The painting is only allowed to remain in Bellenden's Scottish home, however, because of what has been blacked out in it – the figure of the slave, Joseph Knight, whom Sir John had brought back from Jamaica. The 'history' which the painting records has been reshaped to match the absence of Joseph Knight from the household, a black slave who won his freedom in a Scottish court and then disappeared, out of sight, out of history, though in the final section of the novel he is discovered working among the miners in Fife who had themselves only just been legally released from serfdom.

Bellenden is a man trapped in the double narrative of Robertson's account of Scott's patriotism: he is haunted by the Jacobitism for which his father was executed, has married the daughter of the commander under whom his father served at Culloden, and retains as a servant the drummer boy, Aeneas McRoy, who retrieved and kept the company's flag through the years of Bellenden's exile. His inner world is the world of the lost cause, each year interleaved with a series of days of commemoration of past events. The house that he has restored as the family home has been chosen, however, because its situation recalls the house he built in Jamaica, and his Scottish home cannot be complete without the black servant whose kindly treatment would have advertised the progress that wealth makes possible. The immediate impulse behind Bellenden's return to Scotland was a slave rebellion that seemed to him 'like a throwback to another age, a re-enactment of events that should have been consigned to history' (JK, 167), but the return to the homeland is equally a defiance of the expected narrative of history:

> But like the hero in a fairy tale, he could not pass from the unreal to the real (if that is where he was going) without taking with him a token. It would serve as a reminder of where he had been, and what had happened there. It would mark the source of the riches that would continue to flow across the Atlantic and feed his third life. (JK, 167)

Joseph Knight is the 'token', a man who is a mere symbol in someone else's narrative. These double narratives of loss and recovery come into destructive conflict when McRoy and Knight both want to marry the same servant, provoking Joseph's flight and his court case. Bellenden's subsequent and increasingly desperate efforts to find out what has happened to Joseph is also a desperate attempt to re-establish the orderly progression of the history to which he has now committed himself.

The action of *Joseph Knight* takes place in the period of the Scottish Enlightenment, when Scotland's major thinkers – Hume, Smith, Ferguson – developed the stadial theory of a progressive history. In recent times, however, the 'progressiveness' of that Enlightenment account has been challenged by frequent citation of a footnote in Hume's essay 'Of National Characters', in which he suggests that 'there is some reason to think, that all the nations, which live beyond the polar circles or between the tropics, are inferior to the rest of the species',[8] to which he adds, 'I am apt to suspect the negroes to be naturally inferior to the whites. There scarcely ever was a civilised nation of that complexion, nor even any individual eminent either in action or speculation.'[9] Robertson has James Boswell and Samuel Johnson debate this view with prominent Scots over Boswell's dinner table (JK, 181) in 1773. None of them supports Hume's speculation but the narrative of *Joseph Knight* underlines how Scotland's Enlightenment was built on darkness, whether the conditions of the plantation slaves or the blackness of the Fife colliers, and was built on the erasure of narratives, like Knight's, whose life in Africa 'was the beginning of a story that had never happened' (JK, 347). For Bellenden, Knight's life had 'been a journey out of darkness into light' (JK, 276), but for Knight it is a journey between darknesses, a journey unenlightened by the narrative of history. The irony is that the slaveowner is equally trapped by the failure of 'a story that had never happened': to Bellenden,

'Knight was like Culloden – a knot in time he could not untie but could not leave alone' (JK, 277).

For Gideon Mack, the protagonist of Robertson's third novel, *The Testament of Gideon Mack* (2006),[10] Walter Scott's presentation of Scottish history is no less the 'knot in time' which he cannot untie. Gideon, a son of the manse at a time when the Church is becoming as irrelevant to contemporary Scotland as a Walter Scott novel – 'In 1960 the church's pews were all full; by 1970 they were more than half-empty. My father, the Reverend James Mack, stood like a breakwater in the ebb of the decade' (*TGM*, 51) – takes to reading Scott in defiance of his father's contempt for literature: 'My schoolmates were listening agog to *Sergeant Pepper*: I was reading *The Antiquary* (*TGM*, 62). His father, however, secretly follows his son's reading and is able to inform him of the falsity of Scott's conception of history:

> 'He gave a wrong view of history,' my father said. 'A learned and godly man called Thomas McCrie exposed him when he defamed the Covenanters in *Old Mortality*, but McCrie was a minister and people thought him a humourless spoilsport.' He sniffed, his equivalent of a dry laugh. 'Scott had already turned the heads of too many silly women and romantically minded boys with his kind of history. . . . It is a great danger of romance: too many people succumb to it, and forget the one true Author.' (*TGM*, 93)

Gideon feels doubly cheated by his father's condescension – 'This was infuriating. I had waded through millions of Scott's words, and he, who had flicked through a few pages, was telling me that I had been taken for a ride. A *harmless* ride at that' (*TGM*, 93) – and yet, unable to make a decision about his own future (in the 1979 referendum for a Scottish Assembly he votes both 'yes' and 'no'), he will later decide to follow in his father's footsteps and become a minister, even though he has no belief in God. This displacement of himself for the continuation of his father's narrative also results in his stepping aside from his own person to mimic literary characters: thus when he has to deliver a sermon to achieve a church appointment, he models himself on Chris Guthrie's second husband, Robert Colquohoun, out of Lewis Grassic Gibbon's *A Scots Quair*, a book he had 'recently finished reading' (*TGM*, 135). Gideon's subsequent appointment proves that living as literature makes him one of the elect, released from the burden of living, and choosing, as himself.

Gideon has, however, glimpsed a possible alternative narrative in his father's life when he discovers in his library Robert Kirk's *The Secret Commonwealth Elves, Fauns and Fairies*, 'an incongruous item' (*TGM*, 91), which his father sets aside by telling his son that although Kirk was a minister in the 1680s,

> 'In his day superstition and religion still walked side by side. People believed that there was a land under the earth, where the fairies live. Not flittery things like Tinker Bell in *Peter Pan*,' he said, betraying a literary knowledge I hadn't suspected, 'but dwarfish, devilish, thieving folk who could do you great harm.' (*TGM*, 90)

Kirk's book gestures to an alternative reality, one that has been reduced from the claim of supernatural knowledge to mere literary fiction. For Gideon, however, who has taken to living through literature, it can become again real – a door into that ancestral otherworld which is 'locked and bolted to all but a few of us'.[11] It is a door that will open to Gideon when he reads a story by his nineteenth-century predecessor, Augustus Menteith, about 'the Legend of the Black Jaws', in which the ravine carved by the River Keldo is the setting for an encounter with the devil. As though guided by the story, Gideon falls into the Black Jaws, is assumed dead, but reappears to claim that he has been saved by an encounter with the devil; like the Walter Scott heroes who belong to the prudential present but are attracted by the passionate past, Gideon quite literally falls into a narrative that has no place in the modern world:

> O tempora! O mores! Oh holy shit! In the seventeenth century a minister who claimed to have seen and spoken with Satan in the flesh would have been not only believed but, assuming he had given a good account of himself, hailed a hero. In the twenty-first century such a minister is simply an embarrassment. I am not the face the Kirk wishes to show to the modern world. (TGM, 36)

The modern Kirk renounces the seventeenth-century Kirk (both the Church and the author) which made its existence possible, leaving it without purpose in a world where the Devil is no longer believed real: 'There was no plan any more. That was what I had learned in my three days with the Devil. There was no plan. There was no redemption, no salvation, no system of debts and payments. But there was another life' (TGM, 342). 'Another life' – the one to which Robert Kirk's book points, a life beyond the story we call history.

Meeting a devil that can no longer be accepted as real echoes the plot of James Hogg's *The Private Memoirs and Confessions of a Justified Sinner* (1824) and the final judgement by its 'editor' that 'with the present generation, it will not go down that a man should be daily tempted by the devil'.[12] Robertson's novel replicates the structure of Hogg's, the 'testament' being preceded by an introduction written by the publisher-editor and containing the known 'facts' of the case, and followed by a conclusion which provides testimonies by some of those who had known Gideon. The structural parallel with Hogg's novel underlines both the literariness of Robertson's novel and the implication that there are certain kinds of experience marginalised by history which can now only be encountered through literature – Gideon's initials, GM, are those of the devil in Hogg's text, Gil-Martin,[13] and also those of the 'friend' who gave Gideon's father a copy of Robert Kirk's book. The novel is, therefore, necessarily full of textual echoes: not only, as Timothy Baker has pointed out, does Gideon's meeting with the devil echo the confrontation between Balfour and Burley at the climax of Scott's *Old Mortality*,[14] but the place chosen for his death is on Ben Alder, where Alan Breck and David Balfour were on the run in Stevenson's *Kidnapped*; and in the cave where he meets the devil, Gideon, like Alasdair Gray's Lanark,[15] discovers 'a door' which he thinks a possible 'way out' but is, in fact, only a door into hell (TGM, 291), while the evidence of Gideon's meeting with the devil will be, as in James Kelman's *How Late It Was, How Late*, a pair of old trainers,[16] and Gideon's life after death is declared, like Peter Pan's in Neverland, 'an awfully big adventure'.[17]

Having thus recreated a modern version of a nineteenth-century Scottish classic, Robertson structured his next novel, *And the Land Lay Still* (2010),[18] on the book from which Gideon had taken his character as a minister, Lewis Grassic Gibbon's *A Scots Quair* (1932–4). Gibbon's trilogy is an epic of Scotland's development from an agricultural to an industrial society, set in the first third of the twentieth century; Robertson's is an epic of modern Scotland that recounts its journey from the Second World War, fighting for British values, to the establishment of the Scottish Parliament in 1999. And just as Gibbon invented a narrative style in which his central character addresses herself as 'you' – 'You hated the land and coarse speak of the folk'[19] – so the voice we first encounter in *And the Land Lay Still*, in an untitled prologue, addresses itself as 'you':

> *And in the days of early summer you might walk on through the empty hours if there was enough light and you weren't tired. So you walked and you were alone, and later you'd lie down to rest, to sleep in the sun you'd once toiled and starved below.* (ALLS, 1)

We do not initially know who the speaker is: the voice is interleaved between each of the novel's parts and is gradually revealed as Jack Gordon's – 'Mad Uncle Jack' to his nephew James – who was a prisoner of the Japanese in the war, and who has disappeared, abandoning his wife and child and leaving his friend, Don, another war veteran, haunted by his absence. Jack's spectral voice, representative of all the voices lost in war, is a ghostly chorus to the action. This is a narrative structure deeply embedded in twentieth-century Scottish novels – the confrontation between a destructive but apparently historically significant life beyond Scotland, and a domestic environment without significance in the narrative of progressive history. Jack cannot escape his experiences in the Second World War but cannot live through the insignificance of his daily domestic routine in its aftermath.[20] He recognises himself in the Japanese soldier who emerges belatedly from the jungle – a fellow creature 'who had continued to live in a world that no longer existed', one who was 'somewhere else, on another journey that had nothing to do with him, nothing to do with anybody' (ALLS, 376). Jack has escaped out of history to become part of the natural world – 'like the snow, you melted into the landscape' (ALLS, 377).

The antithesis of Jack's historylessness is his nephew, originally named James Bond but who renames himself Peter to avoid comparison with Sean Connery's film character. Peter becomes a minor cog in British intelligence; he is, however, released, but believes himself also retained, a diminished version of Britain's greatest spy, working undercover in Scotland for the British government – 'ghost territory' (ALLS, 283), as his handler describes it – and keeping an eye on the nationalists who might threaten the Union. Trapped between fiction and reality, Bond becomes the collector and disseminator of all the false narratives by which history is distorted to ensure that power remains with those who already hold it – 'power devolved is power retained', in Enoch Powell's much-quoted formulation. Bond is swamped by narratives that may or may not be false, always on the verge of breaking through to a truth that continually evades him. At one point he accidentally overhears a question and answer session with a famous Scottish author:

> Somebody from the audience asked him why he set his books in Italy, France, America and England, but not in Scotland. The writer stroked his chin. Because nothing happens here. The centres of activity, the places where decisions are made, where politics and personalities collide, are elsewhere. London, New York, Paris, Rome. Anywhere but this quiet backwater. (*ALLS*, 244)

And the Land Lay Still presents a country whose history has moved undramatically into a future very different from its past, but does so by recapitulating many of the archetypal structures of earlier Scottish novels. Between Don's two sons, the ironically named Billy and Charlie, there is the conflict of the fearless and the fearful that goes back to George Douglas Brown's *The House with the Green Shutters* (1900); Charlie's child, conceived in brutality, will be brought up by Ellen and her partner Robin, an Englishman for whom 'not being her natural father was not an issue' (*ALLS*, 509), repeating a narrative trope in many recent Scottish writings such as Jackie Kay's *The Adoption Papers* (1991) and Anne Donovan's *Buddha Da* (2003); while Ellen and Robin's relationship also gestures back to all those Scottish heroines – like Walter Scott's Jeanie Deans in *The Heart of Midlothian* – whose marriage to Englishmen was a symbol of the Union. Those relationships now point, however, in a different direction. After the death of Don's wife, he meets again and marries the English nurse who was present at the birth of his son; attending an exhibition of Angus Pendreich's photography, curated by his son Mike, she looks on at the singing of Scottish folk songs and thinks, 'Sometimes the songs are about battles or feuds or murders, and sometimes, as now, they're about the road, and there are occasions when it all seems horribly sentimental to Marjory but it's also what she loves about the land and its people, the clannishness that stretches and twists back into history, the deep-rootedness of it' (*ALLS*, 658).

Robertson's novel twists and turns between the processes of history and a land which seems out of history, both because it is unrecognised by history – merely shadowing an English narrative – and because, in its 'stillness', it is untouched by historical change. Don, looking at one of Angus's pictures captioned as STRATHALLAN GAMES, AUGUST 1966, sees 'white-legged, mud-streaked, wiry men' who 'could be medieval peasants running straight out of history towards the lens' (*ALLS*, 665). The novel's outcome turns on Angus Pendreich's photographs – 'stills' – which manage to capture what is marginal to the news narratives of events, but to make the marginal a commentary on what has been lost in the main narrative. Looking at Angus's photographs of the Trafalgar Square riots in 1990, his son realises that he had not 'gone soft, sold out, missed the point' but that by focusing on the fringes of the action, a unique vision of the world – 'the Angus Angle' – had been produced, as the marginal events of time are transformed into the eternity of art. *And the Land*

Lay Still aims at a similar transformation. Angus's former girlfriend Jean Barbour, a teller of folktales, will tell Mike 'to trust the story' (*ALLS*, 128), and Jack's story will be revealed when he is accidentally caught in one of Angus's photographs: the permanent stillness of the image takes it out of history, suspended between Jack's flight from history and Peter Bond's drowning in it. That image will also reveal to Mike Pendreich an unacknowledged narrative in which he and the characters whom he had assumed to be marginal to his own life are all connected in a story very different from the one they believed themselves to be living through.

When Peter Bond, whose narrative is rendered in ragged rather than justified type to underline just how marginal it is, visits the site of the Pan Am plane crash at Lockerbie in 1988, he is staggered by what he finds: the invasion of Scottish space by others' narratives that underline how little of its history Scotland actually controls. As is often the case with Robertson, a moment in one novel becomes the basis of the next: in *The Professor of Truth* (2013), Alan Tealing's house has become a library of all the evidence he can collect about the downing of the plane in which his wife and daughter had been flying to the United States. His house teems with alternative narratives of recent history: when the death is announced of Khalil Khazar, the supposed perpetrator of the bombing, 'There would be tears I knew, but also there would be laughter . . . A guilty man or an innocent man had gone to his grave: it depended on your perspective.[21] We are in a world where narrative runs riot, as unfettered from the reality it seeks to explain as the bombed plane was from its intended destination.

The global relevance of what might count, in this case, as true or false becomes an obsession for Tealing, a man whose life is suspended in a world without 'grand narratives' but which generates, endlessly, revisited possibilities and competing hypotheses. As a teacher of literature Tealing's professional purpose is to make past narratives endlessly reinterpretable, a fact that he points out to the mysterious and dying 'spook' who arrives at his home to offer him some information that might lead to the 'truth'. Nonetheless, the information sends Tealing, however doubtfully, to a house on the margin of the Australian desert, where the chief witness whose testimony has convicted Khazar is living with a new identity – Parroulet has become Parr – and with a Chinese wife who is also on the run from a destructive history. Tealing's is a life suspended amidst a multitude of narratives to which he can only give meaning by his belief in Khazar's innocence – 'I had locked myself in a cell of delusion, of total blinkered faith' (*PT*, 137) – while theirs is a life without narrative, locked away from the destructive events which have nearly destroyed them. Each knows that they will never be able to pick up the lost narrative of their lives because the truth that would release them would never be believed: the history in which Tealing seeks 'truth' turns into the endlessness of interpretation of the literature he professes. Together Parroulet and Tealing will fight back the bush fire which threatens to destroy Parroulet's house, just as they will have, for the rest of their lives, to fight back the firestorm of conflicting narratives which threatens to engulf them.

James Robertson's novels are poised between the unverifiable truth of history and the interpretive multiplicity of literature: his characters are driven to become a force that will create the truth of history, or to escape from history into the alternative narratives of literature. His characters fight for a 'cause' – the Covenant, Jacobitism, Scottish nationalism – only to discover that there is another, deeper cause that is driving the history that they think they are making, the 'deep, deep truth' that Tealing knows 'would never come out' (*PT*, 251). The ghost of historical truth haunts a world that knows its histories, at some time in the future, will be read only – if at all – as literature, its literature as the expression of a now ghostly and unrealisable experience which cannot help – like Wedderburn's painting – advertising its own unreality. Novels expressive, perhaps, of a Scotland which has existed only in the imaginations of its artists but which, with its reclaimed parliament, is uncertain what kind of history it hopes to rejoin – or whether the ends of that history will produce a narrative of any lasting value.

NOTES

1. James Robertson, *The Fanatic* (London: Fourth Estate, 2000). All quotations are from this edition; hereafter, page numbers will be given in the text, preceded by *TF*.
2. James Robertson (ed.), *Scottish Ghost Stories* (London: Warner Books, 1996), p. ix.
3. James Robertson, *Joseph Knight* (London: Fourth Estate, 2003). All quotations are from this edition; hereafter, page numbers will be given in the text, preceded by *JK*.
4. See T. M. Devine (ed.), *Recovering Scotland's Slavery Past: The Caribbean Connection* (Edinburgh: Edinburgh University Press, 2015), a collection of essays based on a seminar reported in the *Herald Scotland* by Russell Leadbetter, 'Shocking Truth of Scotland's Role at "Very Heart" of Slavery', 3 October 2014, <http://www.heraldscotland.com/news/13182934. Shocking_truth_of_Scotland_s_role_at__very_heart_of_slavery> (last accessed 14 July 2016).
5. Walter Scott, *Waverley*, ed. Andrew Hook (1814; Harmondsworth: Penguin, 1972), p. 489.
6. Ibid., p. 333.
7. Ibid., p. 353.
8. David Hume, *Essays: Moral, Political and Literary*, ed. Eugene F. Miller (1748; Indianapolis: Indiana University Press, 1985), p. 207.
9. Ibid., p. 208.
10. James Robertson, *The Testament of Gideon Mack* (2006; London: Penguin, 2007), p. 51. All quotations are from this edition; hereafter, page numbers will be given in the text, preceded by *TGM*.
11. Robertson (ed.), *Scottish Ghost Stories*, p. ix.
12. James Hogg, *The Private Memoirs and Confessions of a Justified Sinner*, ed. John Carey (1824; Oxford: Oxford University Press, 1969), p. 254.
13. Ibid., p. 129.
14. Timothy Baker, *Contemporary Scottish Gothic: Mourning, Authenticity and Tradition* (Basingstoke: Palgrave Macmillan, 2014), p. 27.
15. Alasdair Gray, *Lanark: A Life in Four Books* (Edinburgh: Canongate, 1981), pp. 376, 378, 381.
16. Robertson, *Testament*, p. 286; James Kelman, *How Late It Was, How Late* (London: Secker & Warburg, 1994), p. 1.
17. J. M. Barrie, *Peter Pan* (London: Samuel French, 1956), p. 48.
18. James Robertson, *And the Land Lay Still* (London: Penguin, 2010). All quotations are from this edition; hereafter, page numbers will be given in the text, preceded by *ALLS*.
19. Lewis Grassic Gibbon, *A Scots Quair* (1932–4; London: Hutchinson, 1946), p. 37.

20. See 'The Body in the Kitbag', chapter two of my *Out of History: Narrative Paradigms in Scottish and English Culture* (Edinburgh: Polygon, 1996), pp. 31ff.
21. James Robertson, *The Professor of Truth* (2013; London: Penguin, 2014), pp. 1–2. All quotations are from this edition; hereafter, page numbers will be given in the text, preceded by *PT*.

FURTHER READING

For an up-to-date list of James Robertson's novels, see the British Council website: <https://literature.britishcouncil.org/writer/james-robertson> (last accessed 22 June 2016).

Baker, Timothy, *Contemporary Scottish Gothic: Mourning, Authenticity and Tradition* (Basingstoke: Palgrave Macmillan, 2014).
Carruthers, Gerard, and Liam McIlvanney (eds), *The Cambridge Companion to Scottish Literature* (Cambridge: Cambridge University Press, 2012).
Craig, Cairns, *The Modern Scottish Novel* (Edinburgh: Edinburgh University Press, 1999).
—— *Out of History: Narrative Paradigms in Scottish and English Cultures* (Edinburgh: Polygon, 1996).
Schoene-Harwood, Berthold, *The Edinburgh Companion to Contemporary Scottish Literature* (Edinburgh: Edinburgh University Press, 2007).

PART V

Postcolonialism and Beyond

CHAPTER 16

Mohsin Hamid: The Transnational Novel of Globalisation

Janet Wilson

Mohsin Hamid's three novels, all written since the year 2000, have established him as a rising star of the transnational novel of globalisation, featuring prominently in what Bruce King calls 'the current golden age of writing by Muslims'.[1] All are forms of the *Bildungsroman* and play out their individual dramas with respect to present-day Pakistan's relationship with the West. They can be read alongside the work of contemporaries such as Hanif Kureishi, Kamila Shamsie and Kiran Desai, who, in showing the human consequences of East-West polarisation, give space and voice to the Muslim subject.[2] In each novel Hamid challenges the interpretative powers of his audience by questioning pre-determined reading positions; and through a literary poetics which draws on the proliferating collectivities and networks of globalisation, in his third novel he hints at a widening arc of international sympathy and understanding.

Hamid focuses on the impact of changing post-imperial US politics, economics and educational opportunity upon the transnational youth of Pakistan: his protagonists are Muslim men who are players in the world of international commerce and banking. In presenting his geopolitical transnational subject matter, he combines documentary realism with fictional modes like allegory, fable and legend, showing a modernist affinity for tropes of impersonality, shadowy doubles, anonymity and mirroring to convey doubt and hesitation, and making use of postmodern theatricality and metafiction. The world of his novels is dominated either by the mass media and its regulating frames of perception, or by global digital technologies whereby cultural exchange occurs in virtual overlapping spaces. Images of media hyperreality following 9/11 in *The Reluctant Fundamentalist* suggest a post-postmodern performativity based on an affective need to respond to this undermining of the 'real'.[3] Hamid's use of the first- and second-person narrators makes audible to the West the voice of the Muslim subject as a representative of Rising Asia, and so challenges readers' assumptions about the 'other'.[4] Through first-person narration or auto-fiction and related modes like testimony, confession or reflective self-analysis, he represents the Asian subject as an insider, so correlating individual with public narratives of contemporary Pakistan, and he co-opts the reader as a character through the 'you' mode of enunciation. All three novels represent the subjectivity of their protagonists through nuance of voice and gesture, and choreograph the reader's response through a call to ethical judgement.

Hamid's first novel, Moth Smoke (2000), introduces contemporary Pakistan and its post-Cold War, East-West geopolitics through the youthful, privileged party set of Lahore. Set in the summer of 1998 when Pakistan unleashed its first nuclear bomb, the nation is convulsed by crisis and a collapse of morality through its rivalry with India, economic meltdown and social division. While the novel's self-absorbed elite benefits from an American education and indulges in a decadent lifestyle, the fate of the protagonist, Darashikah Shezad (Daru), points to the failure of affective ties and presents a parable of national decay. After being sacked from his privileged position in international banking, Daru sinks into apathy, laces his cigarettes with heroin, and falls in love with his best friend's wife. Moral atrophy sets in when he resorts to selling drugs, and he swiftly descends into destitution and self-destruction.

The narrative hinges on Daru's trial for murder, and the demand that the reader assess his character failings in light of an accusation for what is in fact the wrong crime. It is framed by an episode about the break-up of the Mughal Empire: the transgression of Emperor Shah Jahan's anticipated succession when his heir apparent Dara Shikoh was killed by his brother Aurangzeb. Daru's voice, as the condemned man in his cell, introduces Hamid's present-day counterpart to this historical event. The theme of treacherous brotherly love – between the orphan Daru and his wealthy childhood friend, Aurangzeb (Ozi) – and the hinted-at family secret, that their fathers, being 'like brothers',[5] in fact shared the same parent, links the story allegorically to the sub-continent's 'common heritage'.[6] The coda to the Mughal story, 'When the uncertain future becomes the past, the past itself becomes uncertain' (MS, 2), points to the agency of this tainted legacy in the present as Daru's life unravels. As he lacks a secure standpoint from which he can reconstruct events of the past as known and complete, the beginning (and meaning) of his boyhood friendship with Ozi becomes uncertain to the point of unsustainability.[7]

Hamid's postmodern techniques include laying bare the theatricality of the event, here a case awaiting judgement, by using the second-person plural to interpellate the reader, who is dramatically invoked as judge, wigged and robed. His protagonist is already condemned according to the anonymous narrator, because in this trial the witnesses are 'liars all' (MS, 5). The conflicting testimony from Daru's intimates – Ozi, his wife Mumtaz (in love with Daru), and his partner in crime, the rickshaw-driver-cum-robber Murad Badshah – invites assessment of their part in this apparent miscarriage of justice. Like Kazuo Ishiguro in *The Remains of the Day*, Hamid ensures that his cast of unreliable narrators undermines any normative narrative position. The reader is invited to assess their individual subjectivities, exposed as 'precarious, contradictory and in process, constantly being reconstituted in discourse'.[8] Although each solicits a relationship with the reader, metafictional comments undermine their credibility. Badshah, for example, draws attention to the clichéd melodramatic setting of a robbery, breaking the fictional illusion:

> It was a dark and stormy night.
> Do you smile at this introduction? Allow me to submit for your consideration the saying that those tales with unoriginal beginnings are most likely later to surprise.
> So, the night was dark and stormy. (MS, 83)

Sympathy for Daru is encouraged by the suggestion that his murderous impulses are born of tragic heroism – an Othello-like passion complicated by betrayal and loss. Hamid raises the possibility of truth-telling in the conclusion to mitigate Daru's moral collapse and criminality, so reinforcing the narrator's opening verdict, that he is the 'terrible, almost-hero of a great story, powerful, tragic, and dangerous' (MS, 6); the narrative contained in the envelope that Mumtaz delivers to him in the prison cell is 'the story of my innocence. A half story' (MS, 308). This surreptitious intervention into the patriarchal story of crime and betrayal, challenging its discourse of blame, hints at postmodern scepticism towards metanarratives. The tainted Mughal legacy and the verdict of History will be overturned by an alternative, 'truer' version of events made visible by the female narrator who remains loyal to her lover.[9]

Hamid has described his second novel, *The Reluctant Fundamentalist* (2007), set in New York and Lahore, as the mirror image of *Moth Smoke*, in which the USA is restricted to the narrative periphery. In this dualistic narrative of events American perspectives are filtered through the Pakistani gaze and rhetorically the Pakistani voice is privileged in speaking for the West.[10] The story is framed by 9/11 and its aftermath – the US war on terror and India's invasion of Pakistan – which destabilise the protagonist's aspirations in the USA. Demonstrating affinities with *Moth Smoke*'s betrayal of romantic love, questioning of moral codes, and its demand of the reader to decide about the characters, the novel foregrounds the ideology of US economic imperialism as the basis for the hero's identity, aligning his life changes to those in world politics. But threats of political division, hatred and retaliation due to terrorism and counter-terrorism come with gestures toward 'a new global citizen' and a 'cosmopolitan identity' effected through literary and imaginative extension. There is also a ludic quality, as Hamid draws attention to the act of fiction-making through the ambiguity of the first-person voice and different guises and versions of reality.[11]

The protagonist is the twenty-five-year-old upwardly mobile Muslim migrant Changez, who buys into American economic fundamentalism, symbolic of global financial power, then turns his back on this ideology in response to post-9/11 politics. He returns to Lahore from the USA, becomes a university lecturer and leads a radical anti-American student protest movement. Changez tells his *Bildung* during an evening in a tea house in Anarkali, Lahore, to a mysterious, unknown American who may be a member of the CIA. In describing his spectacular rise, first as a stellar student at Princeton, then in joining Underwood Sampson, an evaluation firm that analyses the economic 'fundamentals' of client businesses, he reconstructs his penetration of elite, cosmopolitan circles by drawing attention to his outsider position: he wonders, for example, whether Erica, the woman he falls in love with, finds him either 'irresistibly refined or oddly anachronistic'.[12] The numerous self-adjustments he makes in moulding his behaviour to meet social expectations reflect his alienation and capacity to assume and discard multiple versions of selfhood.

Changez's narrative voice is a mixture of urbanity, politeness and candour; he adapts a faux confessional, deferential manner in his interpellation of the American auditor, which extends to the implied (Western) reader. Underlying his façade is the uneasiness of the outsider, as his hint to the American that 'Your country's flag invaded New York' (RF, 90) symbolises a more rigid nationalism and new exclusions. Other comments such as what counts is 'the thrust of one's narrative . . . not the accuracy of the details', and confessions such as 'I lacked a stable *core* . . .', and '[my] own identity was so fragile' (RF, 136, 168), suggesting the chameleon-like, divided self, also illustrate Hamid's strategy of destabilising interpretation.

Changez's relations with the Americans he meets mirror his intense identification with the elite cadres of Underwood Sampson (the 'US') rather than anchoring him in a more enduring version of himself. Significantly, Jim, his boss and mentor at Underwood Sampson, comes from a background of class dispossession that resembles his own. 'I felt like I didn't belong to this world. Just like you,' he tells Changez (RF, 80). Possibly an alter ego, Jim advises acceptance of change, for '"Power comes from *becoming* change"', seemingly encouraging Changez's volatility and his decision to return to Lahore. The failing love affair with the beautiful Erica, who remains emotionally attached to her deceased boyfriend Chris (/Christ), provokes a similar fusion of identities. Sexual intimacy with Erica transforms Changez into an avatar of self-denial and invisibility as he identifies with the absent 'other' and wills himself into being Chris, becoming his ghostly substitute during lovemaking (RF, 160). Erica's mysterious disappearance, suggestive of melancholia and mourning for the lost lover, Changez's willing loss of selfhood, and the novel's play on names amount to an allegory of the break from capitalist ideology and the dissolution of his relationship with America.[13] The phonic echo and '*regal*' (RF, 19) Erica, an 'empress-in-waiting' (RF, 91), align her with American imperialism and post-9/11 nostalgia, as 'flags and uniforms' (RF, 129) suggest that 'living in New York was suddenly like living in a film about the Second World War' (RF, 130–1). Such temporal disassociation from the present moment and the grand narratives of History, as mediatised images of the past inform and overwhelm the present, suggestive of the waning of affect, is undoubtedly an index of Changez's estrangement and discontent.

The destabilising of self and other in Changez's American narrative, recalling the postmodern blurring of image and reality, is intensified through the media exposure of 9/11. Changez's initial reaction to the attacks on the Twin Towers, what he at first thought was a film on television, then realised was 'not fiction but news' (RF, 82), correlates with the Western hypermediated experience of reality in assimilating the spectacle.[14] While the media consolidate a narrative of military strength based on retaliation and division at this time,[15] he reacts to the over-saturated exposure of events with a mixture of pleasure and anger, with body language suggestive of a growing anti-Americanism: his smile at 'the *symbolism* of it all, that someone had so visibly brought America to her knees' (*RF*, 83), his trembling fury at a newscast showing American troops entering Afghanistan (*RF*, 113–14). Changez's real emotions, ironically triggered by virtual reality, emanate in a new self as he grows a beard and 'others' himself as a Pakistani.

Two of the new forms of realism in the twenty-first-century novel, cultural history and docu-drama, run counter to uncertainties, including the instability of representation, in the post-postmodern period.[16] Hamid's use of documentary realism might be traced to comments in his journalism on the increased ethnic profiling and stereotyping of young Muslims in the post-9/11 USA.[17] In the novel he aligns the personal narrative to the political as the widening gap between self and other is mapped on to the growing public division between 'us' and 'them'. Changez's revised identity and heightened ethnic profile are construed in terms of the Muslim threat to the nation, as incidents such as the insult '"Fucking Arab"' (*RF*, 134), his detainment at US Customs, and being body-searched at airports attest. Afflicted by this resurgent nationalism following the change in US foreign policy, he reaches a turning point in his journey from American cosmopolitan to political dissident when visiting Valparaiso, the novel's third geographical axis, and encountering the works of Pablo Neruda, a poet greatly admired in Pakistan. He finally rejects his prior adulation of American capitalism by imaging himself subordinated as 'a modern-day janissary, a servant of the American empire' (*RF*, 173) and resolving to stop America 'in the interests of . . . humanity' (*RF*, 190).

The novel's post-9/11 political tensions and ambiguous cross-cultural relations are presented through a narrative structure in which the dramatic monologue rhetorically represents an imagined conversation, 'othering' the American as a nameless and voiceless interlocutor, making him a decoy for the reader. Changez's migrant voice, liminal position and capacity to read and speak one culture through another, varying his register and tone between the polite, formal South Asian style of English and the inflections and idioms of American speech,[18] enable him to evoke the American's voice through questions and statements: 'How did I know you are American?', 'What did I think of Princeton?' or 'I see from your expression that you do not believe me', for example (*RF*, 1, 3, 206). The act of narrative manipulation – silencing the Western voice and foregrounding the Muslim one – accentuates the fissures and fractures of Changez's divided personality, and manufactures textually the ambiguity and subtlety of his dissidence and distance, resembling what Roger Bromley describes as the 'intense dialogicity' that comes from writing out of the subordinate migrant position.[19]

As presented from the perspective of the returned immigrant, *The Reluctant Fundamentalist* has affinities with the 'immigration novel',[20] while the global spatialisation of metropolitan destinations (Manila, New York, Valparaiso) is a staple of the diaspora novel. Features of the political thriller or the post-9/11 terrorist genre also appear in the destabilising and enigmatic narrative voice and the problems of precise identification, and uncertainty of action towards the end. In ways similar to the anonymous narrator of *Moth Smoke*, a straw dog who demands a more nuanced understanding from readers, Changez's defensiveness increases as an impasse with his American interlocutor and ideological closure loom. Violence, he claims, is justified because Western counter-terrorists refer to the civilians they have killed as 'collateral damage', but it is not used by his students and, furthermore, he is 'no ally of killers' (RF, 202–3, 205). Such provocative 'bad faith' arguments intensify the doubts about identity and motive (is the American a CIA agent sent to arrest or assassinate Changez because he is a terrorist? Is Changez really a jihadist?), creating new levels of indeterminacy.

In *The Reluctant Fundamentalist* Hamid's achievement is to develop verbal representations of alienated identity into a rhetorical narrative structure through the device of the formal monologue. In staging the experience of detachment and estrangement and magnifying the ambiguity of the unknown 'other' through acts of ventriloquism, he encourages the reader's insight into those spaces between 'the conflicting interests and positions' that are typically associated with the East and the West.[21] But, recalling the enactment then betrayal of brotherly love in *Moth Smoke*, the moment when the stand-off might flare into violence also offers, ironically, consideration of sameness and commonality. As Changez bids the American farewell, he claims, 'you and I are now bound by a certain shared intimacy' (RF, 209).[22]

Hamid's third novel, *How to Get Filthy Rich in Rising Asia* (2013), unlike its predecessors, avoids specific names, national or religious labels, and exact dates to examine universal human themes in an unspecified country of rising Asia in an unknown time. But underpinning its fabular spell, upbeat mood and verbal exuberance is a sharp, satiric take on present-day Lahore. Definitive indicators of twenty-first-century Asian Muslim society with its headscarves, prayers, mobile phones and TV remotes make the eight decades of the novel's time span seem compressed into one contemporary moment, conveying the impression of multiple levels of society and of people inhabiting different worlds simultaneously.[23]

The 'How to' of the title proclaims the guiding conceit: that of the self-help advice book, here to be eagerly consulted by those aspiring to opportunity and profit. Hamid adapts the genre to a satire on poverty, youth and corruption – although his real target is environmental mismanagement in Asia – to include a love story in satiric guise, and meditation on the 'self' and mortality. His protagonist's escape from grinding poverty begins with an entrepreneurial calculation of the profit to be made in providing clean drinking water to a country whose water can cause 'diarrhea, hepatitis, dysentery, and typhoid'.[24] From selling relabelled out-of-date food he moves to passing off illicitly as mineral water boiled water bottled in used containers. The novel's *Bildungsroman* format, the life-story of a spectacular global rise, contrasts with the truncated narratives of the two earlier novels about frustrated young men who wish to break into the privileged circles of the wealthy, and which conclude in expectation of their deaths. The 'how to get filthy rich' formula follows the anonymous hero's life from rags to riches, and cradle to grave, moving through the different classes of society from minor salesman to entrepreneur and market equity trader with the multinationals. Intersecting his elevation to supreme water industrialist, and entry into the galactic 'global network of finance', is an interrupted narrative of romantic love, with the anonymous yet engaging 'pretty girl' who initiates him into desires of a different sort.

These are parallel success stories showing improvisation and self-invention. Hamid's entrepreneur enters the corporate world with 'cooler replenishment contracts', and bribes corrupt politicians in order to become a state-licensed provider, able to augment the public water supply. The pretty girl's trajectory requires trading on her body as photographer's model, gaining public visibility as TV celebrity chef, and accumulating wealth as a designer kitchen showroom owner and retailer of international furniture. Their parallel downward spiral begins when the water empire is snatched away by a scheming relative, the pretty girl is robbed, and both find themselves at a crossroads caused by the onset of ill health, old age and loneliness.

In his postmodern reconfiguring of time and space, Hamid registers the markers of Western global culture alongside the stark poverty and destitution of the rural village where his protagonist is born. In such blighted conditions any prospect of Western privilege is only a dream: the child's scooter, trainers, TV remote and chocolate are only imagined symbols, alternatives to the repetitive and dehumanising grind of the labour of the farmer whose measure of exchange is only 'his allocation of time in this world' (HGF, 7). The whiff of mortality that drives the protagonist's father from his village anticipates the meditation on mortality in the novel's ending. To the planetary symbolism of cities linked into an urban archipelago by fibre optic cables is contrasted 'your' single room, where being human requires a different kind of navigation towards the discomfort of old age and bodily decrepitude. This is made possible when the right kind of company offers 'a wish that you be less lonely' (HGF, 83), and where the imminent cessation of time is offset by the timeless image of 'the pretty girl'. The universalising voice that tells of overcoming lowly birth and limited expectation extends an unexpectedly compassionate conclusion: the softening of death's encroachment by the transformative powers of memory and love.

The self-help manual's format, adapted to the success story, defines the *Bildungsroman* structure of this third novel. Each chapter, written in the historical present, corresponds to a different phase of 'your' life, and every chapter title proclaims a different kind of self-agency: the narrator provides a commentary on the value of advice, meditation on the times, analysis of street credibility, the strategy and luck required. In postmodern fashion the text's constructedness is exposed by authorial injunctions, and meta-commentary on both genre and storyline. Hamid exploits the gap between the formulaic 'Dos' and 'Don'ts' of his chapter headings, and the operations of fate and individual calculation in recounting the decisions that define the path to success. At birth, when self-agency is most limited, biological chance – one's place as third in the family – matters more than 'Getting an Education', while the injunction 'Don't Fall in Love' means putting such emotions on hold, for only when material pursuits are satisfied can the luxury of true love be indulged.

In his third novel Hamid returns to the liberating possibilities of the second-person pronoun, first explored in *Moth Smoke*, in defining a protagonist ('you') whose spectacular success story illustrates far more than the genre of the self-help manual promises. Unlike the autobiographical first person 'I', but similar to the impersonal pronoun 'one', which involves reaching beyond the immediate experience, the 'you' pronoun of the interpellated subject widens the potential for empathetic identification with the space of another. In being conflated with the reader (the 'you' of the narrator's direct address), the protagonist always represents more than himself. In the last five chapters the narrator uses the collective first-person plural pronoun 'we', speaking in generalisations to the shared experience of being human in a global information age, and implying shared concerns and affinities between narrative voice, characters and reader. Through this universalising gesture the narrator reflects on his craft and arrives at a reconfigured postmodern Cartesian world view, the reassembly from a collection of present-day stories of 'the lifelong story of a plausible unitary self' (HGF, 160).

As the protagonist's water-bottling business segues into the mass market, the action shifts to the megalopolis and the country's shoreline and shipping highways which link it to other parts of the world. Spatiality, space flight and aerial perspectives become the new images of the global financial universe around which business nebulae are dotted. If in *Moth Smoke* the reader is elevated as judge, and in *The Reluctant Fundamentalist* is interpellated through the device of the anonymous American auditor, in *How to Get Filthy Rich in Rising Asia* the reader shares the aerial perspectives of the internet and cyberspace as trajectories are traced worldwide. The point of view is literalised as a roaming eye, a drone or unmanned aerial vehicle, which hovers above the earth, peering into multiple spaces and offering simultaneous viewing positions. In its conclusion the 'how to' novel becomes a guide in orienting the reader to the broadening horizons of global technology.

Hamid's fiction has inspired comparisons with Camus's existential, 'confessional' novel *The Fall* (*La Chute*) which uses the dramatic monologue,[25] Scott Fitzgerald's scripts of fast money, big parties and Hollywood-style romance,[26] Jay McInerney's *Bright Lights, Big City*, progenitor of the second-person narrator,[27] and some of Kazuo Ishiguro's novels, Ishiguro being a writer who also 'specialises in voice transitions'.[28] There are resemblances to Aravind Adiga's *The White Tiger*, in which the emergence of a ruthless entrepreneur undercuts the narrative of 'shining India', and the 'I' voice of the murdering narrator illustrates the dark side of neoliberalism. But of these similar versions of the Asian 'slippery' self (HGF, 3–4) Hamid shows a more humane side and encourages readers to believe in the decency of his upwardly mobile characters.[29] Unlike Adiga's raw realism, his narrative experimentation aligns him with American postmodernism, while his many popular and literary intertexts, drawn from TV, Hollywood movies, film noir, modernist writing and crime fiction, contribute to a complex layering of images of masculine subjectivity. Finally, although Hamid's fictional gaze remains set on Lahore and present-day Pakistan, just as Adiga's does on India, so confirming the continued importance of the nation as a nexus of transcultural and transnational exchange, his social, cultural and political discourses additionally produce and articulate Orientally framed knowledge of the West.

Moth Smoke and *How to Get Filthy Rich in Rising Asia*, both based in Lahore, show the assimilation of Western and Muslim values into a new cultural synthesis in which global forces sharpen economic division while also promoting social mobility and new possibilities for individual self-determination. In *The Reluctant Fundamentalist*, where New York is the 'other' to Lahore and hypermediatised filters of the unsayable Event catalyse psychological fragmentation and reduced identity structures, the West's anxieties about the 'other' are presented in ways that suggest a new global imaginary. Although the effects of 9/11 are registered in the past's engulfing of the present through media saturation, and in the present's seeming unrecoverability because already overwhelmed by such images, Hamid's post-postmodern performativity, in which the reader is implicated, works to transcend this effacement of the 'real'. Gestures of affective feeling as 'othering' is on the rise appear unexpectedly, pointing to the overcoming of social and political tensions and creating a fluctuating horizon of empathetic identification.

NOTES

1. Bruce King, 'Losing Paradise Now', *Journal of Postcolonial Writing*, 52.2 (April 2016), 225–31; 228.
2. Margaret Scanlan, 'Migrating from Terror', *Journal of Postcolonial Writing*, 46.3 (2010), 266–78; 267.
3. In the post-postmodern period, witnessing the unsayability of the Event and the ultimate impossibility of interpretation gives way to performative modes; see A. Kelly, 'Moments of Decision in Contemporary American Fiction: Roth, Auster, Eugenides', *Critique*, 5 (2010), 313–32.
4. See Judith Butler, *Precarious Life: The Powers of Mourning and Violence* (New York: Verso, 2004), p. 8; cited by Tim Gauthier in *9/11 Fiction, Empathy, and Otherness* (New York and London: Lexington Books, 2015), p. 6.
5. Mohsin Hamid, *Moth Smoke* (2000; Harmondsworth: Penguin, 2011), p. 232. All quotations are from this edition; hereafter, page numbers will be given in the text, preceded by MS.
6. Muneeza Shamsie, 'Pakistani English Novels in the New Millennium: Migration, Geopolitics, and Tribal Tales', in Janet Wilson and Chris Ringrose (eds), *New Soundings in Postcolonial Writing: Critical and Creative Contours – Essays in Honour of Bruce King* (Leiden: Brill/Rodopi, 2016), pp. 149–67; p. 159.
7. Cf. Laura Marcus, *Auto/biographical Discourses: Theory, Criticism, Practice* (Manchester and New York: Manchester University Press, 1994), p. 276.
8. Kathleen Wall, '*The Remains of the Day* and its Challenges to Theories of Unreliable Narration', *The Journal of Narrative Technique*, 24.1 (1994), 18–42; 21–2.
9. The greater cultural authority of this hidden story is suggested by the fact that Mumtaz's pseudonym, Zulfikar Manto, is a code name for the famous Urdu writer Sa'ada Hasan Manto. See Shamsie, 'Pakistani English Novels in the New Millennium', p. 158.
10. See 'Moshin Hamid in Conversation with Yamina Yaquin', *Wasifiri*, 23.2 (June 2008), 44–9; 45.
11. See Peter Morey, '"The rules of the game have changed": Mohsin Hamid's *The Reluctant Fundamentalist* and Post-9/11 Fiction', *Journal of Postcolonial Writing*, 47.2 (2011), 135–46.
12. Mohsin Hamid, *The Reluctant Fundamentalist* (Harmondsworth: Penguin, 2007), p. 19. All quotations are from this edition; hereafter, page numbers will be given in the text, preceded by RF.
13. See Delphine Munos, 'Possessed by Whiteness: Interracial Affiliations and Racial Melancholia in Mohsin Hamid's *The Reluctant Fundamentalist*', *Journal of Postcolonial Writing*, 48.4 (2012), 396–405; 397.
14. Cf. Slavoj Zizek: 'this fantasmatic screen image entered our reality. It is not that reality

entered an image; the image entered and shattered our reality', in *Welcome to the Desert of the Real* (London and New York: Verso, 2002), p. 16.
15. See Gauthier, *9/11 Fiction, Empathy, and Otherness*, p. 1.
16. See Peter Childs, Claire Colebrook and Sebastian Groes, 'The Need for Real "Truth"', in Childs, Colebrook and Groes (eds), *Women's Fiction and Post-9/11 Contexts* (New York and London: Lexington Books, 2015), p. xvi.
17. See Mohsin Hamid, *Discontent and its Civilisations: Dispatches from Lahore, New York and London* (New York and London: Penguin, 2014), p. 26. He reports his sister saying of New York, 'Now I hear how scared my Pakistani friends are, the abuse they're getting, I'm glad I'm not there.'
18. See Muneeza Shamsie, 'Covert Operations in Pakistan Fiction', *Commonwealth Essays and Studies*, 31.2 (2009), 20–1.
19. Roger Bromley, *Narratives for a New Belonging: Diasporic Cultural Fictions* (Edinburgh: Edinburgh University Press, 2000), p. 122.
20. See Caren Irr, *Toward the Geopolitical Novel: US Fiction in the Twenty-First Century* (New York: Columbia University Press, 2014), p. 60.
21. Morey, '"The rules of the game have changed"', p. 138, alluding to Deleuze and Guattari, argues for a deterritorialisation of Pakistani fiction in order to explore what lies beyond 'the totalising categories of East and West'.
22. In connection with this, see Gauthier, *9/11 Fiction, Empathy, and Otherness*, p. 1.
23. See Theo Tait, 'Review of *How to Get Filthy Rich in Rising Asia*', *The Guardian*, 28 March 2013, <https://www.theguardian.com/books/2013/mar/28/how-get-filthy-hamid-review> (last accessed 24 June 2016).
24. Mohsin Hamid, *How to Get Filthy Rich in Rising Asia* (London: Hamish Hamilton, 2013), p. 99. All quotations are from this edition; hereafter, page numbers will be given in the text, preceded by HGF.
25. Bruce King, 'The Image of the American State in Three Pakistani Novels', in *Totalitarian Movements and Political Religions*, 8.3–4 (2007), 683–8; 685; Morey, '"The rules of the game have changed"', p. 139.
26. Comparisons were inevitably made when the 2013 remake of *The Great Gatsby* was released in the same week as Mira Nair's film adaptation of *The Reluctant Fundamentalist*.
27. Christopher Young, 'Freedom of Speech, the Second Person and "Homeland": A Conversation between Jay McInerney and Mohsin Hamid', *New York Daily News*, 24 October 2013, <http://www.nydailynews.com/blogs/pageviews/freedom-speech-person-homeland-conversation-jay-mcinerney-mohsin-hamid-blog-entry-1.1639343> (last accessed 24 June 2016); Andrew Anthony, 'Review of *How to Get Filthy Rich in Rising Asia*', *The Guardian*, 21 April 2013, <https://www.theguardian.com/books/2013/apr/21/filthy-rich-mohsin-hamid-review> (last accessed 24 June 2016).
28. Parul Sehgal, 'Yes Man: Mohsin Hamid's *How to Get Filthy Rich in Rising Asia*', *New York Times*, 29 March 2013, <http://www.nytimes.com/2013/03/31/books/review/mohsin-hamids-how-to-get-filthy-rich-in-rising-asia.html?_r=0> (last accessed 24 June 2016).
29. See Tait, 'Review of *How to Get Filthy Rich in Rising Asia*'.

FURTHER READING

For an up-to-date list of Hamid's novels, see the British Council website: <https://literature.british-council.org/writer/mohsin-hamid> (last accessed 24 June 2016).

Clements, Madeleine, *Writing Islam from a South Asian Muslim Perspective: Rushdie, Hamid, Aslam, Shamsie* (London: Palgrave Macmillan, 2016).

Elia, Adriano, '"My split self and my split world": Troping Identity in Mohsin Hamid's Fiction',

in Jonathan P. A. Sell (ed.), *Metaphor and Diaspora in Contemporary Writing* (London: Palgrave Macmillan, 2012), pp. 59–79.
King, Bruce, *The Internationalization of English Literature: The Oxford English Literary History*, Vol. 13: 1948–2000 (Oxford: Oxford University Press, 2004).
Perner, Claudia, 'Tracing the Fundamentalists in Mohsin Hamid's *Moth Smoke* and *The Reluctant Fundamentalist*', *Ariel*, 41.3–4 (2010), 23–31.
Weihsin, Gui, 'Creative Destruction and Narrative Renovation: Neoliberalism and the Aesthetic Dimension in the Fiction of Aravind Adiga and Mohsin Hamid', *Global South*, 7.2 (2013), 173–90.

CHAPTER 17

Andrea Levy: The SS *Empire Windrush* and After

Sue Thomas

Andrea Levy affirms Toni Morrison's sense that 'being a black woman writer is not a shallow place but a rich place to write from. It doesn't limit my imagination; it expands it.' Levy's 'Caribbean heritage' is a 'very rich seam' for her as a writer; 'quite simply, the reason that I write,' she states.[1] The seams she works at in her writing are the imperial and post-imperial formation of Caribbean and British lives and the suturing of the historical wounds of transatlantic plantation slavery and its legacies. Her recent novels *Small Island* (2004) and *The Long Song* (2010) have been inspired by commemorative events in Atlantic history: the fiftieth anniversary in 1998 of the arrival of the SS *Empire Windrush*, usually seen as marking the beginning of post-war West Indian emigration to Britain, and the bicentenary in 2007 of the British abolition of its slave trade respectively. 'My heritage is Britain's story too. It is time to put the Caribbean back where it belongs – in the main narrative of British history,' Levy insists.[2]

Drawing on and framing recollection as a method of research and narration, Levy addresses in her fiction how a sharply racialised empire has shaped intimate spheres of her characters' lives: desire, femininity, masculinity, sexual economies, domesticity and imagined communities. Recollection as a form of historical fiction offers a 'counter-memory' of British history and national memory. David Scott, writing on 'the idea of an *archaeology* of black memory', positions '*counter*-memory' as 'the moral idiom and semiotic registers of remembering against the grain of the history of New World black deracination, subjection and exclusion . . . a relation between the idea of an archive, the modalities of memory, the problem of a tradition, and practices of criticism'.[3]

In an interview with Susan Alice Fischer, Levy points to a shift in her creative practice at the turn of the twenty-first century. Her first three novels – *Every Light in the House Burnin'* (1994), *Never Far from Nowhere* (1996) and *Fruit of the Lemon* (1999) – were, she says, 'about exploring aspects of my life, though in fiction. I didn't research it, obviously; it was there in my head for those three books.'⁴ Her Jamaican-born parents, Winston and Amy Levy, arrived in Britain in 1948, her father aboard the SS *Empire Windrush*. The impetus for Andrea Levy to take up writing in her mid-thirties was the death of her father in 1987. She 'wanted to make him visible, record something of his life, and also the experience that we'd gone through with it'.⁵ '[E]xploring . . . with words' helped her work through her 'family background and upbringing' and her 'complicated relationship with colour', 'rescu[ing]' her from an overwhelming sense of deracination by bringing her to identify as black through limning the broader generational resonance of her experience.⁶

In her early *Bildungsromane*, *Every Light in the House Burnin'*, *Never Far from Nowhere* and *Fruit of the Lemon*, Levy draws out the damaging deracinating reach and effects of pigmentocracy, the privilege that has historically been accorded people with lighter skin shades in colonial Caribbean cultures. Levy, who identifies as 'black British' rather than Caribbean,⁷ discovered through writing that she belongs to 'the black experience' of Britain.⁸ Stuart Hall explains that the concept of 'the black experience' 'referenc[es] the common experience of racism and marginalisation in Britain and came to provide the organising category of a new politics of resistance, amongst groups and communities with, in fact, very different histories, traditions and ethnic identities'. In 1992 he locates a 'significant shift . . . in black cultural politics . . . from a struggle over the relations of representation to a politics of representation itself' and 'an awareness of the black experience as a *diaspora* experience'.⁹ Levy's fiction emerged in and has been shaped by this new phase of black cultural politics, as has her sense of affiliation with writers Jackie Kay, Bernadine Evaristo, Laura Fish and Zadie Smith.¹⁰ In *Small Island*, *The Long Song*, and a new story, 'Uriah's War', published in 2014 to mark the centenary of the outbreak of the First World War, she engages with the politics of black representation in the collective memory of post-imperial Britain. She frames her commemorative projects as 'add[ing] the experience' of black people to the 'record'.¹¹ As Alison Donnell points out, 'the recognition and refusal of History, and the affirmation and recovery of histories, has been a defining theme in anglophone Caribbean literature.'¹²

Highlighting the importance of recollection as a 'critical' act in recovering the inner lives of characters in social groups marginalised in national histories, Toni Morrison comments that 'memory weighs heavily in what I write, in how I begin and in what I find to be significant'. Her creative practice is 'a kind of literary archaeology', a 'journey to a site to see what remains were left behind and to reconstruct the world that these remains imply' through the 'act of the imagination'.¹³ The narrative of *Small Island* comprises four first-person memory arcs of time designated 'Before' and '1948' – those of Hortense and Gilbert Joseph from Jamaica and Queenie and Bernard Bligh from England – and a Prologue of Queenie's memories of the 1924 British Empire Exhibition. In '1948' the characters' lives intersect at the Bligh home in Earl's Court, which Queenie has converted to a boarding house to make ends meet.

This is the site of Levy's literary archaeological dig, contextualising the memories of her mother and English mother-in-law, 'war veterans and people who had lived through those times' through reading and archival research.[14] James Procter points out that

> [t]he dwelling place was, perhaps more than the official point of entry, the site at which the regulation, policing and deferral of black settlement was most effectively played out. It was around housing that the national panic surrounding black immigration tended to accumulate and stage itself in this period. ... The threshold of the British homestead took on the significance of a national frontier in this context.[15]

As such, like the 'white female body', it could symbolise 'a national culture threatened with penetration and pollution by the transgressive black settler. At once permeable and impervious, they are sites at which cultural differences are reproduced and regulated.'[16] Levy is also excavating around what Bruce King describes as the 'Windrush legend', a 'mythology' of West Indian 'arrival' and 'struggle' in Britain, 'celebrated' as marking 'the start of the country's new ethnic, racial, and cultural diversity'.[17] Alan Rice notes that Levy 'deliberately broaden[s] out' this 'limited black British historiography'.[18] She engages with Sam Selvon's *The Lonely Londoners* (1956), an iconic comic novel of West Indian migration to Britain in the 1950s, in which women are generally 'objectified' sexually and 'voiceless'.[19]

In *The Long Song* the archaeological sites are the sugar plantation under racialised slavery and the writing scenes of slave narrative. The novel is a response to a question posed by a 'young woman' at the Writing, Diaspora and the Legacy of Slavery conference at Goldsmith's College in 2007: 'How could she be proud of her Jamaican roots, she wanted to know, when her ancestors had all been slaves?' Levy's project was to 'persuade this young woman to have pride in her slave ancestors through telling her a story'. Noting the paucity of West Indian slave narratives, Levy determined to restore black testimonial memory, '[n]ot just the wails of anguish and victimhood that we are used to, ... but the chatter and clatter of people building their lives, families and communities, ducking, diving and conducting the businesses of life in appallingly difficult circumstances'.[20]

Levy's interest in memory's relation to history exemplifies Scott's point that in contemporary memory studies 'memory connotes a sense of immediacy, imagination, and authenticity, an auratic sense of the past's presence beyond the temporal constraints of secular-rationalist historical consciousness ... unlike history, it is openly partial, selective, fragmentary, allusive, nonlinear'.[21] In *Small Island* and *The Long Song* the partial and selective memories of the narrators are a rich source of humour and ironic juxtaposition of points of view. Jeannette Baxter and David James observe that Levy's humour 'moves towards articulating an ethics of empathy'.[22] Like Caryl Phillips's novels, hers develop 'structures of understanding and even empathy across ethnic groups' and an expansive sense of 'history that demands an open engagement with questions of the exercise of power globally and how that power conditions the possibilities for human connectedness'.[23]

Levy's temporal division of *Small Island* as 'Before' and '1948' references colloquial periodisation of history in the anglophone Caribbean by catastrophic hurricanes;

Jamaicans, for instance, speak of 'before Gilbert' and 'after Gilbert', Gilbert being a devastating 1988 hurricane.[24] Levy's allusion to this practice of periodisation positions the wake of the arrival of the SS *Empire Windrush* in 1948 as, metaphorically, a 'human hurricane' making landfall in Britain.[25] In *Small Island* hurricanes, natural and symbolic, are generally associated with processes of uprooting, dispersal, revelation and the parting of family houses. The hurricane has metaphorical and metonymic reaches in plots of maturation, sexual awakening and cross-racial sexual desire and in the dream imagery of characters. Levy pointedly draws out the reach of her use of the hurricane in Hortense's memories of the landfall of the hurricane that ruptured her familial life by exposing her cousin Michael Roberts's affair with a white woman:

> A hurricane can make cows fly. It can tear trees from the ground, toss them in the air and snap them like twigs. A house can be picked up, its four walls parted, its roof twisted, and everything scattered in a divine game of hide-and-seek. This savage wind could make even the 'rock of ages' take to the air and float off light as a bird's wing.
>
> But a hurricane does not come without warning.[26]

Importantly hurricanes figure the providential hand of the author designing the narrative and are an ironised sign of tropical distinctiveness in a tropical/temperate dichotomy that has historically shaped British understandings of West Indian difference from Englishness.

European imperial expansion into tropical regions produced such a 'complex of ideas' about and representations of the tropics that in 2000 David Arnold designated tropicality, a discursive field with which Levy engages deeply.[27] 'The contrast between the temperate and the tropical is one of the most enduring themes in the history of global imaginings. . . .The conventional discourse of tropicality', Felix Driver and Luciana Martins explain, 'might be compared with that of Orientalism, to the extent that both have conventionally been used to define and legitimise essential differences between cultures and natures, both understood in strongly spatial terms.'[28] Like the Orient, '[t]he tropics . . . represented an enduring alterity . . . Broadly speaking, the tropics were represented as a landscape in which the power of nature dominated human existence and to no small degree determined its characteristics and quality.' Tropicality has been structured by a core duality: the tropics as 'pestilential' and 'paradisiacal'. Hurricanes as extreme weather events have generally figured as 'pestilential' in the discourse of tropicality, signs of 'primitiveness, violence and destruction'.[29] Drawn from the pestilential strand of tropicality, Queenie Buxton's elocution exercise, 'In Herefordshire, Hertfordshire and Hampshire hurricanes hardly ever happen' (SI, 248), figures England and disciplined English pronunciation of the names as metonyms of civilisation, modesty and enlightenment and of middle-class aspiration. When demobilised RAF pilot Michael Roberts seduces her for the second time, asking, 'Tell me, you ever felt the force of a hurricane?' (SI, 494), Queenie invitingly repeats the recitation exercise.

Levy pointedly juxtaposes hurricanes, events of 'spectacular' violence, with forms of 'slow', 'attritional' violence that shape the worldly horizons of her characters.[30] In Jamaica the lives and aspirations of Hortense and Gilbert are marked by negotiation of a colonial education, the comparative economic underdevelopment of the region, the legacies of pigmentocracy, the stigma attached to illegitimacy, and a conservative, gendered modernity; in England, Queenie and Bernard are shaped by imperial education, the racism and xenophobia ingrained in it, and a conservative, gendered modernity. The dichotomies that underpin tropicality lend themselves to Levy's comic ironisation of colonial fealty to England and Englishness. In a masculine courting display for Hortense and Celia, for instance, returned serviceman Gilbert holds up a glorified pastoral vision of autumn leaves – 'a blanket of gold', 'leaves . . . float[ing] around . . . like golden rain' – and 'sip[ping] tea and search[ing] for Nelson on his column'. Playfully offering to take Celia to England, Gilbert teases Hortense that she could send them letters about 'the hurricanes and the earthquakes and the shortages of rice on this small island' (*SI*, 94). Hortense and Gilbert make the voyage from tropical to temperate regions and their colonial perceptions shaped by family metaphors of empire (with England as mother) are deflated by grim realities of racism, exclusion and housing shortage.

After enlisting in the RAF, Bernard is posted to tropical India, which he imagines to be a colonial frontier on which he might prove his white, middle-class imperial masculinity. Not passing the eye test to be accepted as a pilot, he serves as an aircrafthand, an erk, dreaming of a personal transformation from 'pallid bank clerk, fretting when the tube got too crowded' to the 'hero' whom he recognises Queenie 'would have liked to live with' (*SI*, 353, 345). The frustration of this ambition shores up a sense of racial and class superiority. Shortly after his arrival in India he is one of a number of workers ordered to remove from a runway two shot-up Hawker Hurricane aircraft, planes that were symbols of British defence, airpower and victory in the European theatre of the Second World War. Levy's description of Bernard's sense of the 'sorry sight' (*SI*, 347) and the process of shifting the wreckage suffuses a surface realism with surreal dramatic irony about Bernard's threatened masculinity, figured as losing his 'footing' (*SI*, 348). He comes to think that he has been a 'poor steward' of the family home (*SI*, 468), a metonym of 'national becoming and community'.[31]

With massive irony on Levy's part, given the Nazi Holocaust – the mass murder of Jewish and Romani people, homosexuals and the mentally ill – he thinks in relation to the 'brown gadabouts' from the tropics settling in Britain, 'The war was fought so people might live amongst their own kind' (*SI*, 468–9). After Queenie gives birth to a child by Michael, this attitude on Bernard's part prompts her to persuade Hortense and Gilbert to adopt the child, an act that, as John McLeod notes, 'paradoxically supports' the 'dominant discourse of racial difference which installs unbridgeable distances in the small island of 1948 Britain'.[32] Bernard's memory arc, 'the narrative perspective of its most explicitly racist white British narrator',[33] is excised from the 2009 television adaptation of *Small Island*.[34]

The spectacular and slow violence renders both Jamaica and Britain 'small', undercutting imperial snobberies before and around 1948. Gilbert thinks of West Indian 'small islanders' as people 'whose universe only runs a few miles in either direction before it falls into the sea' (SI, 131). The adjective 'small' catches up the idea of Little England; it also resonates with Jamaica Kincaid's account of Antigua in *A Small Place*, where the small, too, is tied to absorption in the 'domestic', and to an inability to see a 'larger' interconnected 'picture' and to think strategically beyond the 'present' to a more expansive and liberal 'future'.[35]

In 2007, as part of the bicentenary of the British abolition of its slave trade, *Small Island* – which had won the Orange Prize for Fiction (2004), the Whitbread Novel Award (2004), the Whitbread Book of the Year award (2004), the Commonwealth Writers' Prize Best Book award (2004) and the Orange Prize 'Best of the Best' award (2005) – was the focal point of a mass-reading project, *Small Island* Read 2007. This 'involved the distribution of 50,000 free copies of Andrea Levy's novel, along with 80,000 copies of a glossy A5 readers' guide. It generated 100 separate events (including library talks, book group discussions, competitions, exhibitions), and 60 school workshops.'[36] Designed to promote 'literacy' and 'new forms of creativity' through 'reading', *Small Island* Read 2007 also had larger ambitions: 'us[ing] reading to facilitate learning about the past' and 'bring[ing] diverse communities together through the act of reading and thereby foster[ing] a sense of shared identity'.[37]

Funded largely by Arts Council England and the Heritage Lottery Fund, it was conducted from 11 January to 31 March 2007, primarily in Bristol, Liverpool and Glasgow – all major ports on slave-trading routes – but also in Hull, an electorate that leading abolitionist William Wilberforce represented in the British parliament. The choice of *Small Island* for the mass-reading project, Rachel Carroll has suggested perceptively, was based on the prestige of the prizes it had won and 'its readability', its potential to be 'both "accessible" and "enjoyable"' for a broad readership.[38] The documentation of the event (reader comments and recorded book group and focus group discussions) has enabled searching inquiry into non-academic reading practices. Fuller and Procter found that 'the individual voices of the novel serve to profoundly personalise the historical narrative in ways that encourage readerly identification'.[39] Anouk Lang argues that *Small Island* 'harnesses the powerful effects of character identification in order to overcome the difficulties of cultural and linguistic difference for British readers without diminishing that difference or mitigating its material consequences'.[40] Scholarly studies of *Small Island* Read 2007 show that readers draw out 'informal, vernacular expressions of cross-cultural connection',[41] but also 'hedgings' around the 'fraughtness of ethnicity'.[42]

As Barnor Hesse points out, 'the struggle over the memory of slavery was being fought at the same time as its unrelenting privations on the plantations were being incurred by the slaves'.[43] '[S]lave masters', Simon Gikandi observes, 'turned to writing as a will to power; record keeping, and the archiving gesture, was a form of violent control; the archive was an attestation to the authority of natural history, the key to the ideology of white power. Here, in the archive, the African could be reduced to the world of nature and the prehuman.'[44] July, the protagonist of *The Long Song* (2010), who generally tells her narrative in the third person, is taught to read and write by her mistress Caroline Mortimer, who needs help in the 'administering of the plantation'. 'There was the register of slaves to be taken, compensation to be claimed, always overseers and bookkeepers to be found,' July remembers. July acquires fluency as a reader and writer of English by studying the 'many papers and books that lay about the great house' (*LS*, 160–1).

In narrating her life July, the daughter of field slave Kitty and abusive overseer Tam Dewar, is blunt about the memory of slavery that circulates and is passed down in books published in the period. They are generally 'words flowing free as the droppings that fall from the backside of a mule', 'the puff and twaddle of some white lady's mind' as she expatiates on 'the indolence and stupidity of her slaves ... that most troublesome of subjects' (*LS*, 7–8). Levy sets up July's narrative as a pointed counter-memory of slavery and apprenticeship to the archive of slaveowners, the portraiture they commissioned as a 'presencing of virtue and rank',[45] and the privilege of a white female missionary with the power to misrepresent her in a published article about the adoption of her son, named Thomas Kinsman by his adoptive parents.

Brought up in England and trained there as a printer and editor, Thomas, who has returned to Jamaica as an adult and taken the by then indigent July into his home, ostensibly publishes her narrative as a book in 1898. Theirs is a relationship that pointedly differentiates the conditions of production of the book from those of slave narrative. Barnor Hesse notes that

> the slave narrative was usually a co-production involving the escaped ex-slave *as author only*, with white abolitionists managing the whole enterprise from inception to dissemination. This included directing the framing of the genre, editing the emotional and political fabric of the material, producing the publication, and finally arranging forforewords to be written, which confirmed that the eponymous slave in question really had written the narrative 'himself' or 'herself'. ... The ex-slave in being vaunted for her/his redeemable humanity escaped economic commodification only to be commodified politically [for the abolitionist cause].[46]

Thomas, rather, encourages his mother, from whom he has been estranged through adoption, to write her story as a transgenerational record of family history, a 'lasting legacy'. In his foreword he assures readers that he has been her 'most conscientious editor ... rais[ing] life out of her most crabbed script to make her tale flow like some of the finest writing in the English language' (*LS*, 3). *The Long Song* was well received: it was short-listed for the Man Booker Prize in 2010 and won the Walter Scott Prize for historical fiction in 2011.

In researching her narrative Levy has read against the grain of records of the plantation and of what Hesse describes as 'abolitionist memory', 'the memory of slavery ... as the memory of its heroic and inevitable abolition',[47] a feature, for example, of *Amazing Grace*, a film released to coincide with the bicentenary of the British abolition of its slave trade.[48] *Amazing Grace*, Marcus Wood argues, is 'set firmly on the glorification of [William] Wilberforce, British abolitionists, and the British tradition of parliamentary debate', representing the experience and business of slavery as 'mere catalysts' for 'morally charged' British male agency.[49] Historians have supplemented and challenged abolitionist memory by drawing out repressed histories of slave rebellion and vindicating the agency and humanity of people subjected to enslavement and 'its debasements', 'burdens', 'repressions' and 'cruelties'.[50] Sam Sharpe's Rebellion of 1831, otherwise known as the Baptist War, the violent suppression of the slave revolt by militias, and the persecution of Baptist missionaries by the pro-slavery Colonial Church Union occur in the course of Levy's novel. July, though, concedes that 'at Amity', distant from the rebellion, 'the loudest thing your storyteller could hear was Miss Hannah gnawing upon the missus's discarded ham bone' (LS, 79). Their shamed owner John Howarth commits suicide after witnessing the spectacle of nine male Colonial Church Union members dressed as women torturing a Baptist minister they have tarred and feathered in front of his wife and sons.

Levy's often humorous narrative is shaped by a 'paradigm of resistance', focusing on July's daily acts of insubordination and 'resilience' as she negotiates and manipulates 'conditions of subjugation and dehumanisation'.[51] July is, at times, an unreliable and evasive narrator, especially around life events that distress her. Morrison notes that in deference to 'popular taste' slave narratives seldom 'dwell too long or too carefully on the more sordid details of their [the slaves'] experience'; instead, they were 'silent about many things, and they "forgot" many other things'.[52] July, who is acutely conscious of the potential status of her lighter skin shade, is evasive to Thomas, her son by a manumitted slave, Nimrod, about whether his darker skin led her to give him up for adoption. July's second child Emily, by white plantation owner through marriage Robert Goodwin, is deeply beloved by both parents, and is abducted by the father and his wife, John Howarth's sister Caroline, who return to England after Robert turns sharply against July in the context of his failure to recruit ex-slave labour to work the estate. July pulls her narrative up short, refusing to write in detail about the travails of emancipation and her grief over the loss of Emily. As Anne Whitehead notes, 'a nation is defined as much by what it has forgotten as by what it chooses to remember'.[53] Thomas, keen to locate his half-sister, but apprehensive about unsettling fictions of white racial purity, writes, 'In England the finding of negro blood within a family is not always met with rejoicing' (LS, 308).

Levy's turn to historical fiction with *Small Island* and *The Long Song* evinces a commitment to exploring the common and deeply intertwined Atlantic histories of Britain and the West Indies, inviting national reflections on their reach and meanings in the intimate lives of peoples. Her use of recollection as both a narrative method and a form of critical engagement with the extant archives of those histories offers, like black memory more generally, 'an enlargement of the sources of public memory, a complication of the possible pictures of the past available for remembering, and an enrichment of the possibilities of criticism by which to reshape our present',[54] especially around the legacies of British imperialism and the discourses of race and nation that shaped it.[55]

NOTES

1. Andrea Levy, 'Back to My Own Country: An Essay', in *Six Stories and an Essay* (London: Tinder, 2014), p. 12. Levy quotes Toni Morrison from interview material used by Hilton Als in a profile of Morrison based on a series of interviews, 'Ghosts in the House', *The New*

Yorker, 27 October 2003, <http://www.newyorker.com/magazine/2003/10/27/ghosts-in-the-house> (last accessed 28 June 2016).
2. Levy, 'Back to My Own Country', p. 19.
3. David Scott, 'Introduction: On the Archaeologies of Black Memory', *Small Axe*, 26 (June 2008), vi.
4. 'Andrea Levy in Conversation with Susan Alice Fischer (2005 and 2012)', in Jeannette Baxter and David James (eds), *Andrea Levy: Contemporary Critical Perspectives* (London: Bloomsbury, 2014), pp. 122–3.
5. Ibid., p. 122.
6. Levy, 'Back to My Own Country', p. 11.
7. 'Andrea Levy in Conversation with Susan Alice Fischer', p. 129.
8. Levy, 'Back to My Own Country', p. 11.
9. Stuart Hall, 'New Ethnicities', in James Donald and Ali Rattansi (eds), *'Race', Culture and Difference* (London: Sage, in association with the Open University, 1992), pp. 252, 253, 258.
10. 'Andrea Levy in Conversation with Susan Alice Fischer', p. 133.
11. Andrea Levy, 'Introduction to "Uriah's War"', in *Six Stories and an Essay*, p. 111.
12. Alison Donnell, 'The Lives of Others: Happenings, Histories and Literary Healing', in Michael A. Bucknor and Alison Donnell (eds), *The Routledge Companion to Anglophone Caribbean Literature* (London: Routledge, 2013), p. 422.
13. Toni Morrison, 'The Site of Memory', in William Zinsser (ed.), *Inventing the Truth: The Art and Craft of Memoir* (Boston: Houghton Mifflin, 1995), pp. 91–2.
14. Andrea Levy, 'Small Island by Andrea Levy: Part 3', *The Guardian*, 22 January 2011, <http://www.repeatingislands.com/2011/01/24/small-island-by-andrea-levy-part-3> (last accessed 28 June 2016).
15. James Procter, *Dwelling Places: Postwar Black British Writing* (Manchester: Manchester University Press, 2003), p. 22.
16. Ibid.
17. Bruce King, *The Internationalisation of English Literature* (Oxford: Oxford University Press, 2004), pp. 225, 224.
18. Alan Rice, *Creating Memorials, Building Identities: The Politics of Memory in the Black Atlantic* (Liverpool: Liverpool University Press, 2010), p. 172.
19. Anna Grmelová, 'From Loneliness to Encounter: London in the Windrush Generation Novels of Sam Selvon and Andrea Levy', *Literaria Pragensia: Studies in Literature and Culture*, 20.40 (2010), 76.
20. Andrea Levy, *The Long Song* (London: Headline Review, 2010), pp. 316, 318. All quotations are from this edition; hereafter, page numbers will be given in the text, preceded by LS.
21. Scott, 'Introduction', p. ix.
22. Jeannette Baxter and David James, 'Introduction', in Baxter and James (eds), *Andrea Levy: Contemporary Critical Perspectives*, p. 4.
23. Donnell, 'The Lives of Others', p. 429.
24. David Barker and David Miller, 'Hurricane Gilbert: Anthropomorphising a Natural Disaster', *Area*, 22.2 (1990), 113.
25. Grenadian-born writer Merle Collins makes a distinction between 'natural hurricane' and 'human hurricane' in '*Tout Moun ka Pléwé* (Everybody Bawling)', *Small Axe*, 22 (February 2007), 6. Collins interprets Grenadian history before Janet and after Janet (1955) and before Ivan and after Ivan (2004).
26. Andrea Levy, *Small Island* (London: Review, 2004), p. 52. All quotations are from this edition; hereafter, page numbers will be given in the text, preceded by SI.
27. See Felix Driver and Brenda S. A. Yeoh (eds), 'Constructing the Tropics', special issue of *Singapore Journal of Tropical Geography*, 21.1 (2000); see in particular David Arnold, '"Illusory Riches": Representations of the Tropical World, 1840–1950', 6–18; 9.

28. Felix Driver and Luciana Martins, 'Introduction', in Driver and Martins (eds), *Tropical Visions in the Age of Empire* (Chicago: University of Chicago Press, 2010), pp. 3–5.
29. Arnold, '"Illusory Riches"', pp. 7, 8.
30. Rob Nixon, *Slow Violence and the Environmentalism of the Poor* (Cambridge, MA: Harvard University Press, 2011), p. 2.
31. Paul Gilroy, *Postcolonial Melancholia* (New York: Columbia University Press, 2005), p. 87.
32. John McLeod, 'Postcolonial Fictions of Adoption', *Critical Survey*, 18.2 (2006), 50.
33. Rachel Carroll, '*Small Island*, Small Screen: Adapting Black British Fiction', in Baxter and James (eds), *Andrea Levy: Contemporary Critical Perspectives*, p. 69.
34. *Small Island*, dir. John Alexander (AL Films for BBC TV, 2010).
35. Jamaica Kincaid, *A Small Place* (London: Virago, 1988), pp. 52–4.
36. Danielle Fuller and James Procter, 'Reading as "Social Glue"? Book Groups, Multiculture, and the *Small Island* Read 2007', *Moving Worlds: A Journal of Transcultural Writings*, 9.2 (2009), 30.
37. Melanie Kelly, *Small Island Read 2007: Evaluation Report*, <http://www.bristolreads.com/small_island_read/downloads/small_island_evaluation.pdf> (last accessed 28 June 2016), p. 2.
38. Carroll, '*Small Island*, Small Screen', p. 67.
39. Fuller and Procter, 'Reading as "Social Glue"?', p. 32.
40. Anouk Lang, '"Enthralling but at the same time disturbing": Challenging Readers of *Small Island*', *Journal of Commonwealth Literature*, 44 (2009), 134.
41. Fuller and Procter, 'Reading as "Social Glue"?', p. 28.
42. Anouk Lang, 'Reading Race in *Small Island*: Discourse Deviation, Schemata and the Textual Encounter', *Language and Literature*, 18.3 (2009), 320. See also Bethan Benwell, '"A pathetic and racist and awful character": Ethnomethodological Approaches to the Reception of Diasporic Fiction', *Language and Literature*, 18.3 (2009), 305–11.
43. Barnor Hesse, 'Forgotten Like a Bad Dream: Atlantic Slavery and the Ethics of Postcolonial Memory', in David Theo Goldberg and Ato Quayson (eds), *Relocating Postcolonialism* (Oxford: Blackwell, 2002), p. 146.
44. Simon Gikandi, 'Rethinking the Archive of Enslavement', *Early American Literature*, 50.1 (2015), 92.
45. Simon Gikandi, *Slavery and the Culture of Taste* (Princeton: Princeton University Press, 2011), p. 126.
46. Hesse, 'Forgotten Like a Bad Dream', pp. 146–7.
47. Ibid., p. 150.
48. *Amazing Grace*, dir. Michael Apted (Momentum Pictures and Samuel Goldwyn Films, 2007).
49. Marcus Wood, *The Horrible Gift of Freedom: Atlantic Slavery and the Representation of Emancipation* (Athens, GA: University of Georgia Press, 2010), p. 345.
50. David Scott, *Conscripts of Modernity: The Tragedy of Colonial Enlightenment* (Durham, NC: Duke University Press, 2004), p. 94.
51. Jenny Sharpe, *Ghosts of Slavery: A Literary Archaeology of Black Women's Lives* (Minneapolis: University of Minnesota Press, 2003), p. xv.
52. Morrison, 'The Site of Memory', pp. 90–1.
53. Anne Whitehead, *Memory* (Abingdon: Routledge, 2009), p. 145.
54. Scott, 'Introduction', p. ix.
55. Research for this chapter was funded by the Disciplinary Research Program (DRP) in English, Theatre and Drama at La Trobe University. I want to thank both the DRP and Suzi Hayes, my research assistant.

FURTHER READING

For an up-to-date list of Andrea Levy's novels, see the British Council website: <https://literature.britishcouncil.org/writer/andrea-levy> (last accessed 28 June 2016).

Baxter, Jeannette, and David James (eds), *Andrea Levy: Contemporary Political Perspectives* (London: Bloomsbury, 2014).
Knepper, Wendy (ed.), *Andrea Levy*, special issue of *Entertext*, 9 (2012).
Levy, Andrea, *Six Stories and an Essay* (London: Tinder, 2014).

CHAPTER 18

Aminatta Forna: Truth, Trauma, Memory

Françoise Lionnet and Jennifer MacGregor

The turn to the transnational in literary studies in the 1980s, propelled by the amplified presence in the West of writers whose roots and sensibilities are more global than local or national, has reshaped critical approaches to the contemporary novel.[1] Prominent today in Britain among such transnational figures is the Scottish-Sierra Leonean Aminatta Forna. She has earned a place in the 'great tradition' of novelists distinguished by their intense interest in formal as well as moral complexity.[2] Characterised by the geographical breadth of her subject matter, an elegant narrative style, and a measured concern for the uneven landscapes of justice, ethics, and the changes brought about by the digital circulation of news media and the financial globalisation of national economies, her work consistently engages with the painful histories and unsettling memories of individuals in different parts of the world, individuals who must carry on with ordinary resilience and day-to-day courage in the aftermath of blood feuds and civil strife.

Forna first achieved wide visibility with the success of her second novel, *The Memory of Love*, winner of the 2011 Writers' Prize. Born in Glasgow, raised in Sierra Leone and Britain, she also spent periods of her childhood in Iran, Thailand and Zambia.[3] Her first book, *The Devil that Danced on the Water* (short-listed for the 2003 Samuel Johnson Prize for Non-Fiction), is a memoir that delves into the death of her dissident father, a physician-politician who was framed, imprisoned, and eventually hanged for treason in Sierra Leone in 1975, when she was only eleven years old. Her first novel, *Ancestor Stones* (winner of the 2007 Hurston-Wright Legacy Award), is a fictionalised account of her African female ancestors and their quiet stewardship of the land and the past. With her third novel, *The Hired Man* (2013), she ventured outside her own experience to tackle the outcomes of the 1990s conflict in the Balkans. Forna's insightful, compassionate approach to the troubled histories of disparate regions of Africa and Europe has elicited praise on both sides of the Atlantic. In 2014, she received the Yale University Windham Campbell Prize for her body of work. In just over a decade, her ambitious fiction has earned her a place among the major new literary voices of the twenty-first century.

In conversation and published interviews, Forna has said that 'Creative writing students are often told: "Write about what you know." I prefer: "Write about what you want to understand." And I think that's what lies behind all my writing – I'm simply trying to understand.'[4] It is this need to understand that prompted her to write her first book about her father's involvement in his country's political conflicts. To appreciate the multiple facets of historical 'truth' and the degree to which trauma and its repressed memories affect different populations, she engages with the ambiguities of literary representation. She emphasises human commonalities in her characters by fearlessly broadening her reach to global dimensions. She tackles controversial questions – guilt and complicity, individual integrity and compromise – while maintaining a balanced perspective on the causes and consequences of community breakdowns and civil conflicts. She boldly addresses the need for self-protection while also depicting the quiet authority of those who resist revenge when exacting it might appear most compelling.

Forna's character-driven plots hinge on the entanglement of generations, the link between perpetrators and victims, the ramifications of post-traumatic stress, and the pitfalls of Western humanitarian or economic interventions that interfere with nation-rebuilding efforts. Her thematic and stylistic choices derive as much from her transnational sensibilities as from British realist fiction, postcolonial historical narratives of resistance, and the local traditions of Sierra Leone and the former Yugoslavia, both of which she has researched in great geographic depth and linguistic detail. Attuned to critical debates and controversies about the epistemological value of historical fiction, she exposes the extent to which the past lives on in the present, influencing perceptions of reality and time. Her aesthetic choices convey the flaws of formal representation and the unspeakability of traumatic events. Her work escapes easy labelling, for although she employs realistic descriptions and chronological plot development, she also conveys a multiplicity of interconnected perspectives on actual events and their reverberations. To the extent that she uses a style that simultaneously questions the logic of linear representation and the reliability of individual narrators, she has a post-postmodernist stance that demands historical and geographical reference while also projecting suspicion about the accuracy of any single point of view on that reality.

Her desire to 'understand' the past and its zones of opacity translates into an emphasis on the manifold, collective dimensions of both individual and national memory. She critiques the ideology of individualism understood as the Westernised male belief in the autonomy of the self, and she is more interested in the lives of women whose intertwined stories and interconnected lives provide a narrative model for her own practice. She examines the vital links that tie women's agency and experience to their national histories, echoing but also transforming European as well as postcolonial understandings of nationalism and feminism. As Annie Gagiano notes, Forna and other African women writers 'continu[e] to show a strong ... interest in national communities ... [and] to write women into their nations' histories, present and future [sic], rather than write off their nations'.[5] Steeped in indigenous African feminisms, she engages with history and the macropolitics of nationalism while narrating domestic life and creating characters who seek the private peace and personal growth they know to be inseparable from larger public issues.[6] She does not dwell on historical facts about nation-building and its discontents; rather, she successfully communicates the visceral human experiences of those who, caught in the messy business of wartime politics, struggle to build a peaceable future.

Forna proposes that national and regional affiliations should be cultivated in our globalised world, but she also communicates a sense of urgency about the hazards of narrow ethnic and nationalist programmes that prepare the ground for violent conflicts. Her exquisitely light touch in the portrayal of prolonged suffering renders with acute specificity the symptoms and ghostly presence of trauma among survivors, especially among women whose bodies are easy targets while their contributions to the nation remain woefully overlooked. Forna challenges her readers to take note of damaging patriarchal customs, but her approach is intersectional. She takes into account global factors such as race, ethnicity, class and sexuality when exploring gender issues.[7]

In *Ancestor Stones* (2006), the transformative potential of women's voices is suggested thematically through oral storytelling and structurally by the tension between narrative realism and temporal discontinuities. The chapters work together to offer multiple perspectives on the community, providing a realist account of the colonial, anti-colonial, independent and civil war periods of Sierra Leone. A living and ever-present sense of familial female heritage fosters an intimate connection between Abie, the author figure, and her father's country, its political past and its present predicaments due to globalisation and the intrusions of foreign media that serve up distorted representations of daily life. Successive narrative strands feature five elder, single female citizens, Abie's aunts. Each one remembers her own upbringing in, departure from, and return to her father's village, Rofathane. The aunts' experiences are distinct, yet when read together their stories create a sensitive and personalised history of the country.

Abie is drawn back to this village when she receives a letter in London from her cousin announcing that the 'coffee plantation at Rofathane' is now hers.[8] In the prologue, she explains that her female ancestors' handiwork produced the 'Eden' the first European sailors merely 'took to be nature's abundance' (AS, 6). Blind to a cultural and botanical logic different from their own, these men were unable to read African reality and to grasp that 'it was an Eden created not by the hand of God, but the hands of women' (AS, 6–7). In the book's epilogue, Abie has returned home to London four months later, and she reflects on the healing work her aunts' storytelling has done for her. Between these two framing sections, the aunts' first-person stories appear to have merely been transcribed by Abie, who has however participated in the conversations that drew them out. She notes that the aunts' voices live on in her mind: 'Vibrant and noisy, tumbling through time, jostling for my attention ... Superior by far to any box of disintegrating diaries and lifeless letters' (AS, 315). She trusts the honesty of these voices while recognising that they are more alive and malleable than written words.

The reader, however, is not to rely on the accuracy of the tales 'recorded' by Abie, since memories are imperfect; but they contain essential truths through which she finds comfort: 'What story shall I tell? The story of how it really was, or the one you want to hear?' (AS, 15), as one aunt puts it. The memories are often written as having benefited from years of internal reflection and deliberation, which implies that their truth-value should be viewed with scepticism. This heightens the novel's overall realistic effect while cautioning readers against complacently accepting any single retelling of the past as the truth.

These tales told by Abie and her aunts appear linear and separate from one another, but they are structurally and thematically intertwined, reflecting the novel's call for new collectivities for the sake of the country's future. Instead of following a single aunt's narrative through time, the stories are printed chronologically with each aunt telling a story about her mother, her first time away from her father's home, a highly charged turning point in her adult life, and a private experience of the national conflict. These thematic points can be read as roughly allegorical, the aunts' turmoil or peace corresponding to Sierra Leone's transitional periods: colonisation, rebellion against the colonisers, independence and civil war. However, the storytellers make what Uzodinma Iweala calls 'cameos' in each other's stories and occasionally share characters.[9] Forna foregrounds the inevitable interconnections of the sisters' lives, the porous boundaries of their singular narratives, and the greater truths these produce when told in concert.[10] With its interrelated but distinct voices, the novel troubles the hierarchies of individualism bound up in the great British realist tradition and endorses a collaborative, collective and feminist process as a promising way to the country's political future.

In her wide-ranging second novel, *The Memory of Love* (2010), Forna develops a different style from *Ancestor Stones*, but one that similarly requires readers to examine the book's structure for its implicit critique of both realism and postmodernism. Forna avoids detailing facts about Sierra Leone's 1991 to 1999 civil war, focusing instead on her characters' quotidian life experiences, relationships, personal memories and dreams in the narrative present of 2000 to 2001, in the capital, Freetown. The book consists of the interweaving of both Kai Mansaray's and Adrian Lockheart's points of view with Elias Cole's controlled recounting of his memories. Together these offer three disparate perspectives on the war and its aftermath. Like *Ancestor Stones*, this novel includes characters who cross national borders and oceans and live in the age of rapid international travel and digital communication. The necessity of a hybrid local and global response to the consequences of civil war is highlighted, as are narratives of trauma and processes of healing. But the novel also critiques the power dynamics involved in both global interventions and local nationalist narratives. Plot and structure blend present experiences with the enduring traumas that invade survivors' lives.

Elias, Kai and Adrian know each other professionally, but they have their most profound connections through Elias's estranged daughter Nenebah – Kai's college sweetheart – who changed her name to Mamakay after the war and who dies while giving birth to Adrian's baby. An aged and dying history professor who gained power at the local university as Sierra Leone's government becomes increasingly corrupt,

Elias tells a personal story that his listener and therapist, Adrian, initially believes to be his dying confession. Adrian is a British psychologist who has travelled from London to Freetown to offer help to civil war survivors, and he 'treats' Elias. Elias's stories are told in the first person, and he exercises strict control over narration of the past, often including precise dates. This is unlike sections about Adrian or Kai, which include only vague temporal markers such as 'A memory' or 'A Tuesday'.[11] The memories, as the professor describes them, follow a linear timeline and include verifiable facts, following the form of a nineteenth-century realist novel, rather than the associative, free-flowing organisation more typical of a conversation or therapy session.

The novel echoes Elias's narrative goals by structurally embedding and isolating his stories within their own chapters, thus separating his voice from all other characters' contributing voices, just as he is contained in his private hospital room. Elias's curatorial impulses aim to occlude his jealousy and cowardice, as well as the tragedies they caused. The three main characters of his autobiographical history die prematurely: his colleague Julius, the botanist Saffia (Julius's widow, who marries Elias in the fog of her grief), and Mamakay (his daughter with Saffia). Only Mamakay has the opportunity to expose the lies of Elias's manipulated narrative. His crafting of his story mimics his stalking of Saffia before Julius's death and his increasingly controlling stance once they marry. He 'wished to break her' and 'to catch her out in small lies and evasions' (ML, 291). Jealous of her longing for Julius, he polices her language to control her. Instead of breaking, though, she maintains her autonomy by secretly tending her garden at the home she shared with Julius. Here she grows life and creates beauty in the corrupt nation. Like Abie's female relatives in *Ancestor Stones*, Saffia's garden is made Edenic through her labour. Elias seems to recognise it as an elegy to her former husband with whom she could not have children: 'Standing there, it was as though I had opened a door upon a roomful of silent children: watchful, listening, waiting' (ML, 294), he explains ruefully after sneaking into her private world.

The novel closes with a reference to Julius's handwriting, as Kai drives his nephew and Mamakay and Adrian's daughter over a bridge containing Julius's carved initials (ML, 445). This final detail demonstrates that despite leaving no progeny, Julius's impact on Sierra Leone's future will be more lasting than Elias's attempt to find fame and cater to European interlocutors, such as Adrian. By relying on his journals to tell his 'memories', donating his curated library, and attempting to woo Adrian's sympathies so he will share Elias's version of history with other British professionals, Elias's storyline exposes the untrustworthiness of single-voiced representations while allowing Forna indirectly to denounce the way historical archives are created.

Elias's unreliability as a narrator is made clearer through the novel's critique of foreign journalists and aid workers in Sierra Leone. *The Memory of Love* demonstrates their opportunistic and self-serving tendencies, their similarity to mere tourists. For Mamakay, reporters maintain the cultural capital necessary to create a fiction and turn it into fact for Western consumption by fabricating vignettes of Sierra Leone's war that include teleological timelines and justify predetermined rebuilding goals. Adrian initially universalises his patients' traumas and suffering, ignoring the details of specific experiences in favour of imagining that all sufferers are inherently the same or in need of the same treatment.[12] Kai critiques Adrian's faith in universal reason and psychological treatments, and his nonspecific assumptions of war's effects. Adrian's belief that these survivors in Sierra Leone suffer from post-traumatic stress disorder is proven inaccurate. There is no 'post-' to their trauma; they live side by side with their former attackers, often in poverty and dislocation from their original homes. Despite Adrian's eventual transition from tourist to traveller, thanks to the insights he learns from Mamakay, the novel mostly critiques Western European visitors to Sierra Leone for their unearned global agency, hubris and manufactured visions of the country's history. The novel deftly avoids universalising trauma, while exposing aid workers' tendencies to do exactly that.

Liberation from past trauma is to be found not in Elias's single-authored oral history or in Adrian's initial one-size-fits-all treatment approach, but instead in the collective voicing of personal memories and in the acts of witnessing that enable characters to take responsibility for their roles in the civil war. Forna's technique is to alternate these voices with Elias's. Thus, Kai hears the telling of collective memory as a woman's neighbours recount the traumatic story she, Agnes, cannot voice, but which continues to traumatise her well after the end of the war. Agnes's tale is told by a series of witnesses and neighbours, none of whom hold all the knowledge of her ordeal and all of whom experienced trauma of their own during the war. This powerful episode conveys the complicated nature of 'history' and the community-building effects of creating a 'true' story that is both singular and collective. The omniscient narrator notes that 'Each person told a part of the same story. And in telling another's story, they told their own. Kai took what they had given him and placed it together with what he already knew and those things Adrian had told him' (ML, 306). Agnes's endurance allows Kai to begin to reimagine his own trauma in a less punishing way, and the shared narratives become an alternative to Elias's manipulations of history.

In the second part of the novel, a glimpse at the future is made possible by Kai's own exorcising narration of his past that connects his trauma to that of Adrian's patients, who begin to heal in group therapy. Finding the words to tell his story allows Kai to remain in Sierra Leone and to encourage his friend, Tejani, to repatriate from America. Adrian, meanwhile, repatriates to England, leaving his and Mamakay's infant to be raised by Kai. Only Ileana, a Romanian immigrant, remains, having lived through Sierra Leone's civil war after surviving her own country's violent conflicts. The novel acknowledges that regardless of their nationalities, civil-war survivors share a common experience. In this way, *The Memory of Love* does not simply dismiss global travel and diasporic migration as harmful in favour of local traditions and blind nationalism. Instead, the transnational experiences of the characters signify the possibility of rebirth for Sierra Leone, symbolised by Mamakay and Adrian's infant daughter. The new nation cannot be built only on nationalist pride, but requires connection with and understanding of people from other countries. Global migrations and unconventional kinship structures combine in

The Memory of Love to suggest new possibilities for transnational solidarities while simultaneously crafting a multi-voiced history of Sierra Leone's past.

Forna's most recent novel, *The Hired Man*, is set in Croatia rather than Sierra Leone, but it too addresses the lasting effects of war, the dangers of single-authored history, and the politics of globalisation. Duro Kolak, the hired man and narrator, opens by introducing himself, and suggests the novel will be a testimonial of his experiences during the summer of 2007 with English tourist and real-estate investor Laura and her teenage children, Grace and Matthew. The novel's plot is deceptively simple. Duro's memory appears reliable, his actions transcribed without gaps in an organised, realist style. Yet his revelations, partial at first, only hint at his experiences during the unnamed conflict and siege that haunts his present these sixteen years later. Memories of long-absent people, and the ruins of deteriorating houses and abandoned fields prevent Duro and the residents of Gost from joining Laura in her profit-seeking participation in the globalised economy.[13] Instead, Duro cleverly uses Laura's self-centred neglect of Gost's history for the purposes of maintaining the townspeople's memories of their past actions. He restores the appearance of her house in order to resurrect for his enemies the memory of its original owner, his first love, Anka. The novel's setting in and around Duro's small village does not, however, diminish its global significance. With Duro's help, Laura turns the house into a summer home for international tourists. She blithely balms her own potential guilt at profiting from those who fled their homes during the violence, and imagines that buying cheap property in the post-war recession and marketing it to tourists for a significant personal profit is a boon to Gost's economy (*HM*, 77–8). Her attitude unthinkingly echoes British colonial ideology while reflecting that of neoliberal globalisation. Oblivious to local history, she exploits the country's housing resources. *The Hired Man* offers a critique of capitalism and neoliberalism that positions it as a transnational novel of great subtlety, rather than as a contemporary British travel narrative of encounter with distant cultures.

For Duro, the house provides a means to keep the past alive. His narrative withholds place names, dates, religions, and governmental or political headlines, but his realist account of Gost's violent history is codified for future residents. The exact location of Gost is never given, and Duro merely hints that the origins of the conflict can be gleaned from the village's linguistic and religious differences, thus giving his account human dimensions rather than large-scale national, territorial or ideological ones.[14] He never reveals that he is a Croat, and he describes losing loved ones from both sides of the ethnic divide. He imagines his written testimonial will be read decades later by someone who did not live through the war (*HM*, 43). Rather than asserting one side's primacy, he writes to prevent Anka's erasure after her brother, Krešimir, who had a hand in nearly killing her, sells her abandoned house with plans to leave Gost. '[S]omebody must stand guard over the past. / In Gost, that somebody is me. / The only person I can trust' (*HM*, 43), Duro insists. He emphasises the need for him to guard the past against those who wish to disfigure or destroy it. But he is the only one willing to speak of Gost's often unflattering history. He claims truth for his entire narrative by referencing other inhabitants' desires to forget while he 'remember[s] it all, every grinding minute, hour and day' (*HM*, 43).

After all, who better to document Gost's history than Duro, who imagines himself to be a ruin like the town: unchanging, unsocial and enduring (*HM*, 184).

As in her previous books, Forna respects many of the conventions of the realist tradition while creating a tension within the novel's chronologies between straightforward narration and the untold truths haunting the margins of the story. Laura's presence troubles Duro's sense of time, making the present and the past seem to exist simultaneously for him. He describes his memories as physical entities that coexist in his lived present, yet he remains unable to escape or voice them. He explains that Laura's presence 'opened a trapdoor. Beneath the trapdoor was an infinite tunnel and that tunnel led to the past . . . I seemed to have become trapped in the tunnel, somewhere between a time sixteen years ago and now' (*HM*, 233). Duro's trauma remains long after the siege, locking him and his two enemies, Fabjan and Krešimir, in a triangle of bitterness that he refuses to resolve. The events are located in a previous time, but they cannot be forgotten or passed off as benign. Although Croatia's government is seeking tourist money by papering over the physical evidence of the war and encouraging foreigners to rebuild houses and repopulate businesses, the act of restoring ruins that continue to be sites of trauma merely renews Duro's dedication to keeping the past alive in the present.

He reveals his unacknowledged interest in controlling the narrative as he prepares Laura to appear to be Anka returned in order to haunt Krešimir and Fabjan. He buys her a red hat similar to Anka's and encourages her to drive Anka's old car (*HM*, 144, 239), thrilling at Fabjan's and the townspeople's reactions to her (*HM*, 243). Duro uses Laura's ignorance to undermine her national and linguistic privilege by restyling her into Anka's *Doppelgänger* without her consent, exploiting her as she exploits Gost. When speaking to Krešimir, Duro refers to Laura as 'the woman from England', to imply she could be Anka coming home, and hoping to awaken Krešimir's troubling memories. He notes, '[T]he words left space for doubt to creep in and where doubt existed there was the possibility of something else: the dark child scratching against the walls' (*HM*, 244). Laura's Duro-styled appearance personifies Krešimir's and Fabjan's latent guilt at profiting from threats against their family members, neighbours and friends during and after the siege. The novel juxtaposes these local issues with events in distant places relayed through a newscast Duro watches as he awaits Laura's trip to town: riots in Greece and the resolution of a forty-three-year-old race-based crime in the United States. These news stories connect the aftermath of Gost's hostilities to international ethnic and racial conflicts that have decades-long repercussions. The novel foregrounds these analogies among populations that have endured civil violence and now share similar traumas.

Duro finds commonalities between Gost and other distant places, whereas Laura envisions places outside England as 'other' to her home – she groups countries as distinct as Abu Dhabi and Nigeria together as 'those kinds of places' and seems only to notice herself when she travels, describing a visit to Pakistan by noting its distance from England and the attention she received as a white person (*HM*, 111, 24). She conceives of the world in binary terms; England is at the centre of the globe, while places or communities outside of the wealthy West are peripheral. Duro's engagement with the rest of the world shows instead his awareness of a network of transversal solidarity among similarly affected communities that can relate to each other without the mediations of Western modes of representation.[15] Laura's exploitative actions are revealed through Duro's reactions to her and his ability to find similarities between the citizens of Gost and those who have survived other conflicts across the globe. While Laura dismisses these similarities – she laughs at an 'old slave superstition' in the southern United States that Duro tells her is shared by Gost – Duro sees Gost as part of a network of places affected by ethnicity- or race-based civil violence (HM, 23). He remembers reading books during the siege about the ways other people in 'Constantinople. Delhi. Mafeking. Paris. Dien Bien Phu. Leningrad' survived sieges, and using these discoveries to improve his family's situation (HM, 195).

With Duro's willingness to learn from conflicts elsewhere, Forna implies that countries such as Croatia and Sierra Leone, which have been constructed as peripheral by self-styled Western 'centres', can develop empowering solidarities as 'minor' nations in order to exorcise 'traumas of colonial, imperial, and global hegemonies' and to revitalise and reimagine their national and global identities.[16] By setting the novel in Croatia rather than Sierra Leone, Forna gives herself the right to suggest that the shared experience of trauma can bridge racial, linguistic and national divides, creating strong commonalities. Forna's fearless approach to human rights issues in Africa and Europe places her firmly in the great tradition of British fiction attuned to large moral and ethical questions. Her capacious interest in the transnational dimensions of contemporary conflicts, however, sets her apart as a writer with a truly global understanding of the factors increasingly influencing the formation of individual and collective identities in the twenty-first century.

NOTES

1. See Paul Jay, *Global Matters: The Transnational Turn in Literary Studies* (Ithaca: Cornell University Press, 2010).
2. See F. R. Leavis, *The Great Tradition: George Eliot, Henry James, Joseph Conrad* (New York: New York University Press, 1963).
3. In her hour-long interview with Eleanor Wachtel of the Canadian Broadcasting Company on 16 August 2015, Forna describes her childhood experiences and her choices of subject matter; see 'Writers and Company', <www.cbc.ca/radio/writersandcompany/aminatta-forna-from-sierra-leone-and-llondon- etc-1.3174340> (last accessed 28 June 2016).
4. During a visit to the University of California, Los Angeles, in 2013, Forna repeated this statement, which also appears in various interviews. See, for example, Melissa de Villiers, 'Questions of War' (Review of *The Memory of Love*), *Times Live*, 25 September 2011, <www.timeslive.co.za/lifestyle/books/2011/09/25/questions-of-war> (last accessed 28 June 2016), and Andrew Blackman, '"The Love of Memory": A Review of Aminatta Forna's *The Hired Man*', *The Puritan: Frontiers of New English*, 23 (2013), 102–6; 104; <puritan-magazine.com/the-love-of-memory-a-review-of-aminatta-fornas-the-hired-man> (last accessed 28 June 2016).
5. Annie Gagiano, 'Women Writing Nationhood Differently: Affiliative Critique in Novels by Forna, Atta, and Farah', *Ariel: A Review of International English Literature*, 44.1 (2013), 45–72; 48.
6. She echoes earlier African feminist writers, for example those studied by Susan Andrade in

The Nation Writ Small: African Fictions and Feminisms, 1958–88 (Durham, NC: Duke University Press, 2011).
7. See, for example, Valerie Smith, *Not Just Race, Not Just Gender: Black Feminist Readings* (New York: Routledge, 1998).
8. Aminatta Forna, *Ancestor Stones* (New York: Grove Press, 2006), p. 7. All quotations are from this edition; hereafter, page numbers will be given in the text, preceded by AS.
9. Uzodinma Iweala, 'As It Really Was', *New York Times*, 24 September 2006, <www.nytimes.com/2006/09/24/books/review/Iweala.t.html> (last accessed 28 June 2016).
10. The aunts' shared storytelling is reminiscent of Virginia Woolf's creation of a sense of reality through the collective consciousness of her characters in the high modernist period after the First World War, in stark contrast with the focalisation through the single character of the realist genre.
11. Aminatta Forna, *The Memory of Love* (New York: Grove Press, 2010), pp. 290, 291. All quotations are from this edition; hereafter, page numbers will be given in the text, preceded by ML.
12. For further discussion of the dangers of universalising concepts of trauma, see Michael Rothberg, *Multidirectional Memory: Remembering the Holocaust in the Age of Decolonisation* (Stanford: Stanford University Press, 2009), and Françoise Lionnet, ' "Dire exactement": Remembering the Interwoven Lives of Jewish Deportees and Coolie Descendants in 1940s Mauritius', *Yale French Studies*, 118/119 (2010), 111–35.
13. Aminatta Forna, *The Hired Man* (New York: Atlantic Monthly Press, 2013), pp. 70, 138. All quotations are from this edition; hereafter, page numbers will be given in the text, preceded by HM.
14. Zoe Norridge describes Gost as inspired by Gospić, which was on the border of a former territory called Serbian Krajina that existed from 1991 to 1995. Gospić was held in a siege by the Croatian government and was 'bombarded' from the east by Republic of Serbian Krajina forces. See 'Ways of Knowing Civil War: Human Rights and the Traction of Complicity in Aminatta Forna's *The Hired Man*', *Critical Quarterly*, 56.4 (2014), 99–113; 106.
15. Françoise Lionnet and Shu-mei Shih's concept of transversal solidarity, the 'minor-to-minor networks that circumvent the major altogether' and allow for 'new forms of identification' that transcend 'national, ethnic, and cultural boundaries', is a useful approach to the thematics developed in this novel. See 'Introduction: Thinking through the Minor, Transnationally', in Françoise Lionnet and Shu-mei Shih (eds), *Minor Transnationalism* (Durham, NC: Duke University Press, 2005), pp. 1–23; p. 8.
16. Ibid., p. 21.

FURTHER READING

For an up-to-date list of Aminatta Forna's novels, see the British Council website: <https://literature.britishcouncil.org/writer/aminatta-forna> (last accessed 28 June 2016).

Harrow, Kenneth, 'Suturing Two Worlds: Aminatta Forna's *The Memory of Love*', *Journal of Commonwealth and Postcolonial Studes*, 1.1 (2003), 13–32.
Norridge, Zoe, *Perceiving Pain in African Literature* (New York: Palgrave Macmillan, 2013).
—— 'Sex as Synecdoche: Intimate Languages of Violence in Chimamanda Ngozi Adichie's *Half of a Yellow Sun* and Aminatta Forna's *The Memory of Love*', *Research in African Literatures*, 43.2 (2012), 18–39.

Notes on Contributors

James Acheson is former Senior Lecturer in English at the University of Canterbury in Christchurch, New Zealand. He is author of *Samuel Beckett's Artistic Theory and Practice: Criticism, Drama, Early Fiction* and *John Fowles*, and is co-editor (with Sarah C. E. Ross) of *The Contemporary British Novel Since 1980*.

Daniel Bedggood is Senior Lecturer in English, Cinema Studies and Digital Humanities at the University of Canterbury in Christchurch, New Zealand. He is currently working on two books, one focusing on tropes of travel prevalent in postcolonial literatures, and the other on the revival of the utopian impulse in recent speculative fiction.

Cairns Craig is Glucksman Professor of Irish and Scottish Studies at the University of Aberdeen. His contributions to the study of Scottish literature include his four-volume *History of Scottish Literature*, *Intending Scotland* (an account of Scottish thought since the Enlightenment) and *The Modern Scottish Novel*. He has been involved in the publication of several Scottish journals, including *Cencrastus*, *Radical Scotland* and *The Edinburgh Review*, and is currently the editor of *The Journal of Irish and Scottish Studies* and *The Journal of Scottish Thought*.

Brian Finney is Emeritus Professor of English at California State University, Long Beach. He is author of *Since How It Is: A Study of Samuel Beckett's Later Fiction*; *Christopher Isherwood: A Critical Biography*; *The Inner I: British Literary Autobiography of the Twentieth Century*; *D. H. Lawrence's Sons and Lovers: A Critical Study*; *Martin Amis*; *English Fiction Since 1984: Narrating a Nation*; and *Terrorised: How the War on Terror Affected American Culture and Society*.

Lisa Fletcher is Senior Lecturer in English at the University of Tasmania. She is the author of *Historical Romance Fiction: Heterosexuality* and co-author (with Ralph

Crane) of *Cave*, a forthcoming volume in Reaktion Books' 'Earth' series. She has published widely on popular and literary historical novels, colonial and postcolonial literature, and the literary geography of islands.

Monica Germanà is Senior Lecturer in English Literature and Creative Writing at the University of Westminster. Her publications include *Scottish Women's Gothic and Fantastic Writing* and *Ali Smith* (co-edited with Emily Horton). She is currently completing *Apocalyptic Discourse in Contemporary Culture* (co-edited with Aris Mousoutzanis) and is working on a new book on Bond Girls.

Gretchen Gerzina is Dean of the Commonwealth Honours College at the University of Massachusetts at Amherst. She is the author and/or editor of seven books, including *Black London* (published in the UK as *Black England*), *Black Victorians/Black Victoriana* and biographies of Dora Carrington, Frances Hodgson Burnett and Lucy Terry. She is currently at work on a book on the black wife in British literature and culture, and a mixed-race family memoir.

Dominic Head is Professor of Modern English Literature at the University of Nottingham. He is author of *The Cambridge Introduction to Modern British Fiction, 1950–2000*; *The Cambridge Guide to Literature in English*; *Ian McEwan*; *The State of the Novel: Britain and Beyond*; and *The Cambridge Introduction to J. M. Coetzee*.

Françoise Lionnet is Professor of Comparative Literature and French and Francophone Studies at UCLA, where she directs the J. C. Coleman African Studies Center. She is the author of four books: *Autobiographical Voices: Race, Gender, Self-Portraiture*; *Postcolonial Representations: Women, Literature, Identity*; *Writing Women and Critical Dialogues: Subjectivity, Gender and Irony*; and *The Known and the Uncertain: Creole Cosmopolitics of the Indian Ocean*.

Alison Lumsden is Professor of English at the University of Aberdeen. She is a general editor of the Edinburgh Edition of the Waverley Novels, and has published on Walter Scott, Robert Louis Stevenson and a number of Scottish women writers, including Janice Galloway, Jackie Kay and Nan Shepherd. She is co-editor of *Contemporary Scottish Women's Writing*, and for a number of years was a judge for the Saltire Book of the Year prize.

Jennifer MacGregor is a doctoral student in English at UCLA. She earned her MA in English, with a certificate in Women's Studies, at the University of Pittsburgh in 2012. Jennifer is particularly interested in genres of the novel and narrative representations of time and memory in contemporary anglophone Indian Oceanic literature. She was a finalist for the 2014 Hindi Critical Language Scholarship.

Vijay Mishra is Professor of English Literature at Murdoch University in Perth, Australia. He is author of *The Gothic Sublime*; *Devotional Poetics and the Indian Sublime*; *Bollywood Cinema: Temples of Desire*; and *The Literature of the Indian*

Diaspora: Theorizing the Diasporic Imaginary, and co-author (with Bob Hodge) of two books: *Dark Side of the Dream: Australian Literature and the Postcolonial Mind* and *What Was Multiculturalism?*

Glenda Norquay is Professor of Scottish Literary Studies at Liverpool John Moores University. She has published widely on Scottish fiction and is editor of *The Edinburgh Companion to Scottish Women's Writing*. She is author of *Robert Louis Stevenson and Theories of Reading*, and since its publication has been editing *St Ives* for the New Edinburgh Edition of Stevenson's *Collected Works*.

Susana Onega is Professor of English at the University of Zaragoza in Spain. She is the head of a competitive research team of twenty members currently working on the rhetoric and politics of suffering in contemporary narratives in English. She is author of *The Sound and the Fury de William Faulkner*; *Form and Meaning in the Novels of John Fowles*; *Peter Ackroyd: The Writer and his Work*; *Metafiction and Myth in the Novels of Peter Ackroyd*; and *Jeanette Winterson*.

David Punter is Professor of English and Graduate Dean of Arts at the University of Bristol. His publications include *The Literature of Terror*; *The Hidden Script: Writing and the Unconscious*; *Introduction to Contemporary Cultural Studies*; *The Romantic Unconscious*; *Gothic Pathologies: The Text, the Body and the Law*; *Spectral Readings: Towards a Gothic Geography* (co-edited with Glennis Byron); *Writing the Passions*; *Postcolonial Imaginings: Fictions of a New World Order*; *The Influence of Postmodernism on Contemporary Writing*; *Modernity*; and *Rapture: Literature, Addiction, Secrecy*.

Alan Riach is Professor of Scottish Literature at the University of Glasgow. He is author of *Hugh MacDiarmid's Epic Poetry*; *The Poetry of Hugh MacDiarmid*; *Representing Scotland in Literature, Popular Culture and Iconography*; and, with Alexander Moffat, *Arts of Resistance: Poets, Portraits and Landscapes of Modern Scotland*. He is the General Editor of *The Collected Works of Hugh MacDiarmid* and has co-edited *Lion's Milk: Turkish Poems by Scottish Poets*; *The Edinburgh Companion to Twentieth-Century Scottish Literature*; *The Radical Imagination: Lectures and Talks by Wilson Harris*; and *Scotlands: Poets and the Nation*.

Susan Strehle is Distinguished Service Professor of English at Binghamton University, part of the State University of New York. A scholar who specialises in modern and contemporary fiction, global and American literature, women writers and postcolonial theory, Strehle is author of *Fiction in the Quantum Universe* and *Transnational Women's Fiction: Unsettling Home and Homeland*.

Sue Thomas is Professor of English at La Trobe University, Melbourne. She is the author of *Telling West Indian Lives: Life Narrative and the Reform of Plantation Slavery Culture 1804–1834*; *Imperialism, Reform and the Making of Englishness in Jane Eyre*; and *The Worlding of Jean Rhys*. Her other books include *England through Colonial*

Eyes in Twentieth-Century Fiction (co-authored with Ann Blake and Leela Gandhi) and the edited collection *Victorian Traffic: Identity, Exchange, Performance*.

Sue Vice is Professor of English at the University of Sheffield. Her publications in the field of literary theory include *Psychoanalytic Criticism: A Reader* and *Introducing Bakhtin*, while in cinema studies she has published a monograph on Claude Lanzmann's classic film *Shoah* (a BFI Modern Film Classics volume in 2011). In addition, she has published on the Holocaust in *Holocaust Fiction* and *Children Writing the Holocaust*, and is currently at work with David Forrest on a new project focusing on the novelist and screenwriter Barry Hines.

Janet Wilson is Professor of English and Postcolonial Studies at the University of Northampton and Director of Research in its School of the Arts. She has published widely on the diaspora writing of white settler societies, and religion and fundamentalism. She is co-editor of the *Journal of Postcolonial Writing*, and has co-edited three collections of essays: *Global Fissures: Postcolonial Fusions*; *Rerouting the Postcolonial: New Directions for the New Millennium*; and *Katherine Mansfield and the (Post)colonial*.

Index

Atkinson, Kate
   Behind the Scenes at the Museum, 120
   'Case Histories' (series of novels), 120–2
   Case Histories (novel), 121–2, 123
   Emotionally Weird, 120
   A God in Ruins, 123, 124
   Human Croquet, 120
   Life After Life, 124, 125–6
   One Good Turn, 122–3, 124
   Started Early, Took My Dog, 123

Bakhtin, Mikhail, 78, 100, 107
Bradford, Richard, *The Novel Now: Contemporary British Fiction*, 8, 12n1

Calvino, Italo, *If on a Winter's Night a Traveller*, 13, 37

De Groot, Jerome, *The Historical Novel*, 13, 39, 44
Derrida, Jacques, *Spectres of Marx: The State of the Debt, the Work of Mourning, and the New International*, 107n10

Forna, Aminatta
   Ancestor Stones, 201–2
   The Hired Man, 205–7
   The Memory of Love, 202–5
Foulds, Adam
   The Broken Word, 145–6
   In the Wolf's Mouth, 148–50
   The Quickening Maze, 146–8

   The Truth about These Strange Times, 143–5

globalisation, 28, 48, 100, 103, 177, 199, 201, 205
Grant, Damian, *Realism in Literature*, 13

Hall, Sarah
   The Carhullan Army, 72–3
   The Electric Michelangelo, 73–5
   Haweswater, 70–1
   How to Paint a Dead Man, 75
   The Wolf Border, 75–6
Hamid, Mohsin
   How to Get Filthy Rich in Rising Asia, 182–5
   Moth Smoke, 178–9
   The Reluctant Fundamentalist, 177, 179–82
Hutcheon, Linda, *A Poetics of Postmodernism: History, Theory, Fiction*, 16, 13n17, 21, 48, 54n24, 110

Ishiguro, Kazuo
   The Buried Giant, 114–16
   Never Let Me Go, 113–14
   The Remains of the Day, 110–11
   The Unconsoled, 110–11
   When We Were Orphans, 111–13

Jameson, Frederic, 'Postmodernism, or the Cultural Logic of Late Capitalism', 5, 12n6

Kennedy, A. L.
  The Blue Book, 82–5
  Day, 81–2
  Everything You Need, 79
  On Bullfighting, 80
  On Writing, 83
  Paradise, 80–1
King, Bruce, *The Internationalisation of English Literature*, 21, 177, 187, 204n17
Kristeva, Julia, 107, 125

Levy, Andrea
  Small Island, 189–90, 191–3
  Small Island mass reading project, 193
  The Long Song, 190, 193–5
Lukács, Georg, *The Historical Novel*, 21, 40
Lyotard, Jean-François, 'The Postmodern Condition', 5, 12n7

McEwan, Ian
  Atonement, 18–19
  The Children Act, 24–5
  On Chesil Beach, 20–1
  Saturday, 19–20
  Solar, 22–3
  Sweet Tooth, 23–4
McHale, Brian, *The Cambridge Introduction to Postmodernism*, 5, 12n7, 86, 106
Mantel, Hillary
  Beyond Black, 38–9
  Bring up the Bodies, 37, 40–1, 42–4
  Giving up the Ghost, 38
  A Place of Greater Safety, 37, 40–1
  Wolf Hall, 41–4
Mitchell, David
  Black Swan Green, 31–2
  Bone Clocks, 32–3
  Cloud Atlas, 29–31
  Ghostwritten, 28–9
  MA thesis on the postmodern novel, 31
  number9dream, 29
  The Thousand Autumns of Jacob de Zoet, 32

O'Farrell, Maggie
  After You'd Gone, 62–3
  The Distance Between Us, 64–5
  The Hand That First Held Mine, 66–8
  Instructions for a Heatwave, 68
  My Lover's Lover, 63–4
  The Vanishing Act of Esme Lennox, 65–6

Robertson, James
  And the Land Lay Still, 169–71
  The Fanatic, 163–5
  Joseph Knight, 165–7
  The Professor of Truth, 171–2
  The Testament of Gideon Mack, 167–9
Rushdie, Salman
  The Enchantress of Florence, 134–6
  Fury, 132–3
  The Ground Beneath Her Feet, 130–2
  Shalimar the Clown, 133–4
  Two Years Eight Months and Twenty-Eight Nights, 136–7

Smith, Ali
  The Accidental, 99–100, 102
  Artful, 100
  Girl Meets Boy, 102–4
  Hotel World, 101–2
  How to be both, 105–6
  There but for the, 104–5
Smith, Zadie
  The Autograph Man, 50–1
  NW, 52–5
  On Beauty, 51–2
  White Teeth, 48, 49–50

Tew, Philip, Leigh Wilson and Fiona Tolan, *Writers Talk: Interviews with Contemporary British Novelists*, 42, 128

Warner, Alan
  The Deadman's Pedal, 91–4
  The Man Who Walks, 88–9
  Morvern Callar, 88
  The Sopranos, 89
  The Stars in the Bright Sky, 89
  Their Lips Talk of Mischief, 90–1
  These Demented Lands, 88–9
  The Worms Can Carry Me to Heaven, 90–1
Waters, Sarah
  Fingersmith, 154–5
  The Little Stranger, 157–9
  The Night Watch, 155–7
  The Paying Guests, 159–60
  PhD thesis on gay and lesbian fiction, 161n4
Watt, Ian, *The Rise of the Novel*, 2, 12n5

EU representative:
Easy Access System Europe
Mustamäe tee 50, 10621 Tallinn, Estonia
Gpsr.requests@easproject.com

www.ingramcontent.com/pod-product-compliance
Lightning Source LLC
Chambersburg PA
CBHW061713300426
44115CB00014B/2672